AFTER DANTE

AFTER

PETER COOKSON SMITH

DANTE

DIVINE, DESIGN, AND THE COSMOS

ORO Editions — Novato, California

Trajan's Market, situated on the Via dei Fori Imperiali was inaugurated in 113 CE as part of Emperor Trajan's Forum on the flank of the Quirinal Hill, and eventually completed by Emperor Hadrian. Shops and administrative offices were incorporated by excavating the ridge, connecting the Quirinal and Capitoline hills. The military tower above the market was constructed in 1200 CE. Between the Basilica Ulpia and the temple dedicated to Trajan were two libraries that housed Latin and Greek documents, with Trajan's Column at their center.

CONTENTS

Preface   8

La Divina Comedia:
A Perilous Voyage into the Afterlife   14

A Restless and Creative Seed   38

Encounters of the Turbulent Kind   56

The Roots of Cosmic Observation   72

The Dome of Santa Maria del Fiore   86

Realizing the Renaissance   110

Ascertaining Heliocentrism   150

Mannerism, Monuments, and Markers   166

Calibrating the Cosmos   2276

Deconstructing Paradiso   236

Epilogue   256

Acknowledgments   266

References   268

PREFACE

HE BOOK BEGAN its variegated existence as a series of linked essays loosely focused on the forces that impacted the late medieval age through a divisive tension between the respective responsibilities of church and state that occurred at the cusp of a cultural flowering into the humanism of the Renaissance. This placed the individual as its focus, and represented a period of resurrection and renewal, rich in an exchange of ideas and attainment of knowledge that tended to unify an increasingly secular society with a compulsion toward spiritual ideals. At virtually the same time, Church doctrine stood firmly behind a prevailing school of philosophy inspired by theologians such as Thomas Aquinas. These leaned on a literal interpretation of the ancient theories of Aristotle, and posited a geocentric universe with the earth firmly at the center of existence. The notion of a divine creator that embodied the principle of reason was, on one hand, the liberating inspiration for an outburst of creativity from the beginning of the 14th century that lasted through the entire Renaissance period, and on the other hand unleashed a renewal of the ancient obsession with the Cosmos.

It was the *Divine* that suggested a reinvigorated acquaintance with Dante Alighieri and his epic poetic narrative, *La Divina Comedia* or *Divine Comedy*. The beginning of the 14th century marked not merely a transition between the medieval and Renaissance periods, but encapsulated the prevailing sense of spiritual purpose, celestial power, and philosophical challenge. This effectively laid down a foundation for an unfolding age of arts and sciences within a city culture marked by a rediscovery of antiquity. The creative and ideological realm was therefore endowed with both knowledge and meaning, accompanied by classical references articulated by notions of an "ideal" city form. Pattern books produced by urban thinkers such as Alberti, Palladio, Vignola, and others reconciled artistic considerations with practical aspects relating to the needs of a rapidly urbanizing society. Infiltrating all of this was the persistent imposition of a heavenly will, invoked by the Church to satisfy an often-contested sense of cosmic order, where all natural works were deemed to be of a divine origin. Alberti's architectural treatise, *De re Aedificatoria*, in fact adopted a principle of Aristotle that the "truth" inherent in the balance of geometry and proportion echoed the mathematical structure of the universe.

In an age of apparent ideological certainty, artistic attainment marked a new and challenging humanism representing a philosophy, central to the Renaissance, that embraced an emerging role of citizens as rational and sentient beings. A more contentious aspect of this, dogmatically expressed through church doctrine, was the earth's relationship to the Cosmos and the integral notion of a celestial presence. Just as a progressive culture of learning and new principles of civic design and responsibility dignified the public realm, a resurgent sense of reason and scientific enquiry was pioneering new insights, not only in terms of astronomical discoveries, but about the very nature of the universe. This progressively opened up the frontiers of knowledge that promoted architectural and artistic celebration, exemplified by the construction of the Santa Maria Del Fiore cathedral in Florence, encompassing Brunelleschi's audacious crowning dome that appeared to reach well beyond earthly constraints.

The Renaissance was not merely a period profuse in the exchange of ideas and information, but a vehicle for ordering principles relating to a new urbanism through a rationalism of city design and composition. This effectively mirrored the emerging role of astronomers and mathematicians who sought to establish and explain prevailing symmetries in the natural world. From the enforced dictates of Renaissance theology, scientific knowledge led directly to principles that challenged previously fixed notions of reality. In the process this liberated an unprecedented creative force extending from new design typologies to a concern for human reason through both scientific and divine revelation.

Dante's *Comedia* consists of a cautionary journey that encompasses a mission of exploration and self-examination through three stages of the Afterlife, which focuses in a broad sense on the salvation of mankind and, at a more pointed level, on its unification. It adopts a somewhat literal interpretation of Aristotelian philosophy influenced by the theological reasoning of Thomas Aquinas, and encompasses the planetary epicycles set out by Hipparchus. Dante draws on the fabric of the visible cosmos, stretching its metaphysical features and unfurling them in an imaginative version of space-time. This creates a provocative illusion that transcends an accurate interpretation of nature's laws, even as it challenges the limits of our imagination. The *Comedia's* turbulent encounters represent a metaphor for the state of society, ranging from the consequences of moral abdication, to atonement and eventually the opportunities for redemption. The final encounter in the Empyrean, the highest point in the heavenly *Paradiso,* is reserved for those who respected the essential criteria of a secular state. At the same time it represents an ambitious astronomical construction related to the observable planets, based on certain astrological associations.

This also marked the timely intervention of a new generation of scientific thinkers who drew on theories from ancient schools of philosophy, reinvigorating the debate on planetary movement and re-ordering systems of measurement. From Sacrobosco and Albertus Magnus in the early 13th century to Cusanus and Copernicus two centuries later, this opened up debate on the heliocentric solar system and the movement of so-called celestial bodies.

By the 16th century, the Church had begun to assume an authoritarian role over both the spiritual and secular realm in Italy, but encountered difficulty in implementing reforms agreed by the Lateran Council. It was left to Pope Paul III to commence the Council of Trent in 1537 in response to the challenges of the Protestant Reformation. Many architects and artists left Rome for Venice, which experienced a surge of new construction and city regeneration through designers including Michele Sanmicheli, Jacope Sansovino, Sebastiano Serlio, and Andrea Palladio, transforming the Grand Canal and St. Mark's Square in the late Renaissance period while Bramante and Michelangelo began to carry out work on St. Peter's Basilica in Rome.

Through his paper known as the *Commentariolus,* Nicolaus Copernicus challenged Ptolemy's finite model of the universe along with prevailing Church doctrine, and opened a metaphorical gateway for a sequence of scientifically inclined astronomers. These included Johannes Kepler and Galileo Galilei who, through new discoveries, were able to work at a more precise mathematical level. In the case of Galileo, he was summoned before the Papal Inquisition in Rome for interrogation because of his cautious support for a heliocentric universe in a treatise *Siderius Nuncius*, and was duly found guilty of heresy, narrowly avoiding a sentence of death.

Newton's 17th-century Universal Law showed that the forces of gravity and inertia were universal properties of all matter, and established the relationship between realism and precision, much as Renaissance architects were adopting the notion of symmetry in their architecture and urban design. It was, however, still possible to hold a spiritual perspective as the reason behind gravitational force, and to offer a divine and preordained explanation for the orbital paths of planets within the solar system.

This was followed by further philosophical insights as part of the Enlightenment's scientific revolution, each building on the discoveries of its predecessors, including Descarte's notion of an infinite universe, Immanuel Kant's hypothesis on the formation of stars and planets, and Michael Faraday's explanation of the electromagnetic field. What might be termed "modern physics" commenced with James Clerk Maxwell who developed a consistent mechanical model of the materiality of space that encapsulated a new understanding of electromagnetic forces, light, and radiation. It was, however, Albert Einstein's special and general theories of relativity that proved the laws of gravity and motion take the same form within a four-dimensional universe that equated to three spatial dimensions and a single dimension of time.

Despite fundamental advances in science and cosmology since the early 20th century, and the discoveries that have since acted to verify cosmic theories, we cannot claim that the universe is as conveniently comprehensible as Dante poetically imagined it. There is as yet no grand unified theory that explains nature's fine tuning, and we have to reflect on the knowledge that the universe is made up of necessary atomic matter, dark matter, and dark energy whose composition is indeterminate. While we can describe the patterns that infiltrate the universe that began as a quantum fluctuation, this does not necessarily explain it.

The penultimate chapter, in a reflective way, deconstructs Dante's metaphysical interpretation of the cosmos that was embedded in a belief that moral justice and the omnipotence of God were an integral part of the cosmic narrative, while adopting a central purpose and significance to the laws of nature. As Galileo stated, "we cannot understand the book of nature if we do not first learn the language and grasp the symbols in which it was written."

We have embraced the design language of the Renaissance in terms of its culture, buildings, and artistry, and the aesthetic aspects of this are still open to experience and appreciate on whatever level we wish. This might hopefully be apparent from the sketches that illuminate the text in this book. But such grand design demands an equally grand purpose, and intuiting the constant revelations of cosmology and its significance is an integral part of this. The Copernican Principal initially set off a chain reaction of consternation and refutation, but also a progressive sequence of challenges in navigating ever-emerging realities and discoveries that we are still attempting to understand and if possible stitch together in a comprehensible form. We now look at the cosmos through a mathematical and scientific lens that has opened up a means of making systematic sense of the natural world, even if we remain bemused by assertions such as that attributed to Niels Bohr—"Those who are not shocked when they first come across quantum theory cannot possibly have understood it."

This includes questions as to how and why we ourselves evolved on a small planet conveniently and uniquely equipped with a hospitable biosphere that otherwise has no technical reason to exist. Mathematical rules and patterns infiltrate everything, but while this describes the Cosmos as we know it, it does not necessarily explain it. We must now attempt to find answers that move us along from the certainties of the Renaissance, and to ponder the meaning of existence in seemingly infinite space. Things can be either unknowable or unprovable, and as mathematical truths exist in something of a disembodied state they have to be taken on faith until proven beyond doubt. In this respect the Cosmos might still hold some surprises.

Quantum theory has both physical and philosophical repercussions. Under its rules, as we both inhabit and observe our environment, our interaction with it changes its state and even suggests that the physical world must be explored in terms of probabilities rather than firm assertions. This line of reasoning creates an elusive connection between energy, matter, space, and time. Max Planck, who revolutionized the understanding of atomic and subatomic processes with the fabric of quantum reality, stated that "all matter originates and exists only through a force behind which is an intelligent mind." In other words, the more deeply we delve into the complexity of matter the more we have to admit the presence of some artistic symmetry at work.

This might return us to Dante's Inferno, Purgatario, and Paradiso. The entwined concepts of space and mind signals something of a fissure between science and religion. The transformation arguably began with Plato, but was effectively codified by Dante. This inspired a new era of thinking about the relationship between the terrestrial and celestial realms and marks a transition in Western culture between the medieval concept of a heavenly space, a literal interpretation of its divine structure, and a progressively scientific approach to its understanding.

The Basilica of Santa Maria degli Angeli is incorporated within the fabric of the imperial Roman Baths of the emperor Diocletian, built in 306 CE with the former caldarium marking its entrance. The Basilica was designed by Michelangelo in 1563, the year before his death, and completed by his pupil Jacopo Lo Duca. It is said to be dedicated to the Christian slave laborers who helped to build and maintain the baths. The Basilica incorporates a meridian line sundial on its floor, crafted of bronze and white marble, that marks an intriguing connection between the Catholic church and the blossoming of astronomical science that was proclaimed through the Gregorian calendar.

LA·DVINA·COMEDA: A·PERILOUS·VOYAGE INTO·THE·AFTERLIFE

O human race, born to fly upward,
wherefore at a little wind dost thou so fall.
DANTE ALIGHIERI, *La Divina Comedia*

Venetia, Appresso Giouambattista, Marchio Sossa, & fratelli. 1564

A Divina Comedia or Divine Comedy, the epic poem written by Dante Alighieri between 1308 and 1320, forms a poetic narrative that portrays an imaginative relationship between God, taken to be the benign creator of the Universe, and the souls who inhabit it who are conjured into existence through a celestial force and given spiritual purpose. The poem consists of a heroic journey of exploration but also self-examination that in part pursues the depth and elevated realms of humanity, but at the same time posits Dante as the detached protagonist open to his own beliefs, impulses, and prejudices. The intended purpose of the journey is the salvation of mankind, but can be read on many levels—spiritual certainty and attainment, a vanquishing of barriers, and a conquering of inner demons. Dante's own vision and poetic accomplishment reinforces the sense of mission that purports to carry a message of reform from God to mankind, focussing on the threat of corruption and sin prior to the possible achievement of salvation. In its inspired and imaginative vision of human predestination in relation to the universe, it was made credible in the late medieval and early Renaissance period by the prevailing Christian belief system where philosophical thought was directed toward the human soul and its relation to God.

The medieval "Middle Ages" are generally taken as commencing with the fall of the Roman Empire in 476 CE and the beginning of the 14th century. Outside main centers of learning associated with ancient universities and monasteries, the medieval age suffered from war, famine, and disease. However, a new humanism began to take hold in cities in the first part of the 14th century, focused on education, guilds, and the arts. These were mutually stimulated through new types of political, trading, and religious bodies that celebrated the achievements of classical antiquity, just as it pursued new interfaces with the expanding international order that was spreading across Europe, forging a new modernity.

The main church interpretation of divine creation, derived from the Christian canon through the book of Genesis, was the formation of the Universe and its life forms representing a series of creative acts over six days. The Fourth Lateran Council presided over by Pope Innocent III in 1215, 50 years before the birth of Dante, blurred the issue somewhat by promulgating a canon law that God, through his omnipotent power, "created all things simultaneously at the beginning of time, and then made man from spirit and body." Accordingly, heaven was created on the first day; the firmament comprising air, planets, and stars on the second; the waters on the third; and the celestial luminaries on the fourth. This remained as the most widely held opinion during the Middle Ages, and by the 13th century the only real impulse toward an understanding of the celestial void came from a theology based on an omnipresent God. The heavens themselves were assumed to consist of an ethereal and unknowable realm that changed only with respect to an apparent circular motion. Aristotelian cosmology had, by the time of Dante, become part of Christian theology through the work of Albertus Magnus and Thomas Aquinas.

What Dante sets out in the *Comedia* is arguably a model for an "ideal" society, first through the identification of traits that must be excluded, second the means to counter them, and third the elements that are necessary for its political functioning. It is a call for the unification of society with all parties contributing to the common good through their individual abilities, but also an acceptance that communities must have officials to instill order and provide for the necessities of public life while renouncing any ambitions toward overall power. This well-intentioned but necessarily idealist aspiration is accompanied by a strong assertion that the church itself must be free of the workings of the state, and enable it to concentrate its intentions on ministering to the spiritual needs of citizens.

Dante's writing portrays the late medieval period in Italy, but opens a door to the early Renaissance while examining issues of timeless concern. Love, suffering, struggle, and freedom are imperatives we encounter at a personal level, just as we put great stock in the pursuit of happiness and fulfillment. His use of allegory might well evoke analytical questions revolving around its precise level of interpretation, where there can exist several levels of reference and explanation, quite apart from the literal, even if his rich poetic resonance might detract somewhat from its comprehension.

The availability of classical Greek and Roman texts, that focused on philosophical thought rather than the religious piety of medieval mindsets, created a new emphasis on reason and inquiry related to the natural world. In as much as the *Comedia* reflects, at least in part, the strong medieval belief system set out in scriptures and systematically preached by theological scholars at the time, Dante's profound and poetic communication of this, along with deep introspection as to the fallible state of human will, elevates the stature of the underlying message itself. As a moral focus, reinforced by the authority and conduct of figures such as the Roman poet Virgil, and Thomas Aquinas on his tortured road to salvation, Dante argues that a clear demarcation must exist between the need for a restored Holy Roman Empire and a return to the apostolic values of the Church. Each was seen as having a complementary role in pursuing both justice and ethical standards within society, which should logically extend to eternal satisfaction.

The elusive link between individuality and community hinges on the citizen's ability to make independent choices, and can only be aligned with those who are free to choose. In this Dante acknowledges the philosophical scholarship of Aristotle who argued that the virtuous functioning of communities formed a necessary moral basis for individual re-awakening and salvation. At the same time Dante exhibits an indebtedness to Virgil's *Aeneid* as an epic pilgrimage in pursuit of truth, no matter the trials and hazards associated with the journey. In this sense the underlying discipline of poetic language facilitates a fascinating rapport with the narrative, and its engagement with the horror of Hell, the frustration of Purgatory, and the exultation of Paradise.

The *Comedia* is caught up with the cultural and philosophical context of its time, but this has to allow for the prevailing political tension and the idealistic principles that underscore the poem, in particular the relationship between a God as the benign and prolific presence behind the universe, and his, or her, human creations. This line of thought contends that both the Church and the State have a complementary role in establishing a subtle and possibly an equivocal route to divine contentment, whatever the continual crisis along the path. Dante's familiarity with the *Aeneid* clearly assists him not merely in adopting a new style of narrative verse, but in Virgil's allusions to Christian belief - one that is consistent with appropriate modes of conduct and persistent moral motivation. The *Comedia* therefore

The Palazzo Vecchio and the Uffizi set against the backcloth of the Oltrarno.

stands as a means of conveying both passion and intellectual purpose, but also a conspirational web of double meaning, open to different interpretations and lines of conjecture.

The turbulent encounters in the *Comedia* take place in the year 1320, between Good Friday and the following Wednesday. Good Friday is spent exploring Hell with Virgil as a guide; the next day they ascend from Hell to observe the stars, and arrive at the shore of the Mountain of Purgatory on the morning of Easter Sunday. The *Comedia* ends with arrival in the Earthly Paradise. The "fall" of humanity is equated with what are perceived to be the "problems" in Italian society, with Hell, Purgatory, and the Heavenly Paradise represented by punishment, repentance, and bliss.

The implication of this allows for a certain directness of purpose toward Dante's likely audience in terms of connectivity within the canto form of three-line verses. In the *Comedia* Dante is escorted through the first two realms by Virgil, and thereafter through the celestial barrier beyond the dank material world by Beatrice—a spiritualized ideal of sublime femininity, and a central figure in Dante's poetic imagination, as a guide to the essence of a heavenly reality beyond sordid materiality. Beatrice is shown as a symbolic figure, at once both revelatory and enigmatic, but with an essential role of leading the poet to a divine order of understanding and salvation, from her unrivalled position as the eternal object of Dante's devotion.

The awakening of Dante's own linguistic authority gains from his descriptive power and imagination, but its overriding achievement is to position the work as a means of intellectual challenge rather than indulgence. Dante's use of a vernacular Italian language from the region of Tuscany is calculated to set a powerful poetic standard and reach a wide audience—in effect the poet becomes the vessel of communication, representing a divine as well as a political mission, suggesting an eloquent and enduring meaning that is difficult to express in any other way. It is rooted in a rhapsodic spiritual transmission of belief, imagination, and emotion that embraces the entire universe. To Dante poetry was an instrument to probe and provoke, using it as a tool to grapple with his own frustrations and sense of justice. The intensity and significance of the subject is matched by what can be gleaned from the poetic medium itself. The *Comedia* incorporates several features that allow Dante to accomplish an innovative style of poetry, attuned to each canto. First, the term *comedia* alludes to the somewhat melodious dialect of Florence, possibly to express directly the overall message of humility, rather than the authoritative style associated with Latin—something that was unusual for scholars at that time. Secondly, cantos are used to express the narrative but with some flexibility as to continuity. This challenges the reader to connect the ends and beginnings of successive stanzas in order to decipher the intuitive relationships and contrasts. Thirdly, the adoption of the three-line stanza within the cantos allows the author to incorporate emphatic shifts in the narrative direction along with sudden changes of emphasis and imagery that embellish the underlying meaning and purpose of the poem.

In the portrayal of Virgil and his importance to the *Comedia*, Dante tactically positions his presence as an alter ego—someone who at the same time is an essential part of the poem in the form of an alternative self. This successfully opens up new lines of thought and provides responses that the protagonist himself might wish to state indirectly as a persuasive and even intimate mode of expression—a tactic later adopted by Galileo.

The appeal of Dante, and to a large extent his enduring fascination, is his metaphysical contribution to an enigmatic mix of thought, philosophy, literature, theology, and spirituality. He was born in

Florence in 1265 shortly after the death of Emperor Frederick II and nine years before the death of Thomas Aquinas. This late Middle Age period saw almost constant military struggle, and the defeat of the Florentine Guelphs by the Ghibellines, before a reinstatement of Guelph rule with the assistance of the French, allowing Florence to develop a tentative supremacy over Tuscany. Dante was by all accounts both impatient and presumptuous, possibly reflecting both his willingness to fight for Florence, and his later banishment from the city. His education was largely devoted to Latin, ancient literature, and later philosophical study, allowing him to relish what he termed the "art of grammar" that enabled him to study the classics outside monastic institutions and develop an excellence in prose writing.

It is generally acknowledged by scholars that the embryo for the *Comedia* was Dante's earlier poem *La Vita Nuova* or a book of memory, completed in 1295. This explores the notions of transformation and change, inspired but also convoluted through his encounter with Beatrice, a real life personification of beauty, the daughter of a wealthy merchant, Folco Portinari. She was, however, in many ways a phantom, who exerted a distractive but powerful force on his life. Indirectly this "new life," set in prose and verse, introduces aspects of reason, human nature, and the transience of life evinced by her early death, which Dante sorrowfully suggests as realizing a divine purpose.

Both Dante and Beatrice are presented in the *Comedia* as chosen messengers, so their views are taken as having divine sanction. The poem, occasionally in a rhetorical way, points the way to what is to come— in effect an entré to a more philosophical view of life, essential purpose, and death. More particularly, *La Vita Nova* seems to introduce a realization of Dante's own capacity for ardor and vehemence as a means to adroitly allocate those in or out of divine favor. This includes the damned, who are condemned through moral abdication, and the redeemed, who are considered as being suitably open to ultimate salvation. In the process love is depicted as the source of a new beginning.

The fact that Dante proffers a caricature of himself into the narrative that is often less than positive, while subtly displaying his poetic skills, underscores a delicate collaboration with his audience, but at the same time challenges them. Over the years its many interpretations, with their audacious allusions to human nature and confident references to sacred events, mythology, and history, have permeated into Italian culture. The text also includes passing observations of familiar but incidental details that, in terms of imagery, echo an ancient way of life in the northern Italian city and countryside. While his work is now lauded by the Catholic Church, Dante's poetry contains several layers of meaning and a degree of ambiguity making it open to scholarly interpretation, which perhaps explains the large number of English translations. But we must read into Dante much that is allegorical, only barely disguising repugnance toward the corrupt state of the church, the destructive rivalry among powerful political factions, and the role of the individual in society—all popular topics in the early 14th century.

The *Comedia* is constructed around the simple proposition that humans owe their existence to a creator, and that rather than the humdrum dust-to-dust scenario, eternal happiness will only be achieved when a being returns in sacrificial obedience to the heavenly court. The painstaking path to this comprehension is essentially a search for what is situated as an underlying truth about the concept of "eternity" and the painful hurdles that must be overcome in advancing toward it. That Dante wrote this masterwork during a state of exile from his home city of Florence, and under a lingering death sentence, gives the poem some poignancy. Crisis can bring fear and darkness, but also re-evaluation and resurrection, indicating a persistent pathway to enable the transition from evil to purification and wisdom. If human beings can be casually cast into the biblical version of everlasting fire due to a rather open-ended definition of sin, it was considered only prudent to proffer some ladder, which might permit escape through repentance.

Continuing urbanization encouraged the most powerful and wealthy feudal families to construct tower-house complexes, with unofficial jurisdictions almost independent of the wider urban framework. These consorteria vied with each other as to the size and height of their buildings, and relied on the allegiance of their communal followers and military supporters. The tallest tower in San Gimignano was the tower of the Commune.

Dante in the *Inferno* compared the "crowning towers" on the fortress-like circular parapets built in 1203 around Monteriggioni in the disputed territory between Florence and Sienna, to the giants who surround the deepest pit of hell.

By expressing the city and the state as extensions of the individual citizen, the central issue becomes the identity of the most appropriate mediator between them—the emperor or the pope. In effect, this constitutes a contested choice between the consolidation of the empire and the more debatable supremacy over Christendom. Dante agreed with Aristotle's support for secular government as a moral imperative, and favored the notion of empire. Both Aristotle and Thomas Aquinas, who had an important influence on Dante, advocated that it was in the nature of humankind to learn and communicate with fellow citizens, as being necessary to the attainment and conferring of knowledge, virtue, and the common good. However, this idealistic view might have hidden the unpalatable fact that politics at the time involved monarchies and state governments that were subject to irregular forces and rivalries, not necessarily conducive to peace, happiness, and consensus. In addition, the church's obsession with material wealth, just as much as spiritual affairs, contributed to the tendency to view it as something of an imperial authority over the temporal sphere, creating an almost constant conflict between the respective responsibilities of church and state.

Rejoice Florence, seeing you are so great
that over sea and land you flap your wings,
and your name is widely known in Hell
DANTE ALIGHIERI, *La Divina Comedia*

The *Comedia* is firmly rooted in the city as being a structured entity personified by Florence, while an ideal of empire is exemplified by the divine destiny of Rome with its appropriate scale of central authority, deemed necessary to unify the inevitable competition between the two cities themselves. It was a fundamental facet of Dante's poetic philosophy that to meet the multitude of needs for humankind, society must be unified, and his focus on the city represents the most appropriate geographical entity where a cross section of functions can be effectively structured. The divinity of Rome might, however, have represented wishful thinking, in that the Western Roman Empire had been effectively dissolved in 476 CE when Flavius Odoacer became the first Barbarian to rule in Rome. Several hundred years later it had entered a period that has been called the "Dark Age of the Roman Papacy."

The layout of cities in the Tuscan plain—Florence, Lucca, Pisa, and Distoia—were originally established as Roman colonies, complete with surviving water conduits, thermal baths, theaters and villas. New urban centers were introduced along the ancient east-west road system between the Adriatic and the Mediterranean, and associated with Roman consular roads. Medieval buildings and churches were frequently constructed from the highly decorative remains of Roman architecture—in particular, after Emperor Constantine's edict of 313 CE that permitted the Christian religion. Many small towns became the centers of dioceses, and from the 5th century these embraced extensive hinterlands under the control of bishoprics.

Small hilltop settlements came to characterize the landscape of Tuscany. Between the 12th and 14th centuries fortified towers were introduced, some as high as 230 feet as a reflection of protection, wealth, and dominance. Some towns had many such structures, in particular San Gimignano, which encompassed 72 tower houses. These buildings were built on square plots and had only slit windows in case of disputes between different factions, particularly the Guelphs and Ghibellines, that led to occasional

armed sieges. In some cases extended family *consortieri* constructed several towers that were linked together at an upper level by wooden walkways. The higher the tower, the greater prestige of the family. It was not until the onset of guild government that the height of towers was limited. In the main cities they were demolished to make way for palazzi, and their stones used for new construction. Defensive structures were then built in the form of city walls.

By the 14th century, churches became enlarged with progressively grand architecture. City Burghers, commercial and artisan groups began to formulate free city republics through the introduction of elected consuls, aldermen, and priors, which enabled the broad abolition of feudal rule and a regenerative influence on the cities. During this period secular and clerical power was largely in the hands of either papal or imperial forces, which generated increasing aggression between rival bodies.

When Coluccio Salutati used the descriptive words "Territorial States, Tyrannies, and Powerful Families" to describe Florence around 1400, most central Italian cities had completed major building projects, but the plague and military campaigns had decimated their populations. As a result, public projects were broadly tied to state patronage and directed at fortifications. Certainly by the mid-Quattrocento the larger cities in northern Italy were becoming territorial centers with a concentration of temporal power, demonstrating a shift from older enclaves and civic monuments to domination by new oligarchies and despotic governments.

This was a long way removed from the city of Florence founded by Caesar Augustus in 59 BCE, with a preliminary layout dictated by the nucleus of a gridded military settlement with its precise center now marked by the Piazza Republica. The army camp was itself superimposed on a pre-existing Etruscan settlement as part of a colonization program covering the north and central part of the Italian peninsula in the 9th century BCE. In the 3rd century CE came a cataclysmic shift in city patronage coinciding with the final years of the Roman Empire, from the pagan god Mars to the Christian St. John the Baptist. In 393 CE the first church in the city was consecrated—San Lorenzo. After the decline of the Roman Empire the city was invaded in succeeding centuries by the Byzantines, the Lombards, and the Franks until the unification of western and central Europe under the reign of Charlemagne, who established the stability necessary for a spate of cultural and intellectual activity. After an intervening period of feudalism, the Holy Roman Empire brought together the strengths and aptitude of both Italy and Germany, but also introduced a contrasting and often conflicting balance between imperial and papal spheres of influence. While the wider part of northern Italy remained largely under the reigns of feudal lords, Florence itself became divided into different factions and coalitions while the tightly packed city was encircled by a fortified wall. The excommunication of Henry IV as a religious censure by Pope Gregory in 1080 led to a reorganization of the city's social and political organization into "communes," which adopted a paramount role in orchestrating both the economy of the city and new guilds of artisans.

The medieval city of Florence, where Dante lived from 1265 to 1302, was not then known for its grand civic and religious monuments. With a population of around 50,000 people, Florence represented a mix of narrow streets, with houses and workshops interspersed with vineyards and gardens. Its most prominent spatial characteristic was the array of defensive structures constructed by family clans, primarily

to exhibit their immutable power and intimidating tendencies. The most lavish building at the time and the center for all major religious ceremonies was the Baptistery of San Giovanni. Politics was problematic however. In 1265 Pope Clement IV induced Charles of Anjou, brother of the French King, to intervene in the struggle for control of Florence. The divisions between the two sides, widened by a sequence of victories and defeats, created almost continuous instability between 1260 and 1280 when the two parties reached reconciliation.

The mendicant orders of Dominicans, Franciscans, Augustinians, and Carmelites were largely made up of urban traders and artisans, and expanded rapidly during the 14th century, attracting wealthy patrons. They adopted a deliberately pious lifestyle and followed a path of religious reform articulated by new architectural paradigms applied to sacred precincts. What began in Florence and Pisa spread to the wider Tuscan region, so that churches associated with the various orders in the new merchant cities helped to define new city sectors and characteristic civic spaces in the urban communes. As congregations grew, so church architecture was becoming gradually more sophisticated and monumental. Dante would no doubt have been familiar with Santa Maria Novella in Florence with its mendicant following. However, by the end of the 13th century, elite professional guilds and a proliferating merchant class were displacing the feudal community as an economic force.

Around this time, Florence is said to have embodied an abundance of money, a noble coinage, a wool industry, armament skills, a vigorous building industry, an increase in population, and a civilized way of life. Pope Boniface VIII famously stated in 1294 that "the world was made up of four elements: earth, water, air, and fire," but he also added a fifth element, "the Florentines, who seem to rule the world."

Florence began to assert its physical form and identity after 1290 through several important civic buildings. The first foundation stone for the monastery of Santa Maria Novella was laid in 1279, and in 1296 the small church of Santa Reparata began a lengthy process of transformation into the Santa Maria del Fiore that was not to be completed for another 150 years, with the addition of Brunelleschi's dome. This, together with the almost simultaneous construction of the new town hall, the Palazzo della Signoria in 1299, were to become, in the following century, the most distinctive symbols of the city.

Pope Boniface VIII appointed a new bishop of Florence in 1295, Francesco Manaldeschi, who in turn lost no time in appointing Arnolfo di Cambio as *capomaestro* for the new cathedral. Within 10 years all three had died and work was temporarily abandoned through lack of funds. However, the Palazzo was completed within 20 years in a form that symbolized the ambition of the governing elite, with the gigantic tower asserting the authority of the *Priorate* (the "apostles of the republic") at the same time that private towers over a certain height in the city were ordered to be dismantled.

The doctrine of Purgatory, preached by the mendicant orders in Florence, was that the route to heaven was related to an indeterminate purgation of the soul, suitably reinforced by committed endowments and bequests from wealthy patrons. By 1300 the Franciscans were able to begin work on the church of Santa Croce, while the Dominicans completed the construction of Santa Maria Novella. For both of these, important pieces of religious art were commissioned.

The Trecento was marked by a sequence of catastrophes from plague, floods, and famine, and a group of eminent and concerned Florentine families forming the *signoria*—the seat of city government. The descent of the bubonic plague in Italy was one of the most tragic events in European history, reaching Venice, Genoa, and Florence in 1347 and lasting for

15 years. A substantial amount of civic architecture was carried out in the immediate aftermath of the "Black Death" aided by new technical innovations and working practices. This period marked the rise of the Medici family whose patronage dominated the intellectual tenor of the city for almost 300 years. The major change was in the formal relationship between civic buildings, piazzas, and streets, together with improvements to public spaces and places of public gathering. Design guidelines were introduced for new urban buildings with certain height parameters and an elimination of loggias, which had previously overhung the streets. Residential street blocks varied from six to 30 meters in length, with new palazzos integrated on prominent sites with relatively uniform overall facade treatments.

By the early 14th century, Italy had been transformed into city-states modeled on the old Roman Republicanism. This included Florence, which, along with other republics, formed political centers that collectively combined to usher in the Italian Renaissance. Dante's none-too-subtle analogy in the *Comedia* between the self-indulgent and corrupt city of *Hell* and the existing city of Florence reflected both its power and its perpetual struggle with morality. The various maritime Republics were in an almost constant state of rivalry and warfare reflecting different realms of support for either the Holy Roman Emperor or the Pope, which extended to internal divisions between the Ghibellines who were loyal to the Emperor, and the Guelphs who sided with the Pope. The terms "Ghibelline" and "Guelph" emanated from rival claimants to the imperial crown of Germany and became transposed on northern Italian factions that supported either one side or the other. However, this was also determined by cultural and social alliances between eminent families who indicated a particular affiliation in their coats of arms. Guelphs tended to come from mercantile groups, which included Dante's family, while the Ghibellines were more associated with large estates. While Florence traditionally favored the pope, its main rivals in Tuscany—Siena and Pisa—supported the emperor, which led to a series of disruptive alliances among northern Italian cities. Florence and Venice dominated the central and northern parts of Italy, but abuse of privilege and internecine warfare weakened the country to the point of war with other European countries, which was later to open the door to Habsburg Spain as the dominant power for 200 years.

The *Comedia* cannot be disassociated from this process, as the City of God and the City of Sin constitute the two extremes—one holy and the other pagan. Their Italian counterparts through Dante's eyes were Rome and Florence where the former represented the *civilitas,* the unifying force of both political and spiritual life, while the latter represented a secular impediment. Rome was seen not merely as a city but the dominant seat of world power, based on its glorious history that included its literary and poetic legacy, its promulgation of sophisticated debate, and its central role in Catholicism. All are brought together in the eagle, the symbolic sign of the Roman Empire. Under this scenario, *Purgatory* becomes more than a transitional state between Hell and Paradise, possibly referencing Italy itself, as symbolizing a need to unify and re-connect its impulsive citizens, torn apart by factional strife through a purging of their narrow and self-interested priorities.

ANTIQ CENTRO DELLA CITTÀ
COLARE SOLA L'ORE
A VITA NUOVA RESTITUITO

Rapid growth of Florence was fuelled by its developing role as a banking and trading center that covered much of Europe and North Africa. The defensive Roman-Byzantine wall had failed to contain 13th-century expansion and in 1285 construction commenced on a further fortified structure, covering five miles in length with 73 towers and 15 gates. The city's important unit of international currency was the gold florin with its embossed dual images of the city's fleur-de-lis symbol and its adopted protector, John the Baptist. Economic development in turn encouraged the arrival of feudal land owners from surrounding areas, refocusing established community hierarchies around a new social mobility with a commensurate decline in established jurisdictions, where the realm of grand buildings provided opportunities for extended guilds of craftsmen.

VIA
S AGATA

Anghiari in Arezzo Province, Tuscany.

The steep topography of Sienna encompasses views of the Torre del Mangia from all the radiating streets from the central Campo.

The Palazzo Vecchio in Florence ignited competition with Sienna, which built its own city hall equivalent—the Torre del Mangia—in 1348.

The Palazzo Vecchio in the Piazza della Signoria commenced construction in 1294, designed by Arnolfo di Cambio. Its monumental tower standing sentinel above the Piazza della Signoria in Florence was first developed by a private consortium and then became a major feature in the piazza design, crowned with a decorative belfry in the 14th century. While representing a landmark feature, it presents an almost militaristic presence through its rusticated stone walls and lack of an active interface within the piazza itself, indicating its secondary role as a bastion to protect the ruling city government. The Palagio dei Priori as the seat of city power housed the most important Florentine offices and magistracies, with the tower constructed in 1310. Between 1343 and 1592 various modifications were made and the nine coats of arms of the city communes were added. In 1542 the Medici family, under Cosimo I, moved into the Palazzo Vecchio, with Giorgio Vasari overseeing its transformation.

These fundamental changes were in many ways anathema to Dante who viewed the new innovations in a less than positive sense, and forcefully advocated a return to the more tranquil culture of pre-mercantile Florence. As the son of a banker, Dante was clearly knowledgeable as to the world of finance, the extension of credit and investment. Commerce in fact underwrote the importance of Florence at the time, a much regarded example being Marco Polo who returned from China in 1295 having explored new markets and gained great treasures. Merchant bankers were appointed to collect papal taxes that facilitated trade throughout Europe, and Italian companies financed a great many ventures with long lists of debtors that included both religious and government bodies. At the time of the *Comedia*, political power in Florence was largely under the auspices of three major guilds—wool, cloth, and banking. As business and banking were inadequately regulated, even the concept of trading for excessive profit was subject to condemnation among theologians if this could not be justified according to strict standards. Wealth and debt were to an extent subject to political affiliations and divine providence. It might therefore be said that the expansion of trade and large financial transactions led to a situation of disquiet and agitation between church and state, simply because of their inherent capacity for abuse. However, Dante does not exclude those in the church who received large sums in exchange for piously granting absolution.

San Miniato al Monte located high above the south bank of the River Arno. The site is the oldest shrine in Florence, originally realized as a place of worship over the tomb of the early Christian martyr Minias, now situated in a crypt beneath the choir. In the 1018 CE the site was donated to the Cluniac Benedictines, and a new church was constructed around 1200 CE. It is closely associated with St. Francis of Assissi where legend has it that in 1224, following a vision, he founded a hermitage. The facade is perfectly proportioned and reflects the organization of the internal basilica. It is clad in glazed white and green marble from the workshop of Andrea and Luca della Robbia. Its architecture combines the Florentine Romanesque with the 15th-century Renaissance.

The church was financed and controlled by the guild of cloth merchants and is crowned by their heraldic emblem—an eagle perched on a bale of wool.

Dante's outlook was doubtless propelled by the upheaval and civil strife caused by the continuing conflict and miscellaneous vendettas between the Ghibellines and the Guelphs, which involved, on both sides, periodic confiscations of property, banishment from the city, and destruction of property. The prolonged impasse between Frederick II and Pope Innocent IV in the mid-13th century appeared to be a God-given opportunity to usurp temporal power. Dante himself pointed out the clear advantages of one overall leader to both resolve disputes and ensure peace, while advocating at the same time that the goal of humankind must be distinct from that of the individual. In fact, supposed papal claims to political authority over the city of Rome, and indeed much of Italy, were based on a document that was later found to be a 9th-century forgery.

In the wake of the Roman Empire, of which Dante was a staunch defender for its mission to develop an "ideal" society and construct public works, he acknowledges the authority of the emperor and his capacity for virtuous action while that of the Pope was stated to be the promotion of eternal salvation. Every virtue and sin in the *Comedia* therefore evinces a multitude of political overtones, demonstrated through poetic images and subtle references to known figures in the inspired context of a divinely inspired model of the universe that demonstrates the extremes of corruption and virtue. This approach allows a reinforcement of Dante's philosophical arguments with recourse to an abundance of recognizable references, saintly commentary, and authoritarian interjections. Its not too subtle message is that we must strive to achieve an ideal society, free of preconceptions and open to contemporary but also future political, religious, and social realities that might be projected forward from those of the 14th century.

A·RESTLESS·AND CREATIVE·SEED

Heaven wheels above you, displaying to you her eternal glories,
and still your eyes are on the ground.
DANTE ALIGHIERI

ANTE WAS BORN IN 1265 in the Florentine neighborhood of San Pier Maggiore, regarded at the time as the favored residential area for prominent and influential families. It was also divided by different political interests, notably by pro-papal "Black" Donati and the "White" Cerchi Guelphs, together with the pro-imperial Ghibellines. Coexistence was therefore precarious, and created inevitable instability. As a result there were constant territorial disputes and arguments over economic power, which were eventually to bring about a series of disastrous civil wars.

An ambiguous aspect of Dante's youth was the frequent onset of delirium that some might have put down at the time to the spurious associations of either diabolic affliction or divine intervention. Boccaccio in his biography, while recalling Dante's intellectual feats and his studies of Virgil and Ovid, mentions an often-irascible individual, but also a melancholy and pensive one. At any rate, the emotional undercurrents of overwhelming ecstasy and anguish can be perceived in the *Comedia* by way of its inspired and imaginative vision of human predestination in relation to the universe, and is made credible by the prevailing medieval Christian belief system. Its literary style and articulation celebrates a confident acknowledgment of the route to eternity based on reason and scientific consideration, along with an irrefutable faith in the ultimate benevolence of God. Dante encapsulates this in oblique historical references to his own background, experiences, and political persuasions.

In 1260, the defeat of the Florentine Guelphs at the Battle of Montaperti led to seven years of Ghibelline domination, but two years after Dante's birth the Imperial army restored Guelph rule under the protection of Charles of Anjou. Houses of some of the most illustrious Ghibelline families in Florence were razed and eventually replaced by the Piazza della Signoria.

The Alighieri family profited from the restoration of rule in 1267, although educational establishments generally existed only in monastic institutions. Many Florentine Ghibellines had gone into exile and those who remained were barred from public office before a degree of reconciliation was promoted by the new Pope Nicholas III. Although Dante wrote about the health afflictions that affected his youth, he overcame these to develop great skills as a Latin prose writer. This means of transforming pathological experiences into significant intellectual insights is something that he carried throughout his life and is given credibility by his writing.

Dante's teacher as a young man was Brunetto Latini, a Florentine and a notary who held several political offices in the city, and was a well-regarded man of letters, master of rhetoric, and author of an encyclopedia—*Il Tresor*. It seems likely that this is where Dante, in his formative years, learned the essence of both language and style. Latini was by all accounts a dictatorial teacher, but also to Dante's evident dismay, a highly promiscuous individual of notorious habits, who was later placed in Dante's Inferno among the "unapologetic sodomites."

Following this period, Dante spent some time in Bologna as an external student of philosophy and ethics a new field of study that had previously been dominated by theology. It is most likely that while there he developed an expertise in poetic verse and, with his strong command of Latin prose, would have had the opportunity to familiarize himself with the classic authors, including Ovid, Lucan, and Virgil. Dante, as a believer in the duties of a citizen of Florence, participated in at least one military campaign including the Battle of Campaldino as a member of the armed light cavalry in 1289 on the side of the Guelphs, making reference to this in *Purgatorio*. This brought with it social prestige and political advantages, however ambiguous. Dante, while exhibiting certain doubts about the rate of change that he put down to unnecessary hubris and even self-destruction, famously called Florence "the most beautiful and famous daughter of Rome."

Sketch of Luca Signarelli's portrait of Dante Alighieri.

The Palazzo del Bargello was built in 1255 to accommodate the Capitano del Popolo, but in 1574 it was redesigned to house the Bargello—the chief justice. Its tower rises above the old battlements and balances the campanile of the Badia Fiorentina. This was established as a Benedictine institution in 978 and is now home to the Monastic Communities of Jerusalem situated on the Via del Proconsolo adjacent to the Casa di Dante.

By this time he was a family man, intent on submerging himself in the liberal arts. His marriage to Gemma Donati might well have been a means of compensating for the loss of his famous emotional obsession with Beatrice Portinari, but he had few resources to call on, and his increasing expenses could not be met from his limited rental income. It was this that brought him and his brothers into financial difficulties. In the wake of Campaldino, Dante perceived an opportunity to promote his linguistic and literary abilities in a new kind of book that was to become the *Vita Nova*, an autobiographical poem that recalls the occasion where he met the young Beatrice Portinari who proceeded, quite independently of Dante, to become part of Florence's aristocratic elite before her early death in 1290. Dante claimed that she had inspired his poetry, and he was to place her at the ethereal center of the *Comedia*, notably as the heroine of the Heavenly Paradise. By the early 1290s therefore, Dante had established a reputation as an intellectual, a lyric poet, and an occasional painter, and by the mid-1290s he is known to have attended lectures in theology at the Franciscan Santa Croce and the Dominican Santa Maria Novella in Florence.

Between the years 1293–95 there was an imposed restriction on public appointments unless applicants were registered in a guild, which effectively served to exclude Dante from access to public life. Although he had no recognized profession, in 1295 Dante was enrolled in the guild of doctors and apothecaries, presumably on the basis of his non-professional but otherwise extravagant talents. Shortly after this he addressed the Florentine commune with overtly moral but philosophical words that might be taken as a forbear of the *Comedia*, to the effect that individual virtue rather than wealth must be the prime component of nobility. Dante's public address was a poetic but explicit attack on the degeneration of the magnate class in Florence, which immediately caused a rift with one of his best friends and fellow

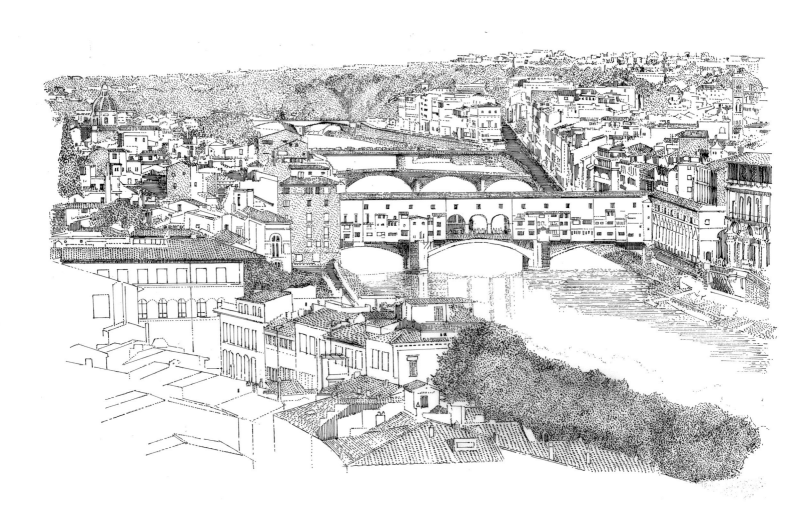

Guelph, Guido Cavalcanti, an Italian poet and impetuous troubadour who is said to have exerted an intellectual influence on Dante's thinking. In fact, it probably reflected more a difference in poetic ideologies, and Cavalcanti went on to become a pivotal figure in Italian lyric poetry, and to feature as an aloof aristocrat in Boccaccio's *Decameron*, something that Shakespeare was to purloin some two hundred years later, as a source for *All's Well that Ends Well*. Dante's association with Cavalcanti was to come back to haunt him when he was accused of using his official leverage to achieve Guido's release from internment a short time before his early death.

In 1300, at the age of 35, Dante was elected to the College of Priors and joined the ranks of the minor ruling elite in Florence, although the political situation he encountered was gradually deteriorating. This coincided with the Vieri Cherchi party's rise to power, through which Dante acted as an administrative ambassador to San Gimignano on behalf of the Tuscan Guelphs against the papal threat of Boniface VIII, the last of the medieval popes and a controversial figure whose contested election to the papacy was motivated by the achievement of pre-eminent aspirations toward a theocracy. The centenary year provided a symbolic opportunity to exercise a spiritual indulgence in the form of forgiveness for sins without punishment to those persistent souls who showed a willingness to repent in the basilicas of Saint Peter and Saint Paul. Dante was only one of tens of thousands who made the pilgrimage to Rome, marking a profound sense of renewal and moral commitment amidst social and political tensions.

By 1301 political violence and persecution between various factions in Florence had reached a critical point, and perhaps planted in Dante's mind the beginning of an indictment of Florence. After the battle of Campaldino, the two groups of the victorious Guelphs began infighting. Dante belonged to the White Faction but the Black Faction, led by Corso Donati, took control of Florence, and purges quickly turned to vendettas. Dante himself was wrongly accused of misusing public funds, which resulted in confiscation of his property, eventually propelling him toward exile from the city. He later, not unsurprisingly, singled out those responsible for financial abuse and the practice of extortionate moneylending, for a special corner of the Inferno where financial irresponsibility is equated with spiritual debt and sin, with souls having to undergo penance before they could enter Purgatory.

Dante's unjustified trial in January 1302 convicted him, along with others, of fomenting civil war in Pistoia with strong links to the opposing factions in Florence and other alliances in Tuscany by vague and unsubstantiated means. He was as a result banished from Florence for two years, and from public office for life. As an added aside he was casually sentenced to death in absentia, which seemingly followed other precedents of Florentine criminal procedure, whereby failing to appear in court was taken as a guilty plea. Thereafter, Dante refused to pay the fine, joining several hundred more affluent individuals who had fled to neighboring cities shortly in advance of similar sentences.

Around the time of Dante's exile in the early 14th century, Florence was one of the largest and wealthiest cities in Europe, seen by some as a successor to Rome, with a policy of large-scale reconstruction and expansion into neighboring areas through military activity. As a means of protection it was in the process of fragmenting itself by building new walls to encircle the medieval city and its citizens, new bridges across the Arno to assist urban growth and renewal, and an ambitious program of church building.

Dante left Florence in January 1302, leaving behind his family with virtually no patron or financial resources. What followed were periods of study and writing interrupted by episodes of political organization, with Florence as a constant focal point. His misgivings stemmed from what he saw as a

growing rivalry with Rome on the part of a group of cities, including Sienna, that were shaping to usurp the destiny of the empire. He went on to compare the refusal of Florence to recognize the empire according to God's will with his own dismissal from the city.

The political system in the wider region around Florence at the commencement of the 14th century was feudal, with large estates controlled by old established families with different political allegiances in Tuscany and Romagna in the upper Arno Valley. Many of those who had been exiled from Florence gathered together in Arezzo, and in 1302 Dante joined them. There he helped to form a coalition between different political factions, and acted as its registrar, perhaps out of a sense of the injustice he had himself suffered. The death of Pope Boniface in the following year had long-lasting consequences for the Catholic Church, marked by the removal of the papal court to Avignon, which attracted a number of exiles and a commensurate outflow of capital. Dante was later to reserve a special corner of the *Inferno* for the less than lamented pope.

After this Dante left for a diplomatic assignment in Verona, as a guest of Bartolomeo della Scala, and there he discovered one of the largest libraries in Europe, the Biblioteca Capitolare, which contained a large number of classical texts. In *De vulgari eloquentia*, a poetic essay probably written in 1304, 10 years after *Vita nuova,* he ruminates on a number of Latin texts acquired from the library. From these he created a conceptual framework for technical references set around disenchantment with the declining role and corruptive influences of the nobility while reflecting on his unaccustomed experience as an exile who had lost the sanctuary of his own city.

A commentary through "minor" texts compiled during Dante's studies in Verona, and his familiarity with the Veneto region, reads as an illustration of his literary invention, growing moral authority, and critical thinking that can be harmonized with the thought that went into the *Comedia. De vulgari eloquentia* is essentially an incomplete treatise on the essence of poetry and language that suggests a penetrating self-examination as a foundation for the *Inferno* in its ethical and political values. It brings together various branches of knowledge drawn from historical references, exploring the principles and attributes concerned with the foundation of language itself as an indispensable attribute of thought that satisfies the very basis of human relations. From this we might assume that Dante's use of the "illustrious" Italian vernacular in the *Comedia* is aimed at satisfying a poetic representation of linguistic expression, at a time of instability when there was a vacuum in political authority on the Italian peninsula. In this sense Dante sets out not merely to avail himself of a specific vernacular language but to construct and define its phonetic details to suit the requirements of his lyric poetry.

Meanwhile, factional strife continued in Florence throughout 1303, and the new pope Benedict XI appointed Cardinal Niccolò da Prato to reconcile the various warring parties through long and arduous negotiations in the Palazzo Mozzi between the Black and White contingents. However, after the cardinal left the city it was set ablaze, and around 1,400 houses, businesses, and palaces were destroyed. New military alliances were arranged and Florence was attacked, unsuccessfully, by troops from Arezzo, Pisa, Bologna, and Pistoia.

At this time Dante was beset by further financial difficulties induced by his exile, and began to

discreetly assemble information on those of his previous patrons who would later reappear through a vengeful designation of their theoretical fate in the *Inferno*. In 1304 his brother Francesco was obliged to negotiate a small loan, guaranteed by a surety bond, to enable Dante to settle his debts and to partially retire from the realm of political comradeship and intrigue by returning to a period of study and writing in Bologna.

It is not difficult to picture Dante's disillusionment with a country beset by feudal rivalry and civil conflict. Although Italy was on the cusp of the Renaissance, cultural and political integrity at the time were both greatly diminished. The feudal values of the nobility had become secondary to the corrupt excesses of the urban market place, while the Church was itself the cause of discord and divisions. The notion of rebuilding a unified and genteel society needed not merely peaceful coexistence, but a philosophical vision fed by a hunger for knowledge and a regulation of power based on a new foundation.

Dante meanwhile began work on the *Convivio*, which entailed an expressive array of his philosophical thoughts threading together discourses on learning, politics, and linguistics, written in the vernacular. In the first chapter he identifies two kinds of defects that impede humankind—one pertaining to the body and the other to the soul. He describes "knowledge" as the ultimate happiness that can be thwarted when the soul becomes the follower of vacuous pleasures, but also if there is no time for adequate contemplation. Dante intended that the various aspects would be presented in 14 ways set out in the same number of *canzoni*—medieval Italian lyrics with various forms of stanzas by means of allegories within the poem to convey hidden meanings below the surface. *Convivio* is expressive, in a similarly way to *De vulgari eloquentia*, and they can be seen as two complementary parts of the same argument. Both are derived from personal experience, explicit references, and frustrations. This encompasses the need for virtuous behavior governed by moral and social issues, hence the requirement for a common language that seeks unification from diversity, directed at a socially and linguistically divided country. Dante's vision was for a reconstituted vernacular, tempered by local references that could become the instrument for a new society. The two book drafts were left incomplete in 1306 when a new Guelph government came to power in Bologna, violently hostile to the Ghibelline faction, and supported by a number of other Tuscan cities.

In 1306 Clement V was elected Pope at the Perugia conclave, the first in a line of French occupants of the Holy See, based in Avignon. While remaining in France he intervened in an attempt to restore peace in Florence, appointing the powerful Cardinal Orsini to oversee this, but with little success. All roads back to Florence for Dante therefore seemed to be blocked, although he explored various ways of obtaining a pardon, possibly by way of his wife's family connections but mainly through adopting a questionable penitential position while emphasizing his honorable part in past military campaigns as part of the Guelph faction. In the meantime he settled in the heart of the Apennine Mountains in Lunigiana, sequestered by the noble Malaspina family of Giovagallo, who embodied almost precisely the values Dante admired and pursued in the *Comedia* that he commenced during this period. This cannot have ameliorated his revulsion at the state of gruesome affairs in Florence and a seeming lack of compassion that can only have been met by Dante with a sense of resignation. By 1308 he had established residence in Lucca, but soon after this all Florentine refugees were ordered to leave the city. It seems likely that Dante might well at this stage have travelled to Avignon, which, through the papal stronghold, had established itself as a vibrant cultural center with a strong intellectual focus.

It seems inevitable that an approach to the *Comedia* at this stage would have become reoriented toward a more potent and assertive intention than the original conception. It points to an insistent moral

Lucca, situated between the Apuan Alps and Monte Pisano, was colonized by the Romans in 180 BCE. In the 14th century Emperor Charles IV gave Lucca a charter of independence, and the Guinigi family constructed the tower with the seven holy oaks, one of the emblems of the city. After 1430 Lucca remained the only independent city in Tuscany until 1799. The first church, established in the 6th century was rebuilt as a cathedral in the early 12th century—the Duomo S. Martino.

direction combined with political ideals, and infused with autobiographical references that suggest the changing narrative events and their implications that he was witnessing. This inevitably incorporated both prophetic and retrospective gestures along with constant changes in position as Dante figuratively battled with shifting situations, autobiographical allusions and scarcely disguised innuendos, as a commentary on current affairs and with a stronger implication as to its message.

Dante completed *Inferno*, apart from small subsequent re-working during the final part of his residence in Lucca, but it is likely he was being prudent in delaying its publication until 1314 at a time when he was trying to regain residence in his home city and retain certain allegiances to the Guelph tradition, while distancing himself from the Ghibellines. The opening of the *Comedia* that offers a glimpse of the terror, disorientation, and even betrayal associated with political and moral disorder, provides a telling introduction:

> *Midway along the journey of our life*
> *I found myself in a dark wood*
> *for the straight path was lost*

In the meantime Dante continued with the written assembly of *Purgatorio* despite various distractions between 1308 and 1313. This represented an essential continuity toward a pro-imperial role of empire above that of the Church, which he associated with an assumption of both spiritual and temporal power to negative effect. Dante's commitment appears to have been inevitably reinforced by the experience of exile, exacting a new enthusiasm for the imperial cause while perversely condemning the reputation of those he considered to be the enemies of Florence. As a direct mark of respect, both *Inferno* and *Purgatorio* are set under the aegis of the Malaspina family, his past and timely patrons.

In 1309 Pope Clement V proclaimed Henry VII of Luxemburg as King of the Romans following a past practice honoring German monarchs, with a coronation date in Rome set well in advance for 1312—an event of great political significance and an opportunity to reassert long held rights over various urban jurisdictions. By long tradition he had to be crowned three times in different places—as King of Germany, Emperor in Rome, and King of Italy in Milan. This brought to a head a problematic issue of imperial rights over the northern and central regions of Italy. It also underscored the complicated sets of alliances and support mechanisms that prevailed at the time whereby both imperial and church power blocs tended to be in a constant state of fluctuation and polarization. However, Henry announced an intention to resolve discord between Guelphs and Ghibellines, and restore equilibrium between Church and empire. He could therefore only have been disconcerted with the unenthusiastic reception of his envoys to Florence in 1310, heralding his attempts at reconciliation. Meanwhile Dante attempted to intervene by using his political skills at written correspondence on behalf of groups who had been exiled from Florence, in a new spirit of unity.

Henry arrived in northern Italy in late 1310 making his way south through a number of cities where he appointed imperial representatives to preside over city councils. The main force behind this was the growing expansion of cities in northern and central Italy, where rural settlements and feudal estates had given way to urbanization and economic growth, with new forms of political control that diluted loyalty to the empire. In the face of this, Henry's imperial forces resorted to the imposition of harsh levies, so that the promise of impartiality began to vanish, and with it his previous prestige along with any capacity to assist the community of exiles. In supporting the emperor's rights to absolute sovereignty, Dante alienated himself further from Florence but at the same time pacified the palatine lords and nobles whose estates had been appropriated, and who continued to host him. In fact, Florence remained under threat and began to strengthen its internal unity, although it expressly excluded its exiled citizens.

By this time Dante was in Genoa in the company of other exiles, where Henry had taken residence in order to prepare for his expedition to Rome. The political arena was therefore in a state of some confusion, and Dante again recommenced his reflections on the role of empire and its providential ordination in the context of changing events. Henry left Genoa for Pisa in February 1312, and shortly afterwards he departed with his refreshed troops for Rome, only to find that the pope had bent to pressure from Philip IV of France and withdrawn his support for the coronation. In response he commenced an armed struggle, briefly occupying the Capitoline Hill before being crowned in the subdued atmosphere of Saint John Lateran without either a proclamation from the pope or recognition from Philip IV. In August 1312 he marched an already depleted army on Florence, laying siege to the town before continuing southwards to invade the Kingdom of Naples as part of an alliance with Frederick III of Aragon. To the despair of Dante, however, before the end of the month Henry fell sick and unexpectedly died near the city of Sienna, some said by poison administered by the Dominicans. His body was taken to Pisa where it was entombed in the cathedral, with Dante attending his funeral, aghast at the sudden collapse of his political vision.

While in Pisa, Dante completed a philosophical and theological treatise on the balance between secular and religious authority, *De Monarchia*, which suggests a benevolent mix of considerations. In this he supports the position of a single secular figurehead, conferred by Divine Providence, be it an emperor or a king with an explicit God-given authority to which the spiritual power of the Church must be subordinate in order to promote eternal unity, albeit with a satisfactory degree of reverence. It is above all a work filled with emotion and passion on the subject of political thought, rooted in the medieval culture of the time and the necessity of separating religion from government.

Dante wrote the majority of *Purgatorio* between 1309 and 1313 through various self-imposed distractions, including the completion of *De Monarchia* that reflects a picture of decline from the virtuous peaks of imperial Rome, and the moral crisis at the heart of the Catholic Church. It ends with Henry VII's increasingly desolate march through Italy and its barren destiny before the solitary pathway to salvation that might well have honed the sense of mission and fervor that created the framework for *Paradiso*.

By 1315, Florence was considerably weakened by enemy forces, and the city issued an order that at least technically revoked Dante's previous banishments. This was made subject to a small payment and a ceremonial acknowledgment in the Baptistery of San Giovanni in return for a restoration of civil rights. Dante refused the offer of an amnesty for what he considered to be a case of injustice in the first place, but determinedly suggested that he would be willing to return if suitably honored. His rebuff to the humiliating process of obtaining clemency and his rebuttal of the offer to appear before the judge led to a further death sentence issued in absentia on November 6th 1315.

This action effectively closed any further opportunity for a return by Dante to Florence, limiting his possible residential options to the potentially alien Ghibelline strongholds in Lombardy. The most favorable of these was Verona under the rule of Cangrande della Scala, the brother of Bartolomeo, a famed military commander around whom many of Henry VII's veterans had gathered. In 1316 Dante took up residence in Verona until 1318. It was here that he wrote the majority of *Paradiso*, some five years before his death. The fact that Dante was to spend much of his remaining years in Verona attests to his ambiguous relationship with Cangrande, which appears to have commenced by means of a letter from

La Loggia di Fra Giocondo and Cangrande's Palace with its characteristic Ghibelline battlements in the Piazza dei Signori, Verona. By the 15th century Verona had effectively lost its independence to Venice, and La Loggia was designed by Giovanni Giocondo, an architect and Dominican friar, to house its remaining government activities. The square is also known as the Piazza Dante with the statue commemorating Dante's stay in the city as an invited guest of the Scala family who made Verona capital of a regional state.In the 12th century Verona was ruled by Ezzelino da Romano, relegated to the Inferno by Dante. His sister Cunizza fared better, being elevated to Paradise.

Pisa's Cathedral and Baptistery were more elaborately sculptured than the religious buildings of Florence and might have been influenced by bold references to naval victories over the Saracens in the 11th century, where the spoils of war subsidized the construction of the cathedral itself. The statue of the Madonna at the apex might be said to sanctify the reputation of the militant Pisans as empire builders, while sensibly ensuring divine protection for their naval fleets. The Baptistery design is said to be a copy of the Holy Sepulcher in Jerusalem. This artful path to salvation cleverly insulated them from intimidation by the Papacy, while fully supporting an energetic process of empire building.

Pisa was an early Roman and then an Etruscan settlement located in the delta of the Serchio and Arno rivers. In the following centuries the city defended southern Italy against the Saracens. In 1091 it was granted an archiepiscopal seat but the city faced increasing competition from Florence, Lucca, and Genoa. The cathedral of Santa Maria Assunta forms the central focus of the Campo dei Miracoli. Building commenced in 1063, commemorating both the victory of the Pisan fleet over the Saracens and the treasure that provided for funding. Building continued for almost three hundred years and therefore embraced a range of prevailing motifs and architectural references. It contains the tomb of Henry VII who died while travelling from Pisa to Rome for his coronation. Dante attended the funeral, supporting Henry's resolve in attempting reconciliation between Church and Empire.

Construction of the Baptistery commenced in 1152 with much of the rich interior decoration later carried out by Nicola and Giovanni Pisano to forge a harmonious and contemplative space.

The Campanile, commonly referred to as the "leaning tower," was the third structure in the cathedral close. The first three levels were constructed by 1185, but subsidence due to unstable soil conditions was already apparent during the following century, and attempts were made to offset the deflection using columns of different height. A further balancing level was added with the tower's completion in 1350, but the angle of

inclination steadily increased over the following centuries despite periodic corrective initiatives. The basic structure is a cylindrical core wrapped in a colonnaded exterior, designed to exert a static function while also creating a stylistic relationship with the cathedral and baptistery. The present-day southward tilt of the tower is 17 feet from vertical but engineering work that commenced in 1988 has succeeded in correcting further increases in tilt through use of counterweights.

Dante supposedly offering a dedication of *Paradiso* in return for a place of refuge and material assistance. This clearly appealed to Cangrande's pro-imperial strengths as well as to his intellectual pretensions.

While the Malaspina family had provided the support for *Inferno* and *Purgatorio*, the final part of the *Comedia* was undertaken largely through the patronage of Cangrande. It is almost certainly a wish to support the position of the latter in his poor relationship with Pope John XXII that explains Dante's attack on the Pope who had supported an offensive against the most prominent Ghibelline lords, and the excommunication of Cangrande in 1318.

The poet's final place of residence from 1319 to 1321 was Ravenna, in the Emilia-Romagna region of Italy. This was through the benevolent auspices of Guido Novello da Polenta, the head of a prominent Guelph family who was schooled in the liberal arts, but well outside intransigent political allegiances. Here he continued to pursue issues of church reform and the necessity of imperial order, while completing *Paradiso*. His two sons and daughter joined him in Ravenna, and possibly also his wife Gemma, with some financial support from the benefices of two churches granted to his eldest son Pietro. In addition, he was surrounded by intellectual friends and colleagues to whom he taught poetry and literary composition. In *Paradiso* Dante fell back on the power of the poetic vernacular that he deemed would change the structure of society. Beatrice is induced to express a faith that "only through change will the real fruit come after the flower." Similarly only through the *Comedia* would Dante be materially restored to honor, and in the process help to transform Florence to a new age of glory, and with it a new supremacy for the cathedral of Santa Maria del Fiore.

Dante's last trip was to Venice as an emissary for Guido Novello, helping to expedite an agreement between the two cities using his skills as an orator and writer. He became sick on his return and died on September 13th 1321. *Paradiso* was completed before his death but had not been published. While Guido Novello had promised to erect an impressive epitaph in Ravenna, a near relative seized power while he was in Bologna, and the proposed grand tomb was never constructed. Ultimately, Dante's destiny was shaped by the strength of his poetry. The *Comedia* would, within several years, come to be the most important work of medieval literature, and is considered to represent the beginning of Renaissance humanism.

The narrative poem was termed *La Comedia*, not for any humorous content but for its healing vision written in the vernacular Italian rather than the scholarly Latin. The poem is rooted in a rhapsodic spiritual transmission of belief, imagination, and emotion that embraces the entire universe, expressed in a dialect that was to eventually form the prime language of Italy. The "divine" adjective was added some 200 years later as an apparent reflection of its metaphysical Godliness, but was also referred to as such by Dante's near contemporary, Giovanni Boccaccio, in his *Life of Dante* some 40 years after his death. It serves to depict a transition from one era to another.

The Accademia della Cursia, founded in Florence in 1583 has as its motto a poem by Petrarch, himself a native of Arezzo, which literally means, "She picks the loveliest flowers." Its proclaimed purpose is to guard the integrity of the popular vernacular language of Tuscany against the predominant but often diluted use of Latin for literary purposes. Dante along with Petrarch are credited with giving the expressive Tuscan language literary status, in particular Dante's treatise *De vulgari eloquentia* together with the *Divina Commedia* and Petrarch's *Canzoniere*. In 1612 the Accademia published the *Vocabulario*, the first dictionary of the Italian language, reinforcing the language of Dante.

ENCOUNTERS·OF THE·TURBULENT·KIND

A man content to go to heaven alone will never go to heaven.
ANICIUS MANLIUS SEVERINUS BOETHIUS 524 CE

ANTE'S GRAPHIC DEPICTION of Florence and his philosophical association of the city with Hell was, in all probability, signaled by the consequences of physical destruction caused by competition between rival factions. Two of the animals artfully introduced into the *Comedia* by Dante as successfully constraining his escape from Hell, were the lion of Florence, symbolic of the city's power, and the wolf, which served as the symbol of papal strength. One of the worst sins attributed to Florence was that of usury, the principal source of the city's commercial success. Florence was not alone in its less than positive depiction in the *Inferno, Purgatory,* and *Paradise*—other Tuscan cities such as Sienna and Pisa were also skewered by Dante for their evidently notorious characteristics including hypocrisy, corruption, falsification, treachery, and theft. If *Paradise* denotes the questionable circumference of the divine universe, then in the *Comedia* Rome is positioned as its earthly center and celestial city, ruled by God.

An important influence was undoubtedly Anicius Boethius, born around the end of the Roman Empire in 477 CE. Boethius was a senator and theologian who translated the writings of the early classical philosophers including Aristotle. His most influential work was *The Consolation of Philosophy*, which examined the philosophical issues of virtue, evil, and universal realities. This had a substantial influence on medieval Christian thought, as a dialogue in prose and verse that conjured up a cosmic order created by a providential God at the center of the universe. Through his equation of providence with fate he concluded that "evil" as a reality could not be forgiven, and would no doubt have sided with Dante in consigning evil-doers to the *Inferno*.

The *Comedia* does not hold back on its condemnation of the church for its pursuit of power, money, and possessions rather than spirituality, although in *Purgatory* Dante allows for the necessity of religious ritual, set among the angels. However, he also comments that the church must be saved from corruption in contrast to the self-denial and austerity of the early saints. In reality both church and empire were malfunctioning with both sides stepping well outside their respective jurisdictions within the earthly paradise advocated by Dante. Intrusion by the church in state affairs and secular politics on the basis of canon law and papal supremacy, sometimes with dire consequences, was widely opposed by the autonomous individual states themselves. Pope Boniface VIII came to personify this ambiguous position, and in fact as a supporter of the Guelph party had a hand in Dante's own exile. Even while Boniface lived there were questions raised as to his legitimate claim to the papal throne, while posthumously he was accused of various malevolent sins and heresies. Succeeding popes became disassociated with Rome, and later from Avignon, which became heavily influenced by the French monarchy. Dante encapsulates their corruption by including popes and cardinals among the souls that are condemned to Hell as being in opposition to God's will, and is a pertinent reminder to us that poets and writers can, when necessary, adequately avenge themselves by means of metaphysical allusions and analogies.

The geometrical topology with its interrelated parts between a Satanic depth and a heavenly stratosphere, blissfully ignoring the realities of finite space, is a clever sleight of hand that allows Dante to describe a higher analogue of a sphere, which identifies three physical dimensions from a particular point in space.

An imaginative notion of the three states of *Hell*, *Purgatory*, and *Paradise* holds within it an assumption that human souls are immortal, which in turn implies the offer of threat and reward but also an elusive lack of beginning or end. Dante positions Hell and Purgatory as parts of the terrestrial sphere whereas Paradise is a heavenly realm. In this Dante accepts the Ptolemaic treatise that posits an immobile Earth as the center of the universe while the nine concentric heavens revolve around it. The tenth heaven is the Empyrean, which overlooks the entire ensemble—the seat of God, and the angelic host. An infinity of steps provide a functional arrangement for the blessed to contemplate God.

A continually contested area between the state and the church was the concept of original sin, which justified papal claims to universal jurisdiction over property and possessions, not merely the stewardship of body and soul. This might have emanated from Saint Peter's claim to having been handed the keys to the Kingdom of Heaven. Misuse of the church's use of excommunication as a political device is challenged in both *Purgatory* and *Paradise*, as flouting the purpose of repentance. Dante conjures up the church as a monstrous body, shackled through its own misjudgments, where the responsible role of the "shepherd" toward its flock is transfigured into a wolf that has the very opposite of intentions, and must be destroyed in order to purify itself.

During the 13th century, the empyrean heaven was widely accepted as the abode of God amidst an accompanying audience of angelic devotees. As a divine entity it was considered as being incorruptible because of its supposed purity, invisibility, and immobility and was therefore a suitable state for the blessed. It was also incapable of demonstrating a rational proof of existence although most theologians were inclined to ignore this.

Churchmen who are encountered in *Paradise*, notably Thomas Aquinas, are without exception those who respected the orthodox notion of a secular state. Emperors who betrayed the empire are equated in *Hell* with those who betrayed Christ. This is deemed to represent the impending state of society when members act against the common good, while *Purgatory* involves a transition from this extreme to *Paradise*, which is the ideal form of society. Dante purports to remind us that through all manner of means, earthly cities are destroyed from within through sins against universal benefactors, but that knowledge of evil is necessary for humankind to be offered an opportunity to embrace a new society. Hell is depicted as a metaphor for the consequences of moral abdication; Purgatory as a merciful opportunity to repent and atone for serious sins and to be satisfactorily purged; while Paradise becomes a heavenly realm suitably fortified against evil, and a culmination of a journey to the presence of God.

Virgil guides Dante through the Inferno, which forms the formidable destination for those who have committed specific sins during their lifetime, and for which they are condemned to eternal damnation.

Copy of Sandro Botticelli's Cone of Hell drawing for the Divine comedy, 1480.

The Mount of Purgatory

The Earthly Paradise

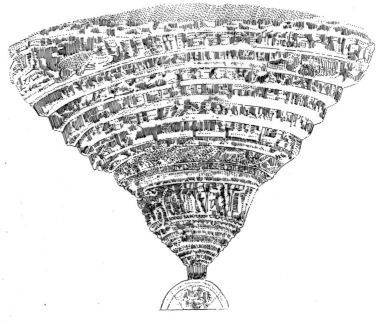

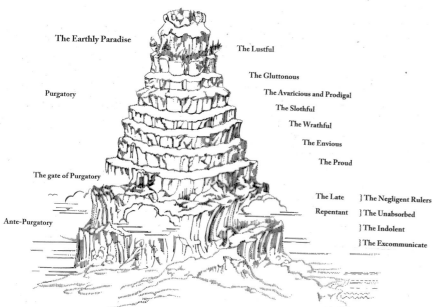

The Earthly Paradise

Purgatory

The gate of Purgatory

Ante-Purgatory

The Lustful

The Gluttonous

The Avaricious and Prodigal

The Slothful

The Wrathful

The Envious

The Proud

The Late Repentant
} The Negligent Rulers
} The Unabsorbed
} The Indolent
} The Excommunicate

THE EARTHLY PARADISE

Upper Purgatory	Disordered Love of God	Excessive Love of Secondary God	Cornice 7 – The Lustful
			Cornice 6 – The Gluttonous
			Cornice 5 – The Covetous
Middle Purgatory		Love Defective	Cornice 4 – The Slothful
Lower Purgatory	Love of Neighbours' Harm (Love Perverted)		Cornice 3 – The Wrathful
			Cornice 2 – The Envious
			Cornice 1 – The Proud
Peter's Gate	Steps	3 Satisfaction	
		2 Competition	
		1 Confession	
Ante-Purgatory	Salvation in articulo mortis	Terrace 2	The Late Repentance
			(a) The Indolent
			(b) The Unshriven
			(c) The Pre-occupied
		Terrace 1	The Excommunicate

MOUNT PURGATORY

60

He then escorts Dante on the tortuous path up Mount Purgatory through seven levels of spiritual enlightenment, where he must learn to reject the earthly realm for the heavenly one before proceeding further.

Beatrice escorts Dante along the route to *Paradiso*, encountering luminaries noted for intellect, faith, justice, and love. The journey ends with a representation of God in the form of the Holy Trinity and the attainment of spiritual fulfillment. Paradise itself is based on the four cardinal virtues of prudence, justice, temperance, and fortitude, and the three theological virtues of faith, hope, and charity. The Empyrean, which represents the highest part of Heaven, is derived from the Latin *empyreus* or firmament, but in Christian literature it stands for the source of pure light and creation.

Hell

Dante's vision of suffering, described in 34 cantos, is seen as an inferno waiting to ensnare people of power who have abused their responsibilities. While this might seem a still common dilemma in the contemporary community, Dante measures this against the insidious consequences to society and its impact on social order. The *Inferno* has been labeled as an algebra of retribution through which the degrees of torment tend to be symbolic of the sins by which the miscreants are condemned. As Virgil is given to state, "piety lives only when pity is quite dead." The moral dimension of order is extended to the rules of sexual behavior, which are stated as being necessary only to preserve the forms of family on which larger units of society are based. Sins for which Dante feels no pity might range from the potentially disruptive such as corruption and treachery, to those of a more personal nature such as lust, hypocrisy, and self-indulgence that inevitably extend their hostile impacts to a wider community. One such unfortunate who was wrathfully relegated to the Inferno in Canto VIII was Filippo Argent, who according to Boccaccio was a member of the aristocratic Adimari family who quarreled with Dante and confiscated his property after his expulsion from Florence.

One might argue as to the pecking order of the most serious sins, and Dante delves into considerable detail in terms of subdivision into sinful categories that emphasize various distinctions along with what are deemed to be appropriate degrees of punishment. This is extended by their identification with actual places including the classical cities of history such as Troy and Thebes that were infamous for their self-destructive tendencies.

The nine circles of Hell comprise Unbaptized Pagans, Lust, Gluttony, Greed, Anger, Heresy, Violence, Fraud, and Treachery, which Dante considers to be the most destructive to the achievement of a principled and virtuous society. Such an approach allows the author to cite and snare a good many identifiable self-indulgent characters invoked from both the past and his contemporary context representing both political and religious backgrounds, who form the allegorical or symbolic subjects of his revelations. The exiled poet with his undoubted resentments conjures up the support of the notably moral and exemplary figure of Virgil who, as a poet himself, guides Dante's path through the innermost parts of *Hell* and *Purgatory*. In this he is identified as having a similar mission to Aeneas, the Trojan hero from Greek mythology and Homer's *Iliad*, in his journey to the "otherworld." This means an acknowledgment of God's existence and divine plan, which had to preclude the inclusion of virtuous philosophers, writers, and scientists of an atheist disposition. Fraud is the most complex of the circles with its villains deemed to be "tyrants" who pervert the political process by prioritizing their own objectives over the public good and the health of public life. The final circle sets out four categories of betrayal—of family, nation, guest, and benefactor, all of which a community is said to rely on for its stability. Dante

Inferno III: 9–21
We are come to the place where I told thee thou shouldst see the wretched people who have lost the good of the intellect. And placing his hand on mine, he led me into the things that are hidden.

In medieval theology, Hell was a place of despair, turmoil, and wretchedness as depicted by Dante from the perspective of Christian idealism. The cosmographical notion is that Earth takes the form of a sphere at the center of the solar system. Below its surface the interior of Hell is a large pit in the shape of an inverted cone with its apex at the earth's center. The nine circles of Hell correspond to the seriousness of sins committed by the damned souls, in the lowest of which is Satan. Eternal punishment is envisaged by Dante in terms of the prevailing Church doctrine that Hell represents a series of inflictions of constant intensity.

Dante arrives at the edge of dark woodland and is forced to retreat by an immediate confrontation with three wild beasts, representing an impediment to Dante's path to righteousness. Virgil appears to assist him, following a route through a high archway with the inscription:

Through me you pass into the city of woe
Through me you pass into eternal pain

The beginning of Upper Hell lies alongside the black River Acheron where Charon, a ferryman, transfers the lost souls to the First Circle of Hell where primary punishment is in loss of Hope. It includes classical poets and philosophers who are committed to punishment as they lived before the first Christian God, including Virgil himself. Steps lead to the second circle where punishment is reserved for the Lustful, and farther down circles devoted to the gluttonous, the hoarders and spendthrifts, and the wrathful. Across the River Styx are the walls of the City of Dis containing eternal fire, guarded by demons, and marking the commencement of Lower Hell. Between the fifth and sixth circles is the realm of bureaucracy devoted to complex tasks that help no one.

Circle six is devoted to arch-heretics of every sect, leading to a descent to the seventh circle, divided into three wings for those condemned for brutality or bestiality, self-harm, and violence against God and Nature. The River Phlegethon flows through the rings and into the Eighth Circle for those condemned of fraud and malice, laid out in a sequence of 10 ditches. Circle Nine is divided into four regions, based on different kinds of treaties.

To exit Hell it is necessary to climb down the body of Lucifer, before reaching the distant opening onto the shore of Mount Purgatory.

The bestiary formed a popular illustrative tradition in the Middle Ages during the late twelfth to the 14th century, and it is not too far-fetched to think that the selective imagery of Dante's Inferno would convey a selection of the more bizarre and threatening beasts to a superstitious and gullible public. Some were conceived from actuality and many from fable and imagination. Ferocious and untamable monsters have always been a fount of wonder and fear, and what could be more fitting than to apply their bestial threats to those relegated to the hell of eternal fear and punishment.

The Romans brought exotic beasts back to Italy, and 13th-century Florence continued to exhibit cages of up to 20 lions or leopards as a symbol of communal power. The bestiary was designed to symbolize situations associated with the Christian world, in particular its perilous vices associated with the human condition, with beasts displaying contrasting powers of behavior, both threatening and benign. The bestiary did not stop at land animals, but sea creatures, birds, and serpents of various imaginative interpretations and dimensions, with some specimens improbably sharing an entire range of characteristics. In classical literature, mythical beasts were attested as being derived from different sources, and illuminated as a visual narrative to accompany liturgical texts that were translated into various languages. The manticore from ancient Greece had the head of a human, body of a lion, and tail of a scorpion, and was well known in European medieval art. Some illustrations were simply based on exaggerated descriptions of wild animals, and their improbable compositional features such as the centaur—a half-human and half-horse creature—or the griffin—an unlikely cross between a lion and an eagle. These images serve to remind us of our less than accurate powers of observation, or, alternatively, of the poetic liberties taken by the artist. Depictions of real beasts were often given the same coverage as the unicorn, dragon, and phoenix that still persist into modern renderings, and ascribe to animals ferocious features to match the required purpose.

purports to remind us that through all manner of means, our earthly cities are destroyed from within through sins against universal benefactors, but that knowledge of evil is necessary for humankind to be offered an opportunity to transcend to a new level.

For the souls who have abused all the known sins set out in the Circles of Hell that make civilized life impossible, an appropriate and in many cases a severe level of justice prevails.

Purgatory

Dante ambiguously positions *Purgatory* on an earthly island, that might easily be available to the living as well as deceased souls. These survive in a state of transition where the relationship between good and evil is finely balanced. Souls must wait for a necessary period outside *Purgatory* until admittance is granted according to their strength of belief. This improbable journey draws on the Old Testament exodus of Israelites to the Promised Land. Access is forbidden to those who fail to approach it with all due humility, and Dante focuses on historical examples of both vice and virtue while at the same time including himself as part of the process. This holds out the tantalizing but perhaps optimistic possibility that with a resolution of tension between church and state, an earthy paradise could be achieved, going as far as supporting the sacrament of confession. Italy itself is portrayed as a riderless horse denoting an emperor who has lost the struggle for control. The sixth Canto of Purgatory includes the statement, "when an emperor does not prevail, tyrants abound." The apparent point is that even in situations where there is a seething dimension of opposing forces, in a properly functioning society virtue brings its own reward in which all should gain benefit. In order to overcome the difficulties involved, there must be mutual support and guidance through a social community which becomes in effect one large family.

Service to society is the subject of the preliminary "ledges," just as the worst sins are those directed against others, and involve pride, envy, and wrath. Pride in particular is identified as the most basic human characteristic, but one where any divine advantage should be placed responsibly at the service of humankind with due humility. As an allegory, the cities of Florence and Siena, which could have turned their common interests to a positive outcome, instead turn to hostility through pride and envy which turns into the most blatant form of factionalism. In physical terms it possibly marked the feudal trend for defensive towers that sparked a comparison between Florence, San Gimignano, and other north-Italian cities that reflected a continuing and assertive power struggle between aristocratic families. In fact certain

PURGATORIO II: 10–81
Mars burns red through the thick mists low in the west over the ocean floor, such appeared to me a celestial pilot in the shape of an angel. Look how she scorns all human instruments and desires nothing other than her wings, between shores so distant.

Dante's Purgatory is set in a mountainous island at the antipodes of Jerusalem. It is guarded by angelic gatekeepers stationed on all the terraces. On its lower sloped terraces are the souls whose penitence is in abeyance as a temporal punishment to expiate one or all of the seven deadly sins on Earth. Dante ascends the terraces with Virgil as a guide. On the summit of the mountain is the Earthly Paradise—a lush Garden of Eden, from which the purged souls ascend to Heaven. Those expiating their sins in Purgatory do not eat or drink, and like those condemned to Hell heal from any wound or injury simply in order to recommence the process.

Exiting from Hell, souls emerge on a seashore under a sky lit by stars according to the four cardinal virtues of Prudence, Temperance, Fortitude, and Justice—to guide arrivals in the correct direction. As dawn rises an angel approaches on a boat propelled by its outstretched wings to transfer them to the steep terraces of Mount Purgatory.

After emerging from the seven terraces the mystic procession ascends from the Earthly Paradise at which point Virgil departs to be replaced by Beatrice who baptizes Dante in a stream before moving on to the music of an angelic choir. Dante wakes and Beatrice asks him to write of what has been revealed to him on his journeys when he returns to Earth.

cities are identified by the names of beasts that are said to reflect the nature of their inhabitants. Even the style of dress is used as a sign of society's corruption, seemingly in reference to a 14th-century decree passed in Florence limiting its extravagance and ostentation. The precise definition of virtue given by Dante is somewhat open-ended, in that condemnation for a lack of virtue at one level, for example anger or rage, might be excused at another because of a change in context or direction.

The ledge of avarice as a major source of corruption is mainly reserved for the clergy as being harmful to the balance of power. If not properly administrated with the dignity of its origins, it is stated that, "the papacy can prove the gravest danger to the soul, as a summit of evil, misery, and shame."

Poets, as might be expected, are given a high profile in *Purgatory*, and help to extend this message to humankind, stirring them to act accordingly. Dante, as a poet and a social and political commentator, passes relatively unscathed through the circle. The role of the visual arts and architecture also convey an expression of unity and harmony as symbols of attainment. The guardians, Calo and Matela, as selfless figures from history, represent respectively the moral and active life. Dante selects the Roman poet Statius to assist with his transition to *Paradise* at the expense of Virgil, both because the former arguably intuited one God but also because of his epic stature in the realm of Latin literature with regard to significant social and cultural issues. Dante also posits language itself as a unifying force, perhaps envisaging his future exalted status as the progenitor of a new dialect that is clearly understandable to all Italians.

The formidable and legendary figure of Matelda is generally identified as the virtuous Countess of Tuscany, known both for her philanthropy and endowments to the church, along with her struggle against corruption within it. She is designated to fortify Dante's procedure towards a state of salvation where Beatrice takes over the mantle of reforming him on his return to the earthly Paradise. This is played out amidst the symbolic instruments of church and state, and the restoration of their correct functions. By admitting to his own sins, Dante necessarily accepts responsibility in order to facilitate his role in the providential process.

Paradise

Dante identifies two rivers in the Earthly Paradise, the first of which erases the memory of sins committed, and the second that restores the memory of virtuous deeds. He finalizes his journey with a restored spirit and a realization of his divine mission. However, a wall of flames forms a formidable barrier to the Earthly Paradise, and must be passed in order to enter the Garden of Eden as a condition of eventual liberation from purgatorial containment.

The admission to Paradise encapsulates the culmination of a process that has led to a universal society where souls prioritize the common good, in effect putting "public" above "private" interests and in this way achieving a heavenly state of cooperation and harmony in a realm beyond physical existence. The blessed who

Paradise XXVIII: 16–45
I saw a point which radiated a light so keen that the eye on which it burns must shut, so piercing is its power. ... And so to the eighth and ninth; and each one moved more slowly as it was more removed from the first, and that one had the clearest flame from which the pure spark was least distant. ... My Lady, who beheld me perplexed and anxious, said: "From that point doth hang heaven and all nature. Look on that circle which is closest to it, and know that its motion is so swift because of the burning love by which it is driven.

In the final part of the Divine Comedy, Dante leaves the Earth and enters the abode of God, encountering a realm of just rulers and holy saints. The 10 Heavens are situated outward from the stationary Earth, and encompass the seven Heavenly bodies, each in its own sphere of Heaven. Beyond them is the Sphere of the Fixed Stars, the Primum Mobile, and beyond the material spheres to the Empyrean. These are arranged in an order based on their spiritual significance. Dante and Beatrice pass through the successive heavens where the celestial souls of the blessed appear to them.

The order of ascent is first to the Heaven of the Moon where Beatrice explains that all are equal in Heaven and therefore not contained in each sphere, reflecting the free will of God. They rise progressively through the heavens of Mercury, Venus, the Sun, Mats, Jupiter, and Saturn where Dante is confronted by a golden ladder, filled by those who have devoted themselves to contemplation and temperance. Gazing down on Earth, the Sun, and the planets, Dante realizes how paltry the Earth appears, before arriving at the Heavenly Gates.

On arrival Dante is presented with a procession proclaiming the "Triumph of Christ," inspiring Dante to pray. He is examined afterward by the three saints, St. Peter, St. James, and St. John, and is later joined by Adam. Dante and Beatrice then rise to the Primum Mobile surrounded by nine concentric rings of fire representing the Angelic Orders that surround God, making way for their ascent to the Empyrean, outside all externalities. "Here your eyes shall see the twofold chivalry of Paradise," says Beatrice who then ascents to her throne in the third circle, while Saint Bernard points out her future inaccessibility to Dante. After this the Light of God shines down, inducing an ultimate salvation before the poet's return to earth.

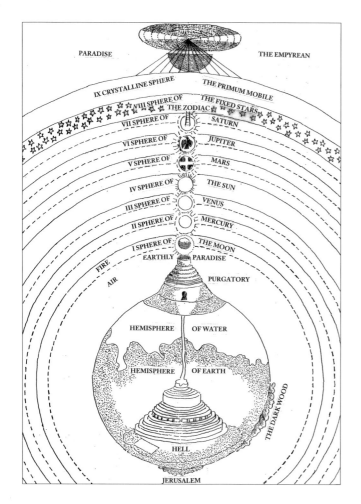

attain Paradise are categorized according to their level of contentment, realized through a pursuit of knowledge, beauty, and science, reflecting an arduous journey from doubt to faith. Its parameters are said to be informed by God and fill the universe, imbuing it with light as opposed to what was seen as the vast emptiness and darkness of space associated with *Hell*. The metaphysical notion of love that moves the sun and the stars reflects Dante's customary belief that astronomy was related to astrology. For this there had to be a pooling of abilities set out in the four preliminary "heavens"—the Moon, Mercury, Venus, and the Sun, according to capacity, rank, talents, and motivation. In this way the actions of humans are taken to equate with the precarious motion of the heavens. Above these in the heavenly hierarchy are Jupiter—the home of emperors and kings—and Saturn, the home of selfless religious leaders who have all but abandoned the world to serve God. Beyond this, in the outer void of space, Dante casts an entire community of religious figures in the form of ascetics, teachers, scholars, followers of a monastic life, and others, all far removed from the secular state and seeking reform against corruption.

Upright representatives of secular authority and martyrs are clustered within the relatively unstructured heavenly realms of Mars and Jupiter, although they also make short guest appearances in Mercury and Venus. Therefore, the notion of a broadly harmonious society is constituted through virtuous groups according to their capacities for motivation. By contrast the first group associated with the Moon passively accept their limitations but with a conviction that never wavers, possibly reflecting the fact that in medieval times the Moon was the most intriguing of all celestial bodies with its waxing and waning associated with inconstancy; the second group associated with Mercury are happy to accept an assigned role, but work to achieve success and honor within a particular role associated with unification and order; the third group are inspired by the forceful impulse of love and charity, and directed toward society as a means of solidifying its compassionate characteristics. The higher places are associated with leaders of various kinds, dedicated to betterment of the community. The Sun is associated with educators; Mars with warriors; Saturn with particularly astute spiritual guides; while the Sun represents an international range of notable scholars who are said to stimulate rather than compete with each other for the enrichment of human knowledge.

The point to be made here is that conflicting ideas can be used to positive effect if knowledge and understanding are sufficiently stimulated. This is perpetuated by two "circles" of thought and teaching, compared by Dante to grindstones that move in tandem to generate the required discharge. One circle orchestrated by Saint Thomas Aquinas, canonized in 1323, contains theological intellectuals including King Solomon, while the second introduced by his contemporary, Saint Bonaventure, is made up of more mystical and prophetic thinkers. Together they put thought and wisdom at the service of society but also impose an important sense of order that promotes the cause of empire.

Dante's melancholic but obsessive distinction between the destinies of Rome and Florence, with the former placed at the center of *Paradise*, is underscored by his insistence that Florence had attempted to usurp the destiny of the empire by entering into the chaos of civil war, and would therefore always suffer from the sins of pride and sedition. His bitterness, stemming from exile, is vented in Canto XVII. This is understandably the central issue of the poem, with a message that, as stated by Beatrice, Paradise is not an abstract vision but one that reflects God's virtues in society, and that those who abuse scripture for their own purposes must be condemned. The notion that crusades, whose righteous mission is to protect a God-given government against infidels intent on destroying it, might then lead to a state where a divine justice will prevail for all. This is of course dependent on the emergence of an ideal society in all its forms.

It might be said that in practice the achievement of a state of grace through good works alone has since proven rather elusive, precisely because of recognized human fallibility in the face of ambitions for power and wealth, and the necessary moral compromises involved. The monastery, even with its sense of order, discipline, and penance cannot be a microcosm of society, but only an autonomous community for its members who must in general accord with the dominant doctrine. In certain situations it might also be argued that pagan rulers have possibly served the cause of divine justice just as well as most Christian monarchs and a large number of elected governments who have been known to casually abuse it. We cannot entirely pin our hopes of a new secular order on those devout souls who renounce themselves from the worldly life in order to devote themselves to contemplation and prayer. Dante's notion of the ideal church representative is one with no ambitions for power or wealth, but with a will to fight inequality and corruption, together with a harmonious conception of the distinction between church and state. The analogy of a "garden" is seen as symbolic of both the fellowship of human society with its gathering together of individual blooms, possibly equating this with "Firenze" meaning flower, but with different qualities and strengths that produce a harmonious whole according to the way in which it is cultivated by individuals who form the basis of society.

There is a compelling argument that as numbers can be assigned to letters, words can take on a divine meaning and, as argued by Pythagoras, they can also assume a predictive form. The number three is, not by coincidence, the number of perfection or "completion" and is taken as God's attributes: omniscience, omnipresence, and omnipotence (in Dante's Latin *omnetrium perfectum*). It is also the smallest number needed to create a pattern. The basic *terza rima* structure of the *Comedia* is set out in three-line stanzas where the first and third lines rhyme, while the second line is rhymed with the first and second sentences of the following stanza. There are 33 cantos in each book, and the trinity is said to hold a divine meaning possibly reflecting Hell, Purgatory, and Paradise, or the Holy Trinity harmony of Father, Son, and Holy Spirit. "Three" is also in ancient cultures said to be the symbol of the soul. Three animals also symbolize the three sins—the Panther for misplaced power, the Lion for ambition, and the female wolf for greed.

Dante remained faithful to the number nine, giving it a recurring symbolic value built around narrative sequences. At the commencement of *La Comedia* nine Muses are on hand to help the process of artistic creation reflecting the nine daughters of the Greek god Zeus. Dante arranges his reception of angels in nine orders in relation to his nine planetary spheres or heavens. The first third represented by the Moon, Mercury, and Venus is devoted to actions that serve others; the second represented by the Sun, Mars, and Jupiter is directed to teaching others; and the final three of Saturn, the Fixed Stars, and the Primum Mobile, as the final stage beyond space and time into infinity, which represents the ultimate mediation between God and Humanity. This corresponds with the nine orders of life relating to the three tiers devoted to the monastic, the clerical and laymen that stretch from the contemplative to the active, with love as the overall binding element for society as a whole. It is given a further significant meaning through nine levels of Hell and nine spheres of Heaven. In *La Vita Nuova* dedicated to a probably unsuspecting Beatrice, he recalls meeting her when they were both nine years old, seeing her again nine years later and being greeted at the ninth hour of the day before her death in 1290. The *Comedia* then becomes a deification of her memory.

Dante discloses both the history and philosophy of antiquity, together with the relationship of the individual to a divine universe and the dynamic nature of the Cosmos. The poet might well have summoned up fanciful imaginary forces, but might just as equally have metaphorically tapped into a stream of consciousness within a cosmos that appeared to be divinely ordained. If the universe creates and sustains life then we might expect it to accommodate its aftermath in some form or other, on the basis that a universe, which is conscious, is one that is alive. Dante's *Comedia* is the most widely translated book after the Bible, possibly because of its chary and psychologically loaded relationship with an afterlife in limbo that has also been woven into or subtly referenced in countless works of literature from Chaucer to Alexander Solzhenitsyn, Primo Levi, and Umberto Eco. The *Inferno* relates to the extremes of horror that in vivid terms mirrors victims of ethnic cleansing, while Purgatory is the supposed test of faith in resolving divisions prior to a fanciful but cautious redemption in Paradise.

It took more than 700 years for the city of Florence to issue a redemption for Dante himself in the form of a pardon, and to confer on him and his heirs the city's highest honor *Il Fiorino D'oro*, belatedly erasing the last remnants of hostility between the city and the poet. His tomb rests in the chapel of St. Francesco, in Ravenna.

Dante's bold and imaginative powers of expression encouraged an equally inspired visualization by sympathetic artistic followers from Michelangelo and Botticelli to William Blake. For example, Michelangelo's drawing of Ganymede, an emblem of mysticism, is influenced by the description of Purgatory. It has also inspired various authors such as James Joyce, Ezra Pound, and T. S. Eliot. The belief system that lay behind the *Comedia* may have long passed, but what remains is the significance and the search.

Statue of Dante situated adjacent to the Cathedral of Santa Maria del Fiore, Florence.

A DANTE ALIGHIERI
L'ITALIA
M·DCCC·LXV

THE·ROOTS·OF CCSMIC·OBSERVATION

For there is no kind of material, no body, and no thing that can be produced or conceived of, which is not made up of elementary particles.
VITRUVIUS, *De arquitectura*, Bk. II, Ch. I

HE *COMEDIA* with its integral allusion to a largely imaginary Cosmos, was compiled at the cusp of the medieval and early Renaissance periods. This permeates the direction of the poem, reflecting ancient astronomical sources that Dante might well have had available to him, dating from antiquity. In particular they were tempered by Aristotelian thought that represented the prevailing belief system.

The ancient obsession with astronomy and its accompanying mythology was probably based on three factors: first, the comfortable association between the heavenly realm and eternal life; second, a practical concern for the perceived implications of planetary movement on climatic and seasonal cycles connected to everyday survival; and third, a link between astronomy and astrology in terms of a predictive explanation and justification of regular and observable events. Philosophers were challenged to apply theories that appeared to satisfy these concerns, and at their center was the perplexing conundrum of planetary motion. With no apparent reason why earth should not be at an ideal central position in relation to the observed heavens, a circular orbit of the Sun at a constant velocity seemed to provide a satisfactory and elegant explanation forcefully justified by philosophers such as Aristotle. Certain inconsistencies could be put aside, or explained through the scientific unworldliness of the times, even as it inadvertently missed the deeper reality. What must have seemed like convincing explanations at the time survived more or less intact until the early Renaissance some 2,000 years later.

To early astronomers who were intent on establishing a justifiable basis for religious and political rituals it was necessary to accumulate detailed inventories for the timing of astronomical events, and the various positions of the sun according to the regular cycles which seemed to be logically associated with the daily rotation of the earth. Formulating any deeper reality with precision was obscured by a need to explain phenomena in a way that simply made sense with what was observed and experienced.

Early Greek philosophers heralded geometry as an exercise in logic. In the 6th century BCE, the Greek mathematician Pythagoras sought out and consolidated ancient Babylonian calculations to establish a famous relationship between numbers, shapes, and sizes that represented the essence of a harmonious universe. Pythagoras and other Greek mathematicians heralded geometry as an exercise in logic. It was in fact architectural interpretation that stretched this out into three-dimensional beauty based on natural harmony. Through this, mathematical thought became a cornerstone of philosophy but also the root of three-dimensional beauty that enabled Pythagoras to theorize that the world was determined according to strict rules. The Nobel Lauriat Frank Wilczek reminds us that it was also Pythagoras who revealed a

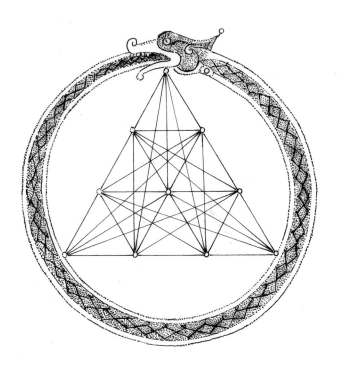

hidden and surprising unity between mind and matter, with numbers as the "linking thread." Pythagoras is also credited with the discovery of the remarkable relationship between arithmetical ratios and musical intervals described by Plato as "the music of the spheres" and proof of an underlying cosmic harmony. This brought together a synthesis of astronomical observation, mathematical ratios, and geometry, governed by the numerical ratios of the musical scale and the structure of the octave. The *musica mundane* was based on the cycle of planets that were thought to exert an underlying rhythm closely associated with that of the human body, and therefore to influence all aspects of life.

Identifying the essential building blocks of matter was an integral part of ancient-Greek philosophical debate. Anaximander, a pre-Socratic scholar from Ionia, born in 585 BCE, influenced many of the early Greek philosophers. He is considered to be the scientific originator of cosmology from which he postulated, with remarkable prescience, that the origin of the universe and the position of all heavenly bodies was the result of a primordial event equivalent to a gigantic explosion. To explain the existence of elementary forces and unification of all opposite constituents, for example fire and water, he conceived a substance called "apeiron"—a primordial organism essential to existence from which everything is derived and to which dying things are returned, although without any preconception of elementary particles. Linked with this was a belief in the fundamental unity of all thing and events. Anaximander's metaphysical speculations included the origin of the universe itself as perhaps the earliest proponent of the "singularity" theory, evolution, and the elementary forces behind climatology. As a continuation of this line of thought he also pointed to the fact that the cosmological process would, at a certain point, have to reverse itself and return to apeiron—perhaps an early indication of our understanding of "dust-to-dust."

Heraclitus, born in 540 BCE in Ionia, observed that "everything flows and nothing abides; everything gives way and nothing is fixed. You cannot step twice into the same river, for other waters go ever flowing on." Empedocles, a native of Sicily, born around 50 years later, assumed the four basic elements of water, air, fire, and earth to explain this, while his contemporary, Anaxagoras of Clazomenae, took a step further by speculating that everything contains the "seeds" of everything else.

Democritus was a pre-Socratic philosopher, born in Greece circa 460 BCE. With his teacher Leucippus he formulated a theory of the universe, rooted in matter and space, which accounted for the apparent order of the natural world. A unit of matter was judged as being the smallest indivisible body of which everything in the natural world was composed, moving in an infinite void and acting to either repel or combine when they collided with another body, allowing for functional adaptation. Responding to

LEFT The Cosmic Ouroboros takes the image of a serpent or dragon devouring itself before becoming reborn from within. The image dates back to ancient Egypt and Greece. Its cosmic representation has come to symbolize the cyclic nature of existence, eternity, and primordial unity.

RIGHT De Sphaera Mundi was an introduction to medieval astronomy written by Johannes de Sacrobosco c.1230 based on Ptolemy's Almagest with additional notes from Islamic philosophy. It represents the universe as a machine, analogous to a clockwork mechanism. This represents a copy of print from 1501.

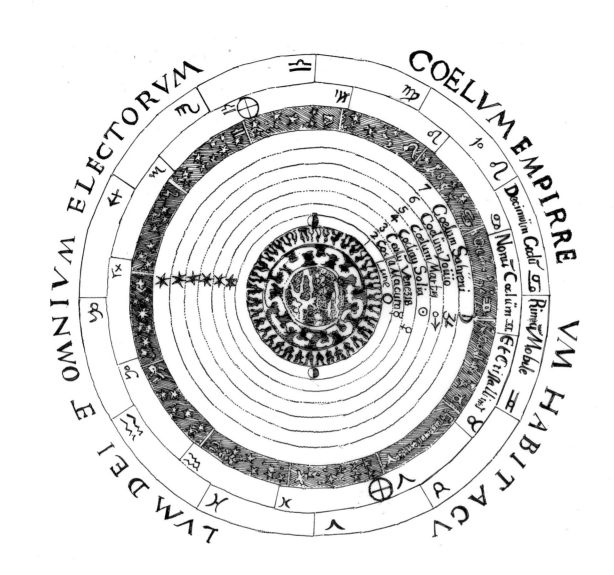

a philosophical challenge, Democritus theorized that in a universe of unchanging material principles, particles simply rearrange themselves. From this came the word "atom" derived from the term *atomos* or indivisible, which invokes an infinite size to the universe, with an equally infinite number of inhabited worlds. Democritus is quoted as saying "Only atoms and empty space have a real existence."

Plato attempted to equate earthly reality as only a shadow measure of absolute reality associated with a divine realm considered to be all-inclusive. As a disciple of the Pythagorean theorem that stars and planets orbited the earth attached to crystalline spheres, he suggested that the world had been created in such a way that it possessed a "soul," understandable and possibly even sympathetic of human reason. In *Timaeus* Plato stated that there was a world of form outside that of the material world that emanated from principles according to a pre-ordained mathematical regularity. The Cosmos therefore had to posses a divine order. On this basis he sought to explain the physical world through a theory that had to embody

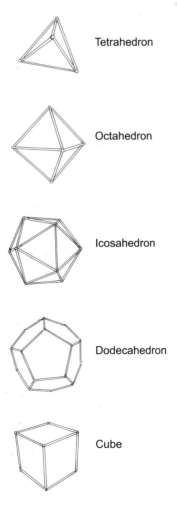

Tetrahedron

Octahedron

Icosahedron

Dodecahedron

Cube

mathematical symmetry, reflected by five perfectly symmetrical objects as a geometric basis for universal design. These came to be known as the five "Platonic Solids"—the tetrahedron, octahedron, icosahedron, dodecahedron, and cube—each distinguished by a different number of faces and vertices. This represented the inspired and even plausible notion of deriving a fundamental structure of matter through form, as each solid is a regular, convex polyhedron. The first three regular Platonic solids are produced by three, four, and five triangles joining together at the vertex. According to Euclidean geometry the maximum number of triangles that meet at the vertex is six, as their angles in combination cannot contain more than 360 degrees, which is all that can be accommodated, so the sixth essentially becomes a surface plane, which cannot produce a volumetric form. A lesser number of triangles can be accommodated within a sphere, which results from an inward curve of the plane. If this is instead curved outward we can in fact add more triangles around a vertex which produces a trochoid or symmetrical "saddle" shape. In nature we can perceive a regularity of these five forms in such things as exoskeletons, and even viruses.

Plato adopted these five polygonal forms as "building blocks" to construct an ingenious theory of physicality through a geometrical approach. As it was reckoned that parts had to be easily assembled to make up a whole, the notion of components was an inspired but largely speculative attempt to explain the nature of the physical universe, which happens to work just as well in terms of modern science with its more sophisticated means of inspiration and creative composition.

The intention was to identify a reality behind what we see, and in his *Timaeus* Plato developed a theory of fire, water, earth, and air elements as being constructed from "atoms" whose characteristics can best be identified with the solids, fire being tetrahedral; water being icosahedral; earth being cubic; and air being octahedral. For a model of the universe as a whole, the dodecahedron with 12 pentagonal faces was identified. This was later boldly adopted in the

17th century by Johannes Kepler as the scaffolding for an elegant but decidedly misguided model of the Solar System that equated the six planetary spheres of Mercury, Venus, Earth, Mars, Jupiter, and Saturn with the five platonic solids based on their relative distances from the sun.

Plato's philosophical conjectures extended to an important treatise on the State—the *Politeia*—that was to become a model for later "ideal" urban archetypes. At the heart of this idea is the enchantment and allure of symmetry, for its distinguishing relationship between mind and matter, and the fact that nature appears to encompass a certain structural elegance. This was something that Renaissance philosophers, architects, and authors were later to return to and further refine.

A school of philosophy under the name of *Peripatetic* was derived from Aristotle, a student of Plato, and dates from 335 BCE when he was teaching at the Lyceum, encircled by grounds that were used as a place for gatherings and discussions. Peripatetic debates tended to be unstructured but directed toward exploring philosophical and scientific theories. Aristotle's virtue was founded on reason and nature just as much as knowledge, and attempted to balance actual facts and observable occurrences with logical and deductive reasoning from the adoption of certain basic premises. However, his preferred notion of a geocentric universe necessitated a complicated explanation for what he discerned to be the "retrograde" movement of the planets, and went further than Plato in dividing the Cosmos into a celestial realm of the Sun, planets, and stars, and an immobile earthy realm at the center of the universe, governed by terrestrial conditions. The attainment of a heavenly realm was therefore pictured by the virtuous Aristotle as exemplifying perfection.

After Aristotle left to return to Athens the Peripatetic School began to decline, possibly because his works were lost or perhaps because his philosophical teaching had become increasingly dogmatic. Interest was rekindled almost a millennium later in the 6th century CE with a better appreciation of classical philosophers, resurrected by a translation of their works into Latin and therefore incorporated in the works of later teachers such as Thomas Aquinas.

Euclid of Alexandria, born around 325 BCE, is generally referred to as the "founder of Euclidean geometry" and author of *Elements*, a treatise of 13 books that rigorously deduced a set of mathematical proofs drawing on the work of Plato. This has been referred to as the most influential textbook ever written. He extended these to works on number theory, conic theory, and spherical astronomy that

Astrolabes date from ancient Greece, and represent handheld instruments made from brass. They were used to mechanically simulate the rotation of stars and produce maps of the sky to assist with astronomical and terrestrial observations, and as a tool for casting horoscopes. One the earliest in use was in Ptolemy's *Planisphaerium*. This enabled him to create a planetary model made up of eccentric circles called epicycles whose centers moved along larger deferments, with points in space around which planets moved in uniform orbits.

provided inspiration for scientific and mathematical research later used by both Galileo and Newton. Euclidean geometry is essentially the study of plane and solid figures on the basis of axioms and theories that he developed. His treatise on optics was applied to both art and architecture creating a classical sense of spatial composition along with the development of linear perspective, which effectively introduced the capacity for a new rendering of religious art.

Aristarchus who lived from 310 to 250 BCE was a scientific descendent of Anaximander and was the first to contradict Aristotle's preferred notion of a geocentric universe. As one of the first accomplished mathematicians to measure astronomical distances, he produced a heliocentric model that positioned the Sun at the center of the known universe, with Earth rotating on its axis. His work also attempted, with primitive equipment, to determine the sizes of the Sun, Moon, and Earth, relative to the distance between them by estimating the shadow cast on the Moon during a solar eclipse. These ideas contradicted those of Aristotle, which tended to prevail until Copernicus reintroduced heliocentric theory some two millennia later.

Eratosthenes, a Greek mathematician, astronomer, and historian was named chief librarian at the Library of Alexandria in 236 BCE. He made the first spherical measurement of the Earth's size using trigonometry to compare the position of the sun's rays and the shadows it cast during the summer solstice. He also calculated the tilt of the Earth's axis and the distance between Earth, the Sun, and the Moon.

The notion that the earth remained as the center of existence was difficult to reject however, and was supported by Claudius Ptolemy—a 2nd century mathematician and astronomer who noted that mathematics applied only to the heavens. Ptolemy attempted to explain Aristotle's geocentric cosmology through his keen observation of the planets and proposed a plausible model, with the Moon, Mercury, Venus, the Sun, Mars, Jupiter, and Saturn following circular paths, named as "deferents" and "epicycles" that were claimed to match their planetary motions. From this he forged the "idealistic" philosophical observations of Plato and Aristotle with the early astronomical science of Hipparchus, the discoverer of the precession of the equinoxes through the spin of the earth, to produce a textbook, the *Almagest*. This was dedicated to the location of all heavenly bodies within a universe composed of "nested spheres" with stars positioned within 48 constellations. The *Almagest* set out the means by which to calculate planetary motion and epicycles, and referenced observations going back to 747 BCE, although it has been suggested by a number of scientists that Ptolemy was quite selective in recording only those observations that supported his model. An obvious difficulty associated with this was that his support for the circular orbits of planets around the earth could not allow for the center of their orbits to vary, and Ptolemy had to determinedly produce several imaginative but ultimately misguided models to deal with this apparent anomaly. However, it was an explanation that went on to satisfy skeptical theologians,

and became absorbed within Western philosophical doctrines until the early Renaissance period.

Ptolemy famously noted that only an exalted role of mathematics could deal with the observable characteristics of the heavens, and as such the eternal was seen as having a sympathetic relationship with theology but not necessarily with the Cosmos. It is therefore of no little surprise that the attainment of a heavenly realm came to philosophically exemplify perfection, and that a simple belief in a circular motion of the planets underscored this. As Ptolomy's model became gradually subsumed into both theological and scientific thought, it became a central part of philosophical doctrines that lasted for some 1,400 years. With only naked-eye observations these theories were mathematically sophisticated, even allowing for the existence of epicycles, but it was not until Kepler's discovery of the underlying laws of planetary motion, utilizing more sophisticated means of observation, that a definitive model came to be accepted.

While the *Almagest* was temporally lost to Christendom, which proceeded to base its creationist theory on the book of Genesis, it was absorbed within Islamic texts and translated into Latin in the 15th century, materially influencing Copernican theory. These theories are a reminder that the search for an underlying eternal reality, even in ancient Greece, partly reflected philosophy and theory, but was also a search for scientific validation through learning and discovery.

The medieval or Middle Ages in Europe, which corresponded to a period approximately between the fifth and the fourteenth centuries, is largely regarded as measuring the transition from ancient antiquity to the Renaissance. Change in the political structure of Western Europe might be said to have commenced with the sacking of the city of Rome by the Visigoths in 410 CE and the fall of the Western Roman Empire. The period is generally divided into classical antiquity, medieval, and late medieval, the latter representing a time of mass migration and the formation of new states. The remains of the Byzantine Empire survived as a considerable power in the Eastern Mediterranean with Rome as its center, employing considerable authority over the Christian world.

The ecclesiastical structure of the Roman Empire survived with a rise of monasticism during the 6th century that began to have a deep impact on political life in the early Middle Ages. The crowning of Charlemagne as Holy Roman Emperor in 800 CE marked a reinvigoration of the Western Roman Empire, with a new form of administration where members of the clergy as well as imperial officers served as officials. The means of education and literacy were almost entirely situated in conjunction with monasteries and cathedrals, and directed toward clerical instruction that reinforced the orthodox Christian faith.

The Franciscan and Dominican Orders remained the bastion of both culture and education up to the 12th century. It was accepted as an absolute truth that Earth and the celestial realm were created by God, and this was naturally perpetuated by the institutions themselves that gave credence to its widespread adoption as an act of faith. Scholars were largely confined to the Roman Catholic Church, which prudently skirted around revolutionary prognostications in favor of less problematic conceptions. This slowly began to change with the creation of universities across Europe, founded by rulers and other noble personages as new centers of knowledge. The earliest in the world, founded in 1088, was Bologna, with the University of Padua founded somewhat later in 1222.

The "Crusades," which began in the late 11th century, might well be considered of questionable integrity, but were widely justified by Western Europeans as an entirely reasonable measure to retake

the Christian Holy Land from its largely Muslim occupants. Islamic scientists and philosophers in the Middle Ages translated many earlier works, compiled planetary tables and textbooks, and constructed astronomical instruments. Classical texts on philosophy and science found their way into European hands in the wake of the sacking of Constantinople in 1453, and many Islamic scholars fled to universities in the city-states of central Italy.

Above all, the period represented major changes between church and society. The late Middle Ages in Europe was marked firstly by a growing scholasticism that introduced an era of intellectual philosophy, and secondly by the growth of cities despite the arrival of the Black Death in 1347, which decimated the population of Europe during the remainder of the 14th century.

Medieval thinking did not so much suggest that the Cosmos was finite, but that with the physical reality of earth at its center, and with the stars situated at its outer limits, it seemed that there could only be an eternal but somewhat ethereal heavenly domain beyond, open to those able to attain its conditional terms of entry. Dante might well have attributed an intelligence to the celestial bodies through speculating that the "soul" is capable of a separate knowledge-based existence as an incorruptible heavenly entity, but devoid of the need for more earthly requirements.

Sacred scriptures were held to contain all that was necessary, and what was otherwise learned from the pagan world was condemned unless it was useful. The *Commedia*, for all its imaginative allusions and references, delineates a complex interrelationship between social, ideological, and cognitive aspects well before the conceptualization of science and religious literature became more intellectually clear cut in the late Renaissance. Natural philosophy and mathematics came to be referenced alongside music and poetry, equating to a rational understanding of the physical universe as it began to be revealed to astronomers. By the 12th century, Cathedral schools had revitalized interest in the Platonic world mixed with an assimilation and re-appropriation of Aristotle's writings along with other works of antiquity from classical sources that supplied Dante with extensive technical references with regard to the natural world. Medieval treatises such as *Physica* and *De anima* in Latin translation together with the Greco-Arabic scientific heritage also provided important material to writers and intellectuals, relating in particular to astrology, alchemy, and medicine.

A supernatural interpretation of heavenly bodies was thought to influence terrestrial events and fortunes. By the late Middle Ages, religious teachers and philosophers such as Thomas Aquinas had absorbed the theories of Aristotle, synthesizing the notion of a Christian heaven with the central theology of the Catholic Church—a cautious reconciliation of faith and reason. This was taken to justify the concern of the church for humankind on behalf of a God who was attributed with the ability to regulate even the prevailing social and political climate. Theologians were apt to use the terms *astronomy* and *astrology* interchangeably, dating back to the philosophy of the School of Athens, where planetary movement was first recorded and it was postulated that celestial motions were attached to a "perfect" universe. Dante notably termed the combination *astrologia*, and in fact a course on this subject was taught at the University of Bologna in the early 14th century. Claudius Ptolemy, who lived 1,000 years before Dante, was honored by him as the preeminent authority on astronomy and planetary properties, and as the author of *Tetrabiblos*, which was used as a university textbook on the mathematical sciences in the 2nd century CE.

The first territorial maps drew on Ptolemy's scientific rules for surveying the heavens, which served to animate Renaissance astronomy, and systematically re-order geographic systems of measurement. A number of mathematical breakthroughs also assisted astronomical calculations, including Leonardo

Fibonacci's 13th-century introduction of the Arabic decimal place system of notation, and Johannes Müller's 15th-century production of trigonometrical and astronomical tables. This allowed a new proportional depiction of space and an integration of nature within the work of artists and illustrators. Medieval cosmological plans and pictures appealed to the mystical imagination but also to a theory of hierarchical patterns marked by architecturally dividing spatial divisions in Gothic churches and cathedrals such as transverse screens or reredos, so that the material world appeared to gradually give way to the transcendental and ethereal. Dante's conception of the circles of Inferno, the stepped grades of Purgatory, and the successive heavenly realms of Paradise, perceptively underscored the medieval distinctions of spaces and light, dedicated to movement and display.

Dante was fully aware of medieval-Christian mysticism, and even the philosophical literature of the Muslim world. Giovanni Boccaccio recollected that Dante was, through an uncommonly held belief in his knowledge of the afterlife, subject to interminable gossip as to his supernatural explorations of the underworld. He had little doubt that events were imparted by heavenly interventions, even modestly attributing his own poetic powers and his recognition of language as the foundation of history and knowledge, to astral influences. Born under the sign of Gemini, Dante remained convinced that the infamous twin figures had ethereally assisted his predestined intellectual qualities, and perhaps his presumptuous search for challenge and social rank. At the same time he considered that people were morally responsible for their actions.

Dante was familiar with the 13th-century writing of Albertus Magnus, a German theologian and member of the Dominican Order, later to be canonized as the patron saint of natural sciences. Albertus, born in 1193, was a scholar and the teacher of Thomas Aquinas. As an informed commentator of the works of Aristotle, which he introduced into the Dominican educational curriculum, Albertus argued in a treatise on astronomy, *Speculum astronomiae*, that an understanding of celestial influences, in particular their cosmic cycles, could influence human, and therefore Christian, precepts. It could be described in terms of mathematical science, but also through a practical application of these instruments as a predictive force for good—*bonum naturae*—with God as the absolute authority who guides human reason through divine revelation. Astronomical references abound in the work, which alludes to supposed planetary properties—for example the ancient associations that equate Mars with war and Venus with love.

Both Albertus Magnus and Thomas Aquinas were students of a medieval culture that regarded astrology as well as astronomy as a respectable discipline, and this was reflected by Dante through astrological references in both *Purgatory* and *Paradise*. He acknowledges in his philosophical conjectures on metaphysical phenomena, that there is a divine intelligence—something that he terms "celestial virtue." In effect, this implies support for a divine law related to the heavens, but also as a means to discover the will of a creator through astronomical observation, and as a force that not only generates life but shapes it just as it does human character. However, Dante also caters for an equally determining factor of free will as something to be guided by virtue as the moral basis that regulates the human state of affairs. The premise of Albertus was that a heavenly afterlife could incentivize and influence goodness in life, and this therefore progressed into a universal ideal of "celestial virtue" reflecting a unity and interconnection of all things. The final word in each canticle of Dante's *Comedia* is "*stelle*" or star, representative of an eternal realm of space associated with salvation. While the discussion is based largely on theology, there are scientific and even cosmological observations with reference to the visibility of stars, the changing position of the sun, and the earthly time zones.

The realm of *Paradise* appears to acknowledge Aristotle's theory that the universe must be of finite size and exist of fundamental elements, so that a body moving toward the heavenly spheres must be fire or air, while a downward motion would be water or earth. The series of concentric spheres that appeared to Aristotle to make up a symmetrical universe with a central Earth, created a cosmic structure for the exalted empyrean domain—a realm beyond physical existence. Such a construction demanded that Dante and Beatrice must ascend, sphere by sphere, to the *Primum Mobile* or "prime mover," and finally to the highest point of heaven with no apparent dimensions. Certain inconsistencies could be put aside, or explained through the scientific unworldliness of the times even as it inadvertently missed the deeper reality. Dante does pointedly indicate the importance of theory and experiment in scientific analysis that is known to have influenced the later theories of Galileo. However, Aristotle's convincing explanation survived more or less intact until the late Renaissance.

The path to Renaissance design was therefore predicated on an impulse to exalt a divine creator worthy of representation through inspired imagery, while at the same time audaciously searching for an explanation derived from the observed working of the Cosmos and what lay behind it. This required a robust relationship between art and science, underpinned not merely by a spiritual connection but by a heroic faith in the elegance and symmetry of natural form, which is to say from the simple to the complex.

THE·DOME·OF SANTA·MARIA DEL·FIORE

Within the form and figure of a building there resides some natural excellence and perfection that excites the mind and is immediately recognized by it.

LEON BATTISTA ALBERTI, *On the Art of Building*

 HE SON OF A WELL-CONNECTED NOTARY, Filippo Brunelleschi was born 56 years after the death of Dante, in 1377. He was to live all his life in the large family house where he was brought up, in the San Giovanni district of Florence near to the Piazza degli Agli. Little is known about his early life until 1398 when, after five years as an apprentice, he was admitted to the Arte Della Selac Guild as a master goldsmith.

Brunelleschi, who became one of the earliest pioneers of Renaissance architecture, was not an architect or engineer by training. However, it was not unusual at the time for artists, sculptors, and painters to have received instruction in the fashioning of gold for both decoration and engraving, and Florence had produced some of the finest artists including Leonardo da Vinci and Donatello. Brunelleschi is known to have developed a strong understanding of the *Divine Comedia* and in particular its architectural dimensions of *Paradiso* with its heavenly constructs.

At the time religion was an all-powerful presence, promoted through architectural and artistic celebration. Its overpowering focus overwhelmed any tendency toward detachment from Christian virtue, with an audacious representation of domes, towers, and campaniles pointing determinedly toward the heavens.

By the time of Dante's death, Florence was at the start of a long era of reconstruction as a result of new trading routes and emerging industries with a new town hall and a ring of fortifications. However, toward the end of the 14th century what became known as the Black Death had visited Florence with particularly severity, and to make matters worse the city was under threat of attack from the north. The major monuments in the city were the result of a continuous sequence of accretions and additions, but Florence had begun to experience a concentrated period of new building work and architectural refinement. The new cathedral of Santa Maria del Fiore was part of a Florentine tradition of ambitious church building, which included Santa Maria Novella for the Dominican Order, and Santa Croce for the Franciscans.

The cathedral had replaced the church of Santa Reparata. It had been designed by the architect Arnolfo di Cambio in 1296 and could be said to mark a visible transition from the Gothic to the Renaissance period. Church design at the time represented an ecclesiastical force within the city, tied into its institutions and sources of financial patronage. Church plan forms were usually based on the model of the Roman basilica—a linear space stretching beyond the alter capable of accommodating large congregations, but which were also designed to serve as meeting places.

Initial control over the design was assigned to five powerful guilds, with sole responsibility for Santa

Maria Novella given to the *Lana* or Guild of Cloth Merchants. The administration of public funds and overall organization was therefore placed in the hands of prominent family representatives who held important posts within the Guild and exercised firm control over their projects, including upkeep and repair. Francesco Talenti was appointed as *capomaestra*, and the plan for the building and dome was prepared by a panel of experts in 1367, along with preliminary specifications of measurements which combined two predominant geometrical elements: the square and the octagon. In part this reflected the octagonal structure of the earlier Baptistery. By 1372 it is recorded that 132 masters and 73 manual workers were active in the Duomo workshop. However, by the beginning of the 15th century the cathedral was far from completion. Its designated site was situated in the medieval center with its tight pattern of fine-grained streets, but was also close to the old city walls. The design challenge was to establish a place of religious worship to an unprecedented scale that created a landmark around which the sprawling urban pattern could be unified and consolidated.

It was against this precarious background that the Guild of Cloth Merchants commissioned a competition for a second set of bronze doors for the northern side of Baptistery of San Giovanni. The year-long process demanded considerable dramatic skill and evolved into a two-way contest between Brunelleschi and a rival goldsmith, Lorenzo Ghiberti. Each contestant was requested to design one panel in bronze based on a subject set out in Genesis 22: 12–13, a scene of God's request for Abraham to sacrifice his son, Isaac, as a test of his faith, which clearly represented challenging design connotations.

ABOVE Brunelleschi's geometric rules behind linear perspective were articulated by Alberti as "legitimate construction," establishing a geometric rationalization with the proportions of the human body used as a unit of measurement. This become a tool for the unified organization of space as a locus of representation in architecture, painting, and sculpture. In the later Mannerist period this began to incorporate more irregular elements in relation to light, distance, color, and the alignment of objects

OPPOSITE TOP The Cathedral of Santa Maria del Fiore. Work began in 1296 to replace the older church on the site—Santa Reparata. The cathedral was finally consecrated after the construction of the dome in 1436.

OPPOSITE BOTTOM Sacrifice of Isaac: Competition panels made by Ghiberti and Brunelleschi for the bronze doors of the Baptistery in 1401.

Brunelleschi's earliest works are best known for their design skill in religious ornamentation and ingenious mechanical composition, including the silver alter in the Cathedral of Pistoia at the time of the plague in 1399. His architectural work in Florence began with the classical church of San Lorenzo in 1418, which together with the loggia of the Ospedale degli Innocenti arguably represented the onset of Renaissance architecture. Brunelleschi's studies of watchmaking had facilitated great mechanical skills, and his sculptural ability together with his pictorial depiction of space helped him to formulate the principles of linear perspective. It was, however, the competition for the Baptistery doors, held in 1401, that was to propel him to prominence in Florence. The Baptistery had been constructed in 960 CE on the site of a Pagan temple dedicated to Mars, and its first set of massive bronze doors had been cast in

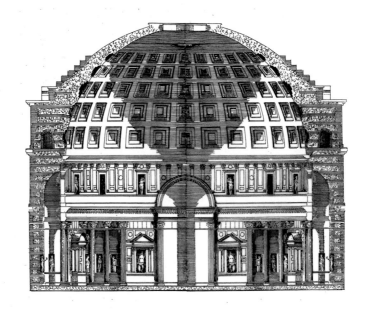

The Piazza della Rotonda with the Pantheon located on its south side. The Pantheon, known as the church of Santa Maria Rotonda, is the most influential building of ancient Rome, constructed between 118 CE and 125 CE. The section is redrawn from Andrea Palladio's *I Quattro Libri dell'Architettura*.

1336 by Andrea Pisano with their ornamented panels setting out scenes from the life of Saint John the Baptist—the patron saint of Florence, and the hub of patriotic communal festivities. Dante noted in the fourth canto of *Inferno* that "Baptism is the portal of the faith" and in Florence all children born within the city walls were baptized at San Giovanni.

The guilds represented the civic core of Florentine Society, promoting their various interests and laying down stringent requirements of admission into their ranks. They also played a significant role in city planning, shaping the main city quarters, exercising control over all civic and religious buildings, and administering public works. The Wool Guild was one of the most powerful, reflecting the strong economic momentum of the wool trade, and entrusted by the city with the undertaking of innumerable building projects.

Ghiberti worked slowly to perfect every detail, while Brunelleschi applied a more rapid and purposeful approach. His final submission was the most theatrical while that of Ghiberti was generally agreed to be the most dignified. In Brunelleschi's relief the composition is dramatic, centered on the intervening figure of the angelic messenger, while Ghiberti's is more oriented to the powerful story itself. Brunelleschi's panel, in its configuration of space, gives an indication of his architectural inclination and a new conception of *civitas*, while Ghiberti introduced a flowing technique to the graceful positioning of figures and elaborate composition. Brunelleschi's casting of his plaque was solid but was not cast as a single piece, so that several parts had to be soldered on, while Ghiberti's was hollow and therefore utilized one quarter less bronze.

Both panels are now housed for comparison in the cathedral museum. Brunelleschi's biographer, Antonio Manetti, states that the jury awarded the commission jointly to both competitors, but that Brunelleschi then withdrew due to his lack of complete control over the project, and thereafter chose to eventually redirect his capabilities toward architectural design.

After the competition Brunelleschi left Florence for Rome along with another ambitious sculptor Niccolò Donatello. The "Eternal City," was a place of ancient ruins with a population that by this time

The inscription reads: M·AGRIPPA·L·F·COS·TERTIVM·FECIT

had shrunk to less than 20,000. There he studied and surveyed the classical remnants, and in particular old established vaulting techniques, setting out his measurements and mathematical ratios using a cryptic code in order to conceal his findings. These included the classical orders, which were governed by Greek and Roman rules on proportion that regulated architectural form. Of special interest to Brunelleschi must have been the Pantheon with its colossal dome, built in 126 CE as a museum and dedicated to Romulus—the mythical founder of the city. The dome of the Pantheon spans 142 feet with a circular oculus at the crown of the cupula that admits light to the internal space, and allows those inside to contemplate the heavens. The Romans, who erected some of the most advanced engineering structures, including the Pantheon, understood the principles of compression and tension, and the forces that must be counteracted by a reduction of the load through a containment of horizontal stress. This was a fundamental problem that had to be resolved in the future construction of the great dome of Santa Maria del Fiore.

The octagonal drum of the cathedral had already been constructed and this increased the height by around ten feet, so that vaulting for the cupola would have to begin at a higher level than any other comparative structure. Furthermore, its octagonal shape called for an unorthodox approach to overcome the technological problems involved. The dome itself embodied a strong religious significance through its relationship to liturgical practice, so that it shaped worship and the necessary acoustic resonance of church ceremony, including the Byzantine "divine liturgy," which denoted the Eucharist or Holy Communion. Plans for the dome itself were not examined in detail until May 1417, when Brunelleschi was paid the sum of ten gold florins for drawing up geometrical aspects of the proposed dome, and a preliminary model was commissioned at a scale of 1:16 which he might have thought would put him in good stead for detailed work. Instead, in August 1418, the board of the Opera del Duomo announced a competition for the main dome of the cathedral with a prize of two hundred gold florins. The construction of the new cathedral had by this time already taken more than one hundred years, interrupted by competing demands for material and labor. It was the largest cathedral in the world, standing as a daunting sentinel over the older medieval center.

At a meeting of the Opera in July 1420 a detailed document was agreed, setting down all aspects of the structure and its interconnections along with features of the exterior. It was to remain as the overriding building program for the dome with intermittent modifications. The dimensions of the dome's height, width, and curvature had been previously established by a decree of 1367 after the vaulting of the nave had been completed, with a ratio of 2:1 between the dome's height and the diameter of its base. An interesting issue is the extent to which the original cathedral designers could have imagined the construction of a dome with such unprecedented dimensions, having incorporated it within their initial concept. A scale model had already been completed according to the stipulations of the Commune of Florence to a design by Neri di Fioravanti, but with no clear knowledge of how to construct it according to the adopted plans.

The continuing process took around 18 months, and a second competition then focused on the difficulties associated with constructing a dome without "centering"—that is to say, dispensing with a temporary supporting structure. An important aspect of this, relevant to later Renaissance structures, was a conviction, later disproved by Galileo, that there was an accurate correspondence between the static structure of a model and the actual building. It is in fact quite possible that had it not been for the ingenious structure of inner and outer shells and the "empty" spaces within the cupola, specified by Brunelleschi as part of the design process, the dome would have collapsed under its own weight.

Brunelleschi's solution was a reversion to his acquired knowledge of Roman masonry construction, and the creation of a double shell that consisted in laying out brickwork of different shapes in horizontal rings with vertical elements inserted between them. The octagonal shape of the cupola meant that the horizontal brick courses could not be continuous, and a herringbone pattern had to be adopted. This was described together with spherical vaulting, by one of Filippo's exalted colleagues, Leon Battista Alberti, in his later treatise on architecture.

Technically, the Board of the Opera was responsible for construction, but Brunelleschi's technical conceptions and obstinate insistence on a solution that did not require either an armature or centering, created little room for maneuver, particularly in terms of the dome's steep inclination. For the competition submission he insisted on constructing a brick model of the cupola with the help of several experienced artisans, together with sculptors and artists to adorn the facade and portals. The model was built in the courtyard of the cathedral, open to onlookers, and took five months to complete.

The committee assembled for an evaluation of proposals in December 1418, but Brunelleschi's proposal was greeted with some skepticism. The solution looked ingenious but unbuildable, particularly as no technical details were produced to elaborate the intricate steps involved. In something of a repeat of the Baptistery competition the two remaining finalists were Brunelleschi and Ghiberti. The latter by this time was a prosperous goldsmith who was, after some 17 years, still casting the giant Baptistery doors amidst many other commissions for shrines and statues. The initial competition result was nebulous and other factors, including the arrival of a new Pope in the city, Martin V, who stayed for more than one year, diverted attention away from the dome. While the scheme was being debated, Brunelleschi was commissioned to undertake several projects including the Ridolfi Chapel in the church of San Jacopo Sopr'Arno, which allowed him to test some of his ideas at a practical level. Other projects including the Hospital of the Innocents and the Sacristy of San Lorenzo were themselves masterpieces of design that were built almost simultaneously with the cathedral dome. Several commissions involved the design of cupolas that were relatively small in scale, and also without the wooden centering which normally supported an arch, allowing Filippo to refine his approach to the cathedral cupola.

In the final event both Brunelleschi and Ghiberti were appointed as joint *capomaestros*, although the promised prize was not awarded. However, only Brunelleschi had the architectural knowhow, technical competence, and capacity for invention to take the project forward, and remained secure in the knowledge that he was indispensable. Construction tentatively commenced on August 7, 1420. Perhaps the most ambiguous aspect of the proposed program was the open-ended nature of the design, it having been agreed that when construction reached a specified height above the drum, only practical experience on site would be able to dictate the more detailed technical approach. This would, in any circumstances, have presented an indeterminate means of resolving a clearly impending problem, and a great deal of reliance was allowed to rest on Brunelleschi's ability to customize and adjust the process as necessary.

A number of subsidiary building sites were established for the storage of timber and marble, together with accommodation for the artists and forges for making and repairing metal works. Timber in the form of white fir, which fulfilled the specified requirements for length, came from the forests of the Casentino, now a national park between Arezzo and Florence. The River Arno begins its course to the Tierrenian

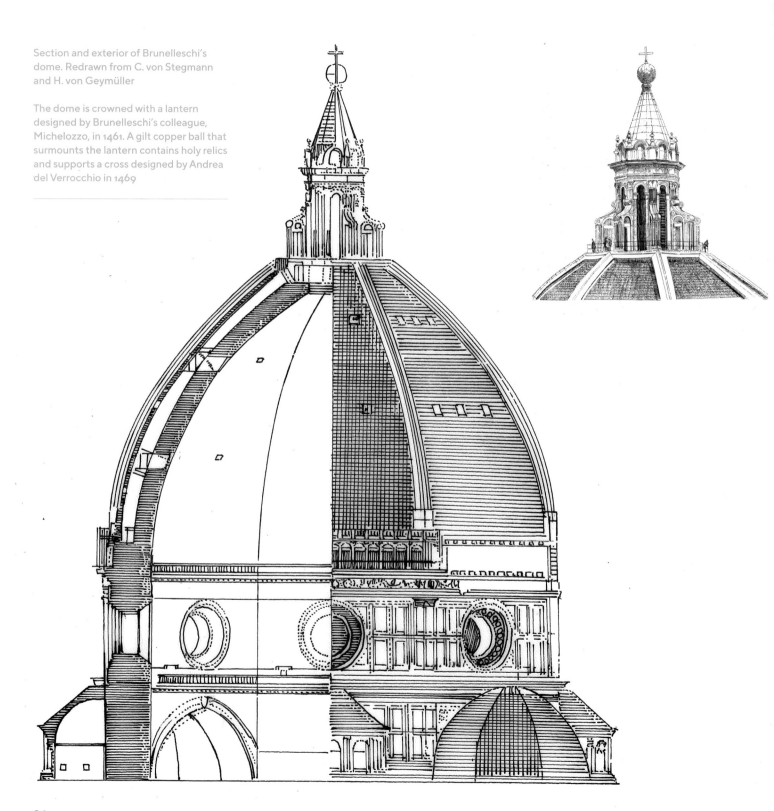

Section and exterior of Brunelleschi's dome. Redrawn from C. von Stegmann and H. von Geymüller

The dome is crowned with a lantern designed by Brunelleschi's colleague, Michelozzo, in 1461. A gilt copper ball that surmounts the lantern contains holy relics and supports a cross designed by Andrea del Verrocchio in 1469

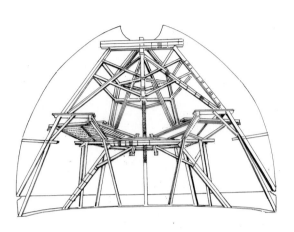

Sea from this area making it possible to float the long tree trunks down the river. The wooden chain needed great strength, and oak for this was chosen from the Apennines.

The quarries of Trassinaia, north of the city, provided sandstone, which was cut into large blocks and transported by ox-driven carts. The best of white marble was obtained from Carrera, closely supervised by Brunelleschi to ensure its quality, and transported to the building site via a combination of sea-going ships along the coast from Pisa, and then by barge along the Arno before being loaded onto ox-carts. Bricks were produced from local kilns supervised by a master brick maker and supplemented from various other producers as there was a requirement for several million bricks over the course of construction at a rate of approximately 400,000 a year.

Progress was interminably slow. Between 1423 and 1440 Florence was on an almost continuous war footing with Milan and Lucca, and funds intended for construction were deflected to defense until the Florentine victory at Anghiari. After this, economic decline ran parallel to the Medici's ascendency to wealth and power.

Brunelleschi gradually transformed the original plan into a more formal conception, related to the already established dimensions but one that more clearly corresponded to the required external massing and internal spaces. In conceiving the cathedral and the city as a unified whole, Brunelleschi is accredited with the development of linear perspective through which he pursued an ideal of a rational spatial structure and a proportional relationship between its parts and their relative position. This was achieved by reintroducing the principle of the vanishing point that was known to the ancient Greeks, and which acted to plot actual lines of sight. From Brunelleschi's experience of surveying ancient sites he formulated a means to convey a schematic reconstruction using the Baptistery of San Giovanni as a focal point with the assistance of an optical device, assembled from simple materials.

In 1425 Brunelleschi was prior of the San Giovanni district, which adopted the Baptistery to be depicted on its coat of arms. It was therefore this building that he chose for his exploration of perspective, initiating an accurate way of representing space and demarcating a shift from two to three-dimensionality through applied optics. Brunelleschi's famous experiment with the depiction of the Baptistery and piazza was based on the "illusion" of reality, and the fact that all horizontal lines at right angles to the observer converge toward a point of infinity. By means of a drawn perspective, a reflecting mirror and a hole that reflected the vanishing point of the drawing where all the parallel lines of the perspective converged, Brunelleschi demonstrated a realization of space in relation to building plans that was to have a major impact on both urban design and artistic representation over the next two centuries. The optical instrument to render the Baptistery in perspective used a painting and a mirror, while clouds were reflected by means of a polished material to represent the sky.

Accurate observation is at the heart of both deriving and depicting objects positioned in three-dimensional space. Filippo Brunelleschi formulated a technique by which to represent the alignment of horizontal lines and vanishing points. The comparatively simple principles of linear perspective created a means to accurately compare the same scene based on different viewpoints. Geometric perspective had an immediate impact on art, architecture, and urban design. It introduced a new element of accuracy and realism to representation, lending an authority to artistic composition and a means by which patterns of three-dimensional space in an urban environment could be articulated, compared, and understood. In the process it illustrates the basic idea of relativity as something that can be represented in different ways depending on the stance and position of the viewer. A rotation of views creates a symmetrical and valid depiction of the subject as the perspective is changed, without altering its fundamental composition.

Geometric perspective was, for the first time, used to accurately represent a precise architectural appearance of a three-dimensional structure in the urban landscape from any number of viewpoints, each presenting the same information but in a slightly different way relative to the position of the observer. However, the totality of views achieved from the sum of each perspective representation include certain characteristics that are common to all and can be said to be invariant, although all views are equally valid. In effect, the vanishing point at the horizon allows the observer to visualize infinity. Relativity is therefore at the core of what is being represented, as a rotation of views allows observation of many complementary facets of the same subject. A description of it requires an accumulation of all perspectives and an interaction between subject and observer. The comparatively simple principles of linear perspective introduced a new authority to urban design composition and the means by which patterns of three-dimensional space in an urban environment could be articulated, compared, and understood. Design and artistic rendering, therefore, complemented advances in mathematical analysis and even astronomy.

The design of the Santa Maria del Fiore dome reflected the cosmic order, not in a literal sense but in terms of balancing the spiritual dimension to which all the participants in the new astronomy subscribed, with the physical manifestation of this within an architecture that sought to reach far beyond physical space to the heavenly paradise. This was deemed to be distinctly purposeful, the earthly realm being associated with the transient elements of earth, water, fire, and air, while the heavenly realm offered the more promising prospect of eternity free from the afflictions of time.

The visible surfaces and the dome itself thereby articulate the spatial organization of the building complex, including the Baptistery and Giotto's Campanile. The profile of the dome, sitting above empty space at ground level, balances its essential verticality against the longitudinal nave, while from external views it appears suspended above the city, expressing its outer shell that remains identical from all viewpoints. As the most recognizable symbol of Florence, it is also one of the most difficult to interpret, and Brunelleschi was eternally secretive about the mechanics of the cupola's construction and its structural complexity.

From 1433 Brunelleschi was handed sole control of the project, breaking a long-standing practice in terms of corporate building work. The lantern itself was begun in 1438 and completed 33 years later in 1471 with the installation of Verrochio's copper ball on top of the lantern. The eight projections of the buttresses that reinforce it are aligned with the ribs of the dome itself, and serve a structural purpose by strengthening their junction.

The Form of the Cupola

An "understanding" of building construction in the late medieval age was directed mainly toward what was visible within the structure, and which areas were going to be occupied. Technical limitations required innovative solutions to problems as and when they arose, and a degree of spontaneous reaction to periodic changes in design. Structural adequacy was considered largely through transfer of loading from vertical or inclined supports to horizontal or curved members. Building form, even for prestigious and religious buildings, was frequently an expedient envelope for the artistic decoration of the interior. Such buildings were intended to last long into the future with the minimum of planned obsolescence and the maximum decorative indulgencies. As a result, structural design represented a combination of acquired knowledge, use of construction models, recourse to precedent, and, perhaps ultimately, faith. As a former student of theology, Brunelleschi was not above evoking "inspiration from above," but was equally able to affirm the transcendental value of "knowledge defeating false judgment." Brunelleschi is known to have visited Sienna where he temporarily worked on fortifications and aqueducts as part of military engineering efforts, and this undoubtedly had a favorable impact on both his knowledge and immense confidence.

The initial construction program stated that masonry was only to be raised without centering up to a height of 17.5 meters. The eight-sided cupola with its "pointed-fifth" curvature profile was based on a circle, divided into five equal parts but dependent on a precise structural solution. It required an effective coordination and time-management strategy whereby certain activities had to be carried out simultaneously, while others could be in sequence—for example, work could be carried out on all the eight segments of the octagonal structure at the same time, but masonry "rings" had to be completed in succession. This necessitated a "slack-line" arrangement of brick courses that lie on the surface of an inverted cone on an axis with that of the dome to ensure an uninterrupted arrangement with no weak points. A herringbone pattern of brickwork then permitted the gradual convergence of the individual segments without centering. This was formed by placing bricks on sloping beds, but in a spiral formation, akin to a single helix skeleton.

The equipment designed by Brunelleschi was technically ingenious, while also embracing a whimsically elaborate appearance. It was practical in its use however, and in this sense not overly complicated. Some of the tasks to be met were daunting, particularly the necessary hoisting and positioning equipment, and this meant innovative solutions. The installation for raising massively heavy loads for the cupola construction was an ox-powered hoist located on the cathedral floor, which could reverse the ascent or descent of loads at different speeds while maintaining the rotation system of the oxen. This was based on a worm-screw mechanism with two horizontal gears. Other devices were used to transfer loads to different work points that involved the use of revolving cranes with load-positioning devices.

Brunelleschi, like many of the more accomplished architects and designers, evolved inspired ideas through high confidence in his own abilities. Practical geometry and intuition along with the accumulated experience handed down through generations of *capomaestros* seem to have been sufficient. His almost secretive protection of technical ideas and design solutions was quite within the standards of his time, particularly when both innovation and a broad level of creativity were obvious challenges. At the time of a cultural renaissance, full of new and unforeseen opportunities, his genius was to devise spontaneous measures to resolve an almost constant series of practical matters in a resourceful way. The burdens would be many and the risks perilous, but the rewards would be profound. Brunelleschi inspired many followers including Michelangelo who studied the structure of the cupola and later reinterpreted this, albeit at a somewhat smaller scale, on the dome of Saint Peter's in Rome. Giorgio Vasari also adopted the model for the Basilica of the Madonna dell'umiltà in Pistoia. The dome of the Chapel of the Princes at San Lorenzo for which Brunelleschi, and Michelangelo one hundred years later, designed the two sacristies, lies almost adjacent to the cathedral piazza, and includes a smaller octagonal dome crowned with a lantern.

The form of the cupola and its polygonal plan announce, at one and the same time, a simplicity of form that belies the complexity of its structure. However, the practical experience of master builders could only be taken so far. Brunelleschi's presumptuous design, without supportive centering and with dual shells that arose from his own extraordinary intuition, was calculated without the availability of mathematical tools. At the time there was also little real knowledge of compressive and tensile stresses,

and therefore the resistance properties of the cupola's masonry.

The expressive design displays aspects of the divine in its innovative and complex construction methods that remained modestly hidden within its inner recesses, behind a double skin that challenged both known and unknown structural forces, but with a conscious sense of purpose. The dome acts as a dominant element in Florence, subjugating everything else in the city within its force field—a reminder of the eternal amidst the temporal. It exudes a force that appears to lift it above the roof of the city, with a lantern *tempietto* sitting at the crest of white marble ribs that unambiguously point toward the heavens, even as its red tiling blends in with the surroundings.

The cupola itself serves to organize and celebrate the volumetric massing of the internal space while its expressive external dominance celebrates a powerful transition from the medieval Gothic to a new Renaissance, reflecting both new realms of thought and spatial design. In 1475 a tablet with a small aperture was placed on the southern opening of the lantern allowing a ray of sunlight to be directed to the chapel of the cross where a gnomon is located showing the time by the position of a shadow. It is small wonder that Domenico di Michelno's painting of Dante, clutching the *Comedia* some years after his death, position him straddling a space between the "circles of hell" and Santa Maria del Fiore that might indicate a plausible pathway to the perfections of *Paradiso*.

In 1520 the wooden choir beneath Brunelleschi's dome was replaced with a marble and bronze design by Baccio Bandinelli in anticipation of the edicts issued by the Council of Trent, situated below the cupola with its evocative paintings by Vasari and Federico Zuccaro that depict the "dome of heaven" encompassing the resurrection and last judgment. A potent source of design influence was Dante, through the octagonal structure that descends in concentric layers to encompass such interpretive references as a celestial choir, the Elect, Hell, and Christ sitting in judgment encircled by saints.

The Visual and Symbolic Image

The cupola has been both a subject of technical and scientific interest, and an artistic inspiration since its inception. Technical drawings of the levels and sections of the cathedral and its prominent cupola were compiled some years after construction. Only then was it possible to obtain a clear understanding of the structure, enabling maintenance to be carried out and structural repairs to be undertaken along with a periodic replacement of parts.

Artistic interpretation of the cathedral and its famous dome is of particular interest for two main reasons. First it has attracted a continuous widening of artistic techniques from the time of its completion, through oil paintings, water colors, woodcuts, and engravings that collectively reflect a range of very different representations, both realistic and stylistic, in conveying its architectural characteristics utilizing Brunelleschi's own perspective technique. Second, is the compositional and graphic depiction in relation to the urban setting—the panoramic scenes from prominent viewpoints where the iconography of the city characteristics tend to focus on the cathedral around which are clustered an ensemble of iconic buildings, spaces, and streets. In this way the cupola becomes an

The decorative facade of the Cathedral was invigorated with divine representations. Various ordinances were passed by the commune that regulated the surrounding buildings in relation to the cathedral, stipulating the curved outline of buildings to match the profile of the apse, and in the process creating an overall spatial correspondence that facilitated civic activity and clerical display.

imposing sculptural element, establishing a sense of focus and equilibrium to these urban compositions. It does not simply reach for the heavens, it dissolves the distance, challenging its celestial sacredness and inviolability in the same way that Dante celebrated its spiritual virtue in *Paradiso*, and Galileo later questioned its cosmic primacy and basic laws. In simple design terms the cathedral represented a reconstitution of Gothic and Classical styles, indirectly introducing a uniquely Florentine Classicism.

The cupola, like the cathedral itself, by virtue of its overall form and situation, establishes a set of delineated relationships through its visual connectivity and landmark status both within the city fabric and from afar, blending in just as equally as it stands out. This is also affected by the changing quality of light and shadow in relation to the adjoining streets and squares throughout the day as the sun moves across the sky. It is likely that had Dante been able to see the finished cupola he would have agreed with Leon Battista Alberti's criteria in *De re aedificatoria,* that such an accomplishment expressed a new political dimension in the city's newly commenced program of regeneration and development.

Brunelleschi was a Dante scholar, and was particularly interested in the interpretation of his works at a period in time when the *Comedia* was being read as much for its political and religious text as for its cosmological explorations. After its completion it became customary for celebrated architects such as Michelangelo and Bramante to compile both commentaries and occasionally visual interpretations of the three realms of Hell, Purgatory, and Heavenly Paradise. These then found their way into future editions of the *Comedia*, although Michelangelo's were lost at sea in a shipwreck. Behind this might well have been a substantial undercurrent of humanist dissent and a desire for reform.

Antonio Manetti, an energetic humanist and biographer of Brunelleschi, some 40 years after his death, conceded that the cupola's structure contains "the seeds of many mysteries which lie concealed." Manetti claims that various parts of the cupola construction were drawn to full-scale, laid out on a flat site, and used to make construction templates. He also refers to *Sphaera mundi*—the sphere of the Cosmos, a medieval text drawing on ideas from Islamic astronomy written by Johannes de Sacrobosco, and based on Claudius Ptolemy's *Almagest*—a Greek astronomical treatise on the apparent motions of the stars and planets, and an influential scientific text, first printed in 1515 and used in many Italian universities. This creates a certain correspondence with Dante's image of the Inferno's dimensions as a gigantic amphitheater of separate circular realms.

Brunelleschi believed in natural laws that governed the physical world while God ruled the operations at a cosmic level, concerned with beauty and truth. The cathedral dome is in fact akin to a mandala—a symbolic representation of the Universe, displaying a divine symmetry between its interconnected parts. The far-reaching influence of the cupola design gained Brunelleschi the high honor of a burial in Santa Maria del Fiore, memorialized in marble and with an inscription over his tomb that states, "The body of that man of great genius, Filippo di Ser Brunellesco, Florentine."

Minor cracks appeared to form on the cupola within two centuries of its completion, first surveyed by Gherardo Silvari, architect of the Opera di Santa Maria del Fiora in 1639. Shortly after this a committee was established, comprising eminent architectural authorities, to investigate the cracks and various recommendations were made. Over the course of the 18th and 19th centuries the cracks were further

The old sacristy at the church of San Lorenzo was undertaken between 1421 and 1428, and represented Brunelleschi's first ecclesiastical building, with decorative interior elements by Donatello. It was intended as a funerary chapel for the Medici family, and exhibits an elegant interplay of internal forms with an overall symmetry, dictated by a desire to create a space in the form of a cube under a hemispherical dome that preceded Santa Maria del Fiore but was almost as symbolic. Brunelleschi's design drew on medieval monastic buildings to achieve a simple typology in the form of a cross with a cupola above the crossing between the transcript and the nave, with the aisles demarcated by arched colonnades and classical orders that shaped

the ceremonial nature of the central space with oculi that permitted light to focus on the religious activity while its resounding acoustics underscored religious authority. At the same time, this reflected continuity with the antecedents of antiquity, and a symbolic link with imperial Rome. The supreme precedent for this was the Pantheon in Rome—in itself a temple to all gods commissioned by Marcus Agrippa and completed in 120 CE, and which created a model for Renaissance church construction, symbolic of heavenly power. Its open oculus admits light into the central space, creating one of the earliest examples of interplay between the ideal unity of two geometric forms—the circle and the square.

Brunelleschi's dome dominates
the roofspace of the central city
of Florence

studied but there was continued disagreement as to their cause, and therefore the best applicable remedy. In a report from the 1990s, almost 600 years after its construction, the cupola was stated as being in a good condition, mainly due to the lateral thrusts exerted and the vertical setting of the Cathedral piers. The main cracks were found to be quite stable, because of the tensile stresses caused by the weight of the cupola on the structure of the octagonal drum.

The redevelopment of the ancient church of Santo Spirito in the San Frediano neighborhood of Florence and dedicated to the Roman martyr "Santa Felicità" was intended to commemorate the Florentine victory at Governolo over the Milanese, but it was not until 1446 that work began. It represents a late work of Brunelleschi. His idea was to eliminate plans for large chapels and he instead proposed a series of niches that ran around the church. The earliest project for Santo Spirito dates from 1428 through an urban plan that included a large square next to the River Arno, however, the plan was blocked by opposition from owners of houses and land between the church and the river. The plan is based on a proportional aggregation of equal metrical elements, something that became typical of Renaissance architecture. The church is raised above the piazza creating an essential sense of place and a transition in terms of scale and threshold space without monumentality.

The Pazzi Chapel dating to 1443 is attributed to Brunelleschi although subject to alteration and refurbishment over the years including the front portico, which gives it an unintended monumentality. The structure was intended as a chapter house to the Church of Santa Croce and represents an extended replica of the old Sacristy, enlarged from a square plan to a rectangular form. The dome above the central square reflects that on the old Sacristy, with a lantern that was restored in the 19th century.

Statue of Filippo Brunelleschi, Santa Maria Novella

REALIZING·THE RENAISSANCE

Man was born to be useful to himself and others; and our primary and proper use is to turn the powers of the soul toward virtue, to recognize the causes, and order of things.
LEO BATTISTO ALBERTI, *De Iciarchia*

Title page redrawn from Bartoli's first edition of Alberti's *De re aedificatoria*.

 ENAISSANCE THINKERS tended to harmonize humanism and virtue with physical and spiritual beauty, linking scientific discovery to a sense of universal order, but also in line with an artistic and aesthetic ideal. The result was an almost continuous progression of scientific ideas, development of philosophical thought, and a questioning of natural phenomena that went back to Plato and Aristotle.

The term Renaissance suggests a resurrection or renewal, but it was also a period rich in the exchange of ideas, relevant to design invention and execution, and marked a transition from the Middle Ages into modern history. In the early Renaissance period regularization of the urban planning frameworks, unless enforced through compulsory measures, was to a large extent dependent on reconciling new growth with the city's legacy of medieval streets and spaces. These had, over the centuries, become defined by the large defensible palaces of the nobility, and warlords who often held land as ancient fiefs. The older quarters with narrow streets offered little noticeable division between the sacred and secular.

The Renaissance liberated creativity from being merely a physical medium to a concern for the spirit of *Disegno,* whereby design carries a complex and inventive capacity marked by precise detail and realism. Through constant refinement, the receptive mind can thereby create an ideal—the divine nature exemplified by the greatest practitioners. It underlies Vasari's verdict on the Florentine Renaissance as the model for great art and a locus of intellectual concern for works of visual representation, literature, and philosophy intertwined with religious commentary and devotion. The concept of *Disegno* carries a reference to both theory and practice in terms of art, sculpture, and architecture linked to philosophical and scientific exploration but also the capacity for invention, uniting the visual arts and systematically establishing their relationship, as a group, to other fields of knowledge. In the process this sustained an underlying organizational order, subordinating art and design to a particular set of rules for architecture and urban design where certain representations were equated with particular settings. Buildings took many years to construct, extending well beyond the lifetime of their architects, and the remnants of faded grandeur of older styles was all around most Italian cities in the ruins of Roman remains from antiquity as a constant reference.

The path to Renaissance design was predicated on two aspects—an impulse to exalt a divine creator through representative imagery, while at the same time seeking an explanation of the Cosmos and its significance. Thomas Aquinas observed that art depends on nature, but nature depends upon God, so that all natural works had a divine origin. This fostered a robust relationship between art, philosophy,

Originally a woodcut illustration of the Ptolemaic universe, in its redrawn and modified state it is taken to represent a break in the medieval Cosmos as a peasant peers out from the medieval world to the revolutionary new world of the Renaissance.

and science, underpinned not merely by a spiritual connection but by a heroic faith in the elegance and symmetry of natural form.

The philosophy of humanism originated in northern Italy during the 14th century, with the individual as its focus. It reflected a culture that was becoming increasingly secular, while also recognizing the Catholicism that was important to daily life. Renaissance thinkers tended to unify humanism and virtue with an aesthetic ideal, linking this with new scientific discoveries that brought a sense of universal order. In the process this liberated artistic creativity from being merely a physical medium to a concern for society drawn toward the Divine.

Christian scholastic studies between the 14th and 16th centuries at Italian universities, particularly in Padua, followed an *Averroistic* doctrine—a school of medieval Islamic teaching—influenced by Aristotle, that examined Christian doctrines through a "unity of the intellect" where philosophical and religious worlds were regarded as separate entities. Dante recognized Averroes's theory as a basis for his secularist political philosophy set out in *De Monarchia*, arguing that mankind shares a common intellect. At the heart of this was the question of individuality, whereby faith could be followed despite the contradictions or pretentions of human reason. The intellectual function of the mind was not therefore entirely disassociated from logical and ethical values independent of the senses. Personal thought could be at least partially shared and developed, so long as there was a correspondence of knowledge, experience, and human sensibility, and where this "cosmic connection" created a compulsion toward a universal good.

The flowering of Renaissance art and architecture was marked by the rediscovery of antiquity and its assimilation with emerging cultural and city-building realizations. An understanding of both are deemed necessary for a more articulated presentation of space that stemmed from a new ideal of physical harmony, through an emphasis on geometrical proportion and the reinvention of perspective as a reflection of a universal order. This primarily commenced in the 15th century, gathering even greater momentum through the next. Architects and urbanists embraced a new ideal of artistic representation that evolved from late medieval practitioners who had been subject to the spiritual direction of the church. In its conveyance of moral principles, this began to place an increasing emphasis on the arts.

The mid-Quattrocento defined the essential core of the early Florentine Renaissance, beginning with the Duomo and coming to maturity in the palaces of the Medici. This came about despite a long period of political upheaval associated with the prevailing peninsular politics of the Papal States. It was a time when the power of art, design, and engineering projected a sense of community and articulated the urban identity. The city's artists and artisans were organized under talented and charismatic leaders in large collaborative workshops where traditions and techniques were passed through generations. Architects had a high status and many sculptors and goldsmiths extended their artistic experience to building design. This was a city densely dominated by the sacred symbol of Brunelleschi's cupola and Arnolfo di Cambio's tower. Santa Croce was located to the east and Santa Maria Novella to the west. These represented long and often complicated chronologies, between their commission and completion as church and palace landmarks.

The Palazzo Medici marked the commencement of the Medici urban quarter and its assembly of building sites. Together with Brunelleschi's San Lorenzo these displaced many older buildings and monuments creating a conjunction of old and new. The latter included new works of art inspired

The Palazzo della Ragione was the medieval town hall and palace of justice in Padua, built in 1219 and reconstructed in the early 17th century by Andrea Moroni. Its importance as a center of civic display and grandeur is a measure of the importance placed on these aspects by the Parduan Commune. Together with the Palazzo Vecchio in Florence and the Palazzo Pubblico in Siena it marks the artistic creativity and dominance of these three cities, but also the scope of secular patronage, while the buildings also express very different characteristics. The Palazzo della Ragione now separates the two active city markets in the Piazza delle Erbe, and the Piazza dei Frutti.

Stone carving from the Palazzo della Raggione

The San Lorenzo neighborhood of Florence was, by 1444, the Medici quarter, following construction of the Medici Palace, designed by Michelozzo di Bartolomeo. It was the residence of Cosimo the Elder—elected "Father of the Country" by the people of Florence, and Lorenzo the Magnificent, before the Medici family moved to the Palazzo Vecchio in 1540. The design exhibits the principles established by Alberti and Brunelleschi. It clearly distinguishes the division of floors, with a stone rustication to the ground floor progressively flattening out on the upper levels with a rhythmic pattern of cadenced arches and double-lancet windows. In plan form it exemplifies the square-shaped buildings organized around a central arcaded courtyard that were developed in Florence during the mid-15th century.

The Convent of St. Mark was assigned to the Dominican brotherhood in 1427, and 10 years later Cosimo the Eder appointed Michelozzo Di Bartolomeo to restore it. In the 15th century it was one of the most important cultural centers in Florence. From 1491 Savonarola was prior, which allowed him to preach the ideals of poverty and absence of possessions that influenced the local population. However, his vitriolic attacks on Lorenzo de'Medici and the Papacy, and his support for a theocratic democracy against the wishes of the Church, led to his execution in the Piazza della Signoria in 1498. The convent is associated with St. Anthony, archbishop of Florence. It was suppressed in 1866 and is now a museum dedicated to the fresco work of Beato Angelico.

by the humanist culture of the time, some of which began to depict medieval Florence itself as an appealing backdrop. The Palazzo commenced construction in 1445 and took around 15 years to build with its somewhat forbidding cubic mass of rusticated masonry, rounded Renaissance windows, and an overhanging cornice, which became a model for palace design elsewhere. In the center of its courtyard was Donatello's bronze statue of *David*, possibly reinforcing the association of the Medici with republican iconography.

At the same time, Florence was consolidating its political relationships through its hegemony over neighboring towns such as Pisa, Padua, and Arezzo, while it was also extending its trading, business, and banking strengths across and beyond the Mediterranean. As a result, the city was becoming more cosmopolitan, drawing in workers from outside the country. The relationship with the city's outer region was asserted in particular by the Medicis who formed the lynchpin of Florentine politics throughout the Quattrocento, after the time of Cosimo the Elder's return from exile in 1434 until the second expulsion of the family in 1494. The palazzo itself served as a de facto center of politics within the Florentine state and as a reception vehicle for international visitors, reflecting the worldliness of the Medici wealth and position well beyond the city walls.

The Loggia dei Lanzi in Florence was constructed in the Piazza della Signoria, Florence's principal civic piazza, by the guild hierarchy in 1383 as a covered space in which ceremonial functions could be performed as part of new civic values. Benched seating was provided so that the citizenry could participate in the public life of the city. Carved reliefs of the seven virtues were set into the spandrels of its arches and protected by a projecting canopy.

Statue of Michele Di Lando in the Loggia del Mercato Nuova, a wool carder who led the Ciompi Revolt in Florence that won guild representation in 1378.

Giambattista del Tasso's stylist design for the Loggia del Mercato Nuova in the 16th century was intended as a modern forum on the site of the medieval one. It was constructed on a major civic thoroughfare leading to the Ponte Vechio, with an existing inscription that lauds its magnificent structure and outward vistas that included Cosimo's new residence, the Palazzo Pitti. It also includes motif references to Michelangelo's Biblioteca on which Tasso was an assistant, and other hints at Etruscan details. Statues in the niches represent notable Florentine personages.

The Medici Chapels at the heart of the San Lorenzo complex in Florence. The Chapel of the Princes has a baroque-style interior by Matteo Nigetti.

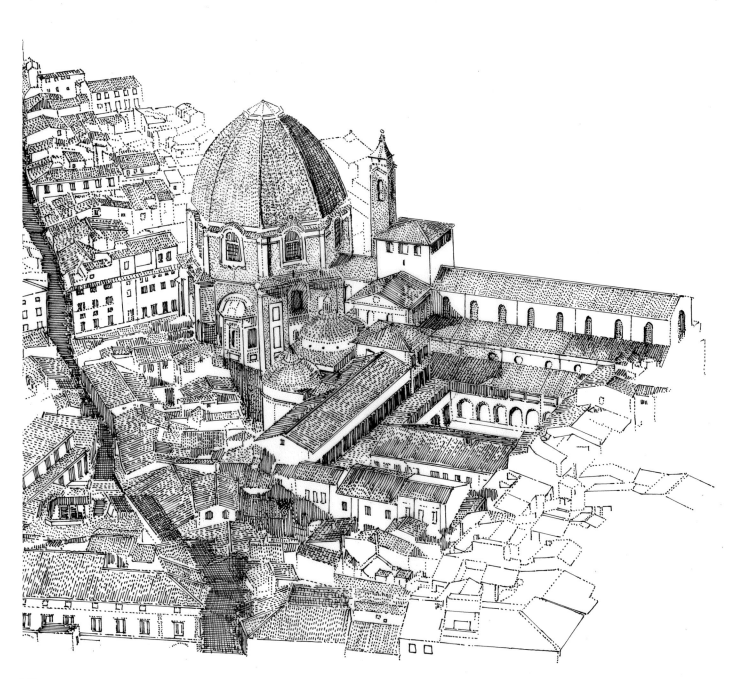

From 1419 and the suppression of the confraternities with their threatening political alliances, such grand-scaled urban design became the focus of political intrigue, aristocratic financial support, and adroit planning. The planning of the two basilicas of San Lorenzo and San Spirito in Florence was an exercise in replacement rather than restoration, which made use of new religious buildings as foci for new buildings and piazzas. Urban regeneration involved demolition of houses, shops, and warehouses, and with this came a transition from medieval to Renaissance urbanism. This was advantageous to the Medici and other property owners who perceived opportunities to build or enlarge properties of their own, including a Medici Palace that was intended to be built directly opposite San Lorenzo but that was later redirected to the Palazzo Pitti.

The church of San Lorenzo is the oldest church in Florence dating to 393 CE. The new church of San Lorenzo was constructed on the foundations of its earlier Romanesque structure built in 1060, and its organization corresponds to a proportional module based on a square form. The facade was left bare after Michelangelo's later appointment by Pope Leo to implement the design was cancelled because of the high cost involved.

The redevelopment of the ancient church of Santo Spirito in the San Frediano neighborhood of Florence and dedicated to the Roman martyr "Santa Felicità" was intended to commemorate the Florentine victory at Governolo over the Milanese, but it was not until 1446 that work began. It represents a late work of Brunelleschi. His idea was to eliminate plans for large chapels and he instead proposed a series of niches that ran around the church. The earliest project for Santo Spirito dates from 1428 through an urban plan that included a large square next to the River Arno. The plan was blocked by opposition from owners of houses and land between the church and the river however. The church is therefore raised above the piazza creating an essential sense of place and a transition in terms of scale and threshold space without monumentality.

The underlying philosophy of the Renaissance was concerned with a theory of knowledge, and it was this that shaped its physical constituents. Many cultural figures embraced the doctrines of the Florentine Academy founded by Cosimo de'Medici in 1462, with a philosophical and spiritual goal rather than a strong political direction. The artistic and creative realm was therefore endowed with meaning and substance, and interpreted according to prescribed doctrines. Within these the concepts of individual intellect and empirical observation were directly connected with design initiatives, scientific knowledge, and a new sensitivity to the world of form. Hence its sensual character, and a renewal of ancient and classical references in both the arts and society.

Lorenzo de'Medici, through skillful diplomacy, helped achieve peace between the Italian states and bring about an era of prosperity to Florence, although power remained vested in the republican *Signoria*. His proactive involvement with the visual arts is extravagantly recounted in Vasari's *Lives of the Artists*. Lorenzo visited Rome in 1471 during the election of Pope Sixtus IV and was guided around the monuments by Leon Battista Alberti. Following this he acquired a site on the Piazza San Marco in Florence that became a place of repose, where Michelangelo acquired his sculptural experience. Further interventions were proposed around San Marco and the Innocenti Hospital, along with internal improvements to the Palazzo della Signoria. Two new palaces—the Palazzo Cocchi and the Palazzo Scala—were both designed by Giuliano da Sangallo, the author of a book on architectural design, the *Codex Barberini*. Up to his death in 1492 Lorenzo embarked on a series of construction projects designed by Michelangelo and the sculptor Bertoldo di Giovanni for cultural and ecclesiastical projects, including the sacristy of Santo Spirito, with a campaign to build new streets for which tax incentives were included.

One of Lorenzo's last Medici villas was the Poggio a Caiano, one of the most original, located on a hill overlooking the city and corresponding with Alberti's guidelines in *De re aedificatoria*.

Renaissance art was marked by a shift to representational forms and classical events with precise detail and realism. An idealized naturalism reached its culmination in the High Renaissance of the early 16th century through such figures as Michelangelo, Leonardo da Vinci, and Raphael, before giving way to a more dramatic representation. This emphasized the philosophy of humanism that originated in northern Italy during the 14th century, with the individual as its focus, echoing a culture that was becoming increasingly secular.

Central and Northern Italy's position at the core of the Renaissance is centered around the classical style, uprooted and revived from an ancient past and recalibrated to fit, in varying degrees, a rapidly urbanizing Europe. Classical insertions began to occur in a range of physical and social spaces, facilitating community involvement in their deciphering and application, depending on whether they were directed toward the secular or the spiritual. This involved an increased appropriation of fashionable architectural mannerisms, often regardless of historical association, combining an amalgam of interpretations that later evolved into the occasional architectural excesses of the baroque. However, this was not so much a matter of emulating the past but in establishing a physical connectedness with antiquity, drawing on the vast inheritance of visual objects associated with city places. Inigo Jones, the architect of several highly regarded classical buildings in England, notably commented that this was the result of a long habit of self-restraint rather than reinvention, where a refined style itself signified the overriding factor in conceptualization.

If science is about reason, art is about imagination. Each is about the power and ability to produce form through a correspondence between the divine and the human mind.
LEON BATTISTA ALBERTI

New design trajectories were articulated in the writings of Leon Battista Alberti, an architect, mathematician, poet, artist, and philosopher who adopted an approach that embraced a new humanist outlook corresponding to the existence of the city-state. Born in 1404 in Genoa after his wealthy father and other members of his family, like Dante, had been banished from Florence, he later studied canon law in Bologna and only returned to Florence at the age of 30, where he spent much of the remainder of his life. Alberti's arrival in Florence in 1434 with the court of Pope Eugenius coincided with the advanced construction of the Duomo, and what has been termed an artistic renaissance of quattrocento Florence. The artistic works of the period by Ghiberti, Donatello, and others stimulated his systematization of "painter's perspective" that he shared with Brunelleschi to whom he dedicated *Della pittura*, and which was later developed by Leonardo da Vinci.

After his move to Florence, Alberti began composing verse in the expressive vernacular Tuscan style, popularized by Virgil. Almost a hundred years after Dante, he helped to gain its popular acceptance as the primary literary prose language of Italy. In one such literacy dialogue, *Della tranquillita dell'animo*, Alberti conducted a discussion with other Florentine humanists under Brunelleschi's cupola, metaphorically encapsulating an essential harmony and tranquility but also exploiting the atmosphere of this great space and its impact on community identity. He reverted to Latin in his written work as it was aimed mainly at wealthy architectural patrons.

Piazza Maggiore—the central square of Bologna surrounded by the city's older religious and administrative buildings

The Fountain of Neptune located in the Piazza del Nettuno in Bologna. The four main sources of political power in the city are inscribed on the base.

Statues of the Virgin erected in public spaces often became shrines for informal worship reinforcing the influence of the sacred within older neighborhoods. The Orsanmichele was originally constructed in 1285 as a loggia for grain merchants in the city, and the site of the painted Madonna of Impruneta, which had become the focus of wide veneration for its supposed capacity to work miracles. Public offerings were converted into alms and distributed to the needy and by 1380 the entire ground floor of the Orsanmichele had become reserved for veneration purposes necessitating the relocation of the market. Francesco Talenti redesigned it as a church in the early 14th century. In 1406 the external piers of the loggia were allocated to individual guilds, with a series of 14 niches on the external walls to contain images of their patron saints in order to fulfill their obligations in relation to the ritualized devotional cycle of the oratory. The most important guilds secured the prime positions and only these were sufficiently wealthy to commission the best artists. The Banker's Guild commissioned a bronze statue of St. Matthew by Ghiberti; the Armorer's a statue of St. George by Donatello; and the Stonemakers and Woodworkers a group of four crowned martyrs by Nanni di Banco. This was part of a wider program to refashion the city's central streets, so that by 1425 the assembly of saintly statues was complete, some gilded or colored, which heightened the sense of paternal watchfulness over the city's orphans and widows.

Donatello's marble statue of St. Mark situated in a niche on the wall of the Orsanmichele, Florence, 1411–13.

The confraternity received a large amount of riches from wealthy citizens and in 1352 at the end of the plague an oratory or "tabernacle" was designed by Michelozzo in polychromatic marble and stained glass to receive hundreds of votive candles devoted to the altarpiece for the Madonna created by Andrea Orcagna.

In the 14th century an ordinance authorized that private properties in Sienna's central Campo must install bifurcated windows, common in medieval Italy and modeled on those of the Palazzo Publico, to provide for a unity of fenestration.

The main focus of his work was the city as a spatial and social structure, with its variety of public and private buildings, and essential connectedness. Alberti drew on values from a society whose primary forces and complex ideals were in a state of ferment, and craftsmanship was a fundamental part of construction that exhibited its burgeoning humanistic values. On the other hand he considered urban planning as being expressive of political activity and necessary territorial organization that was to condition the nature of Tuscan architecture.

Major spatial change came about through the growth of trade and commerce, and led to population growth at much higher densities, which induced a consolidation of agricultural tracts or wasteland for development, with the urban perimeter defined by reinforced city walls that protected the populations within. It also necessitated sturdy city gates that provided opportunities for imposing entrances or triumphal arches that added to civic status.

The Palazzo Ducale overlooking the valley of Urbino. It was designed by Lacuna and Francesco di Giorgio between 1467 and 1477, and transformed the ancient fortress as part of a program of renovation and expansion under the reign of Federico da Montefeltro. Over the course of 38 years Federico became an enlightened architectural patron to whom Alberti dedicated De re Aedificatioria and under whom Bramanti received most of his architectural training. The design extended the older building fabric, connecting it with the cathedral. The two, slender, medieval military towers were designed with an arcaded frontage to allow Federico da Montefeltro to look over his territorial possessions while fortifications were repositioned along the city borders.

According to Alberti the notion of an ideal city demanded a biaxial symmetry as part of a systematic approach to urban design, particularly in the relationship between building form and open space. This allowed for the delineation of buildings along streets with the capacity to define central spaces, carefully assembled to orchestrate a new public realm of well distributed squares, arcaded frontages, and civic or religious buildings requiring a prominent setting. The only reason to deviate from an idealized regularized form was an insurmountable interface with the medieval fabric, where new classical forms collided with an ancient and unstructured urbanism. An exception was the incorporation of palazzos, founded by powerful merchant and banking families who bought up adjoining properties in order to underscore their status. A new monumentality was introduced in 1427 through a tax on landed wealth that induced a greater consolidation of building mass.

Incentivized by the adversity of exile and the premature death of many family members, Alberti claimed that this led him to develop virtues that were doubtless associated with his first employment in the service of Cardinal Aleman, the papal legate in Bologna, and Alberti's later role as an "apostolic abbreviator" in the Papal chancery. There he was encouraged to exercise his latent preoccupation with architectural theory and practice, focused on urban placement, nature, and proportion from his experience in both painting and mathematics. At the same time he acted as an almost permanent secretary to the Papal Court for more than 30 years, bringing together classical learning with emerging scientific thought as an enlightened commentator and practitioner.

The papacy bolstered Alberti's approach to proportional harmony with ideological support, directing his design to religious buildings and the residential palaces of cardinals. By the mid-15th century this resolution of formal yet understated design had begun to influence domestic architecture, particularly large private palazzos, so that palace courtyards began to emulate church cloisters, reinforced by a recasting of civic buildings in the mid-Renaissance period. Important streets began to display dignified facades with regularized fenestration and restrained ornamentation that minimized business activity along their frontages. This in turn acted to increase internal privatization through courtyards and walled gardens that transformed but also dignified the character of city streets.

130

Alberti articulated an essential harmonious correspondence between the microcosm of humans and the macrocosm of the universe. He concerned himself not merely with a classical architectural order, but with the multiple issues raised by a changing society and through a philosophical and literary focus. His belief that the city was the central component of civilization led to an exploration of civic design in terms of the relationship between ancient and modern, symbolism and order, following classical traditions. The notion of society's structure based on status and fundamental distinguishing characteristics was essentially practical rather than idealistic, and it was prudent to accept the prevailing oligarchy between those who governed and the remainder of citizens whose positions in society were attributed according to their class and commercial hierarchies.

The philosophical movement of Humanism embraced poetry, the visual arts, and spiritual renewal that became associated with the Renaissance, marked by a flowering of creative thought whereby each part contributed to a larger ideal. Whereas medieval philosophy was characterized by faith in an absolute truth, the Renaissance embraced an interdependence of philosophy through scholarship as a means of reasoned understanding, whether through Alberti's architectural and urban order, or Vasari's observation of new artistic trajectories. In these we can discern not so much an unquestioned ideal of piety but a practical respect for the values of nature and its vital forces.

Alberti's writings are in one sense idealistic but are also the result of a devotion to contemplative intellectual values that evolved during his years of service to senior figures within the papal chancery. As a humanist, a rationalist system of thought based on classical learning might be expected to demand its own set of standards, reinforcing the connection between knowledge and virtue. With Alberti this turned to a consistent reconciliation of artistic considerations with practical aspects and ethical ideas reaching back to the moral philosophy of Cicero and Aristotle in fusing his civic-minded humanistic concerns with the needs of a rapidly urbanizing society.

The intellectual context for urban design cannot be separated from the ongoing theological debate as to the place of humankind in the universe. The *Renaissance* itself is represented in physical terms as the encapsulation of an architectural classicism, with its refined design principles codified by a

Equestrian statues by Giambologna. Left is the statue of Cosimo I in the Piazza della Signoria; to the right is the statue of Ferdinando de'Medici, the first Grand Duke of Tuscany in the Piazza SS Annunziata.

small number of urban thinkers and enlightened protagonists. These in combination transformed an ancient design vocabulary into a refined style directed largely at the developing cities of northern and central Italy, as expressions of their growing commercial wealth. Palladio's succinct summary a century later was that well-chosen and correctly used materials are necessary for architecture to be "convenient, durable, and beautiful" in order to determine its identity. In Italy's northern cities it was marked by material physicality, sculptural extravagance, and impressive placement of monumental landmarks. These articulated both the economic activities of trade and exchange, but also a mutuality with the hinterland and countryside that provided sources of food and raw materials.

> *I think no prudent man in building his private house should willingly differ too much from his neighbors, or raise their envy by his too great expense and ostentation; neither, on the other hand, should he suffer himself to be out-done by anyone whatsoever in the ingenuity of contrivance, or elegance of taste, to which the whole beauty of the composition, and harmony of the several members must be owing.*
> LEON BATTISTA ALBERTI, *De re Aedificatoria IX*

The classical city held within it an orderly if frequently disrupted social life. Alberti accepted the organic pattern of streets and spaces in the older urban quarters that inevitably evolved and changed according to informal and periodic planning circumstances that added to urban variety, diversity, and practical convenience. However, he applied a more doctrinaire approach to urban design with a concern for spatial perspective according to building outlook, consistency of form, and ordered frontages that merged individual buildings into the wider public realm. Principal facades were elaborated in precise accordance with an ordering matrix that achieved harmony and symmetry on different levels according to Vitruvian principles of progressive refinement, from use of the Doric order at ground level to Ionic and Corinthian orders above. These in turn were linked with a system of squares that had designated functions, primarily for market and public gatherings, not withstanding their practical ability to store materials in times of siege. Squares served an additional purpose as formal spaces within the wider spatial structure, with fixed proportions and ceremonial entrance points from street approaches.

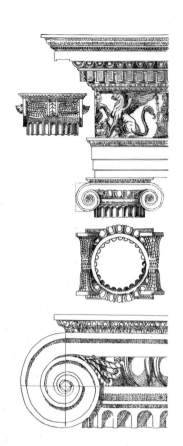

Francesco di Giorgio Martini's study of the relationship between the human body and a fortified city was described by him as binding the body to the city, reflecting for the first time the notion of the Ideal City and the unifying principle for urban space. The core of the new Renaissance city became the cathedral square with symmetric proportions and a harmonious relationship between the porticos and loggias. The head becomes the fortress and the arms the added fortifying walls that separately surround and bind the rest of the body to the city.

A copy of Jacopo Vignola's analytical illustrations from Regola delli Cinque Ordini d'Architettura, 1562. This and other handbooks reformulated earlier design handbooks, and both articulated and promoted consistent ideals that could be explored in terms of an urban design that encompassed both symmetry and artistic representation.

The mathematical relationship between microcosm and macrocosm became associated not merely as a canon of ideal beauty but of universal harmony. In representing the human form and proportions, the deeper implication was that this represented the perfection of creation reflected in the mathematical rules set out by Vitruvius, and interpreted by Leonardo Da Vinci in the "Vitruvian Man."

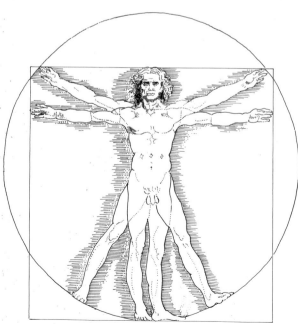

During the long medieval period geographical maps held little of scientific value, and were largely compiled through a pictorial representation of heterogeneous places and mythical features rather than a measured and unified approach. Maps of the Empyrean Heaven tended to indicate only the vagaries of the pre-Copernican world, and it was not until the early 15th century that scientific cartography began to set out reasonably accurate and verifiable city plans.

Alberti was responsible for the only measured plan of Rome during this period, combining medieval techniques to acquire a new empirical approach that heralded modern geographic information systems. An understanding of surveying and mapping was described by Alberti in *Descriptio urbis Romae*, setting out the surveyed features of the Eternal City, and establishing the basic principles of triangulation as part of cartographic exercises. This involved the use of an astrolabe, a modification of an ancient astronomical measuring device, which created a new exactitude and marked the beginning of a scientific approach to city mapping. Such an approach became increasingly common in the late 15th century when maps were combined with pictorial perspectives to provide spatially accurate depictions of city views such as the 1470–82 perspective depiction of quattrocento Florence where certain buildings are made to stand out in three dimensions.

In this way Renaissance architecture achieved a sense of unity by means of correspondence between the parts and with an exactitude of proportions. It also introduced the notion of geometry related to symmetry in the attainment of beauty in all constructed edifices. At the core of this philosophy was that congruity could only be achieved by an acceptance that nothing could be added, reduced, enlarged, or taken away without impairing the harmony of the whole—a quality Alberti called *concinnitas*. The necessity of complete form and proportion was considered to be intimately connected to the inner measure of harmony that flourishes in nature itself through a critical correspondence of parts that is instantly recognizable and is the source of aesthetic authority in building, just as it is in music.

The architectural language established inventive variations on different building types, but with a marked continuity of style and practice drawing new purposes from the classical past. Antiquarian study was part of an accepted scholarly process so that aesthetic considerations overlapped with political, social, and religious agendas, and the role of buildings as symbols of power in the cityscape that ranged from voluptuous merchant houses to stately palaces. Those in Venice were built with brick but faced with white stone or Istrian marble, and adorned with a proportional arrangement of fenestration elements. Elsewhere, building forms mainly utilized local materials and design references that inevitably reflected status and ambition such as the massive stonework on the Florentine palazzos.

An idealist ethical and artistic approach to civic design, together with high technical skills, combined both theoretical and practical sides that inter-related in an unfolding humanism. This helped to establish a set of applicable rules that posited rational goals for design, and helped to encapsulate the essence of the human spirit. Like Dante, Alberti considered that human destiny must be placed unreservedly in the hands of humanity itself, and no part of life could be discordant with the rest. Also in a similar way to Dante, Alberti aspired to a system of government that met the interests of all citizens in the preservation of liberties, along with a condemnation of civil strife. His humanist outlook tends to suggest a philosophy that blended together Christian dogma with a sense of reason aimed at a level above material acquisitions.

In 1447 Nicholas V was elected Pope as a reflection of his diplomatic skills, and Alberti was appointed as an architectural advisor and a canon of the Metropolitan Church of Florence. Nicholas V viewed urban design and architecture as divine forces and eternal monuments to a new Christian empire, in accordance with the papal claim to the resurrection of Rome's earthly significance, bridging the distance between heaven and earth. In this sense the Renaissance became a persuasive means of legitimizing spiritual and secular authority with a convenient attribution to all that was holy. This entailed a stylistic merging of medieval and classical sources that personified the Renaissance ideal.

Alberti drew on his own profound antiquarian knowledge to set out a classic treatise on architecture in 1452—*De re Aedificatoria*. This comprised ten books on the "Art of Building" to which he made constant additions right up to his death in 1472. It marked an intellectual means of relating urban design to politics and morality, based on Alberti's own research, practical experience, and observations that deal with various subjects in no apparent order. It was published in 1485, 13 years after his death, and dedicated to Lorenzo de'Medici, but was reproduced in the more familiar vernacular form a century later. This became the first printed book on architecture, patterned after the Roman architect Marcus Vitruvius who dedicated his treatise *De Architectura* to the five Greek classical orders according to different classes of buildings and his theories on town planning with a focus on strength, utility and beauty. *De re Aedificatoria* addressed architecture applied to city making as part of a new culture of learning that adopted a contemporary classical vocabulary. The 10 volumes set out design approaches to lineaments, materials, construction, public works, works of individuals, ornamental work applied to various types of building, and an approach to restoration. In Book 9 of *De re Aedificatoria*, Alberti acknowledges that in nature, as in human life, there are many kinds of beauty, but however dissimilar these are there is an imprinted sense of quality through a dignity of form that reflects a "divine" origin.

Gradually the new stylistic vocabulary was adopted further afield, transmitted by architectural followers, scholars, and textbooks where classical orders were assimilated and interwoven with local traditions. Design inventiveness referenced political, social, and cultural change, but architectural principles also began to reflect new scientific and cultural currents across an expanding field of discourse and discovery. The design of religious building in particular offered a means to celebrate the privileges of the observed universe rather than invoke fear of it.

In its clarity of expression Alberti's treatise built on the legacy of Brunelleschi through both design and innovative building technologies related to the practice of architecture. Alberti dedicated his treatise *Della pittura* to Brunelleschi as being symbolic of artistic progress and representation through *ingegno*, which can literally be described as a combination of creative abilities. In passing he described Brunelleschi's cupola as being large enough to cover all the Tuscan people with its shadow. Largely through this, both design and utility came to be seen as necessary civic responsibilities.

Alberti's ideas of civic design encompassed a high degree of symmetry in terms of planning and design. He interpreted this as being in accordance with the fundamental laws of nature—that is to say, the quality of being made up of similar but not identical components as part of a consistent and identifiable whole. It could be applied to the axial grouping of principal public buildings around a central square such as the Annunziata in Florence, St. Mark's Piazza in Venice, ceremonial spaces such as the Loggia della Signoria in Florence, and Alberti's own ambitious plan for St. Peter's and the Vatican Palace in close collaboration with Nicholas V.

Santa Maria Novella is a Dominican Church dating from 1278, and forms a defining spatial element in the Piazza Novella. The interior is designed in the Gothic style of the late medieval period. Alberti's symmetrical design of the facade for Santa Maria Novella in 1458 was based on reconciling pre-existing medieval ornamentation within a classical scheme made up of polychromatic marble with overall proportions that fit within a square frame.

San Biago church designed, on a central plan format, by Antonio da Sangallo Montepulciano, Sienna.

Palladio later referred to Alberti as the "second Vitruvius," and his elegant drawings and versatile designs reflected a refinement of applied detail applied to an orthodox classicism. Bernini's work also drew on Alberti's anthropomorphic studies on the relationship between human proportions and architectural forms in his conception for St. Peter's Square in Rome.

Buildings were divided into three groups for which certain principles were set out: public buildings, including churches and halls of justice that were considered important to the dignity of the public realm; houses of leading citizens, which required a harmonious disposition and avoided ostentation; and modest housing for the poor, which avoided a negative correlation with wealthier city quarters. Taken as a whole these elaborative guidelines reflect both the theoretical and the technical, devoid of any reference to religion but displaying a strong affiliation with classical antiquity. Alberti and other humanist scholars tabulated the mathematical dimensions of the ancient architecture of Rome. Just as Brunelleschi had recorded historical structures, Alberti perceived that the study of architectural antiquities revolved not merely around design directions but was a means of bolstering the educational ideals of humanism. Classicism itself came to be interpreted as a recognizable canon related to detail, harmony, and proportion that could be mixed with expressive Byzantine and Gothic forms to create a representational urban design. Through this, Florence evolved a "culture of supremacy" represented by its architectural edifices.

In order to achieve this elusive concept of harmony and proportion in built structures, Alberti attributed great importance to a simple model, with reference to Brunelleschi's inspired approach to structural design and coherence. To support this he set about understanding the elements of ancient and contemporary construction from architects, shipwrights, and even blacksmiths, including the assimilation of knowledge on the correct placement and stability of building materials that logically contribute to the design process. He placed much design emphasis on pillars and columns, from the wooden versions that originate in nature to their marble equivalent that create a supporting framework, both in relief and detached form.

An ideological objective was to both reinterpret and synthesize the design and harmonic proportions of the architectural orders, codified by Vitruvius according to numerical ratios, with a more naturalistic and anthropomorphic focus. Having established the logic of the orders, mathematically based on optimum human body measures, he then dealt with the symmetrical positioning of each part in terms of optimal proportions that had a design ancestry going back to the articulation of Greek temples. This elaborated on the numerology of Pythagoras, employing numerical rules for dimensional ratios to various parts of buildings, spaces, and symbolic references that he termed beauty in architecture or *concinnitas*, derived from antiquity. It reflected a subject of considerable interest to a newly aware society in the early Renaissance, equated by a unification of aesthetic criteria with scientific measurement and practical principles that formed the basis for consistent composition, and a necessary correspondence with building elements. For example, Alberti was attracted to the expressive potential of polychrome marble that he used to compositional effect, such as on the facade of Santa Maria Novella in Florence, to express both character and functions.

In all architecture there does not exist any work which requires greater talent, care, skill, and diligence than that needed for building and decorating the temple.

LEO BATTISTO ALBERTI

In examining the concept of artistic beauty, respectful of the harmony of nature, Alberti reflected a growing intellectual interest in classical antiquity, including its literature and regulatory values. This approach was defined as "planning rationally and executing practically," which implied a command of design, optics, and mathematics placed at the service of the community, only partly echoing and supplementing Vitruvius who stated that fine public buildings were necessary both to the republic and the empire. A further essential point of difference was that Alberti advocated a rationalized Tuscan architectural tradition based on proportionality and a symmetrical relationship between the various building parts according to both regulatory principles and human needs, determined by a sense of social purpose. Decoration was to be restrained and made subordinate to the wider values of form and fit, and extended to the urban ecology including its physiology and hygiene. These can be considered inseparable from the plans for human settlements and townships that Alberti recognized should achieve an environmental balance with the surrounding area, but also be reasonably self-sufficient in terms of crops and water. It was also argued that in an age of rivalry and warfare, cities should be necessarily defensible.

Gradually the new stylistic forms were adopted further afield, transmitted by architectural followers, scholars, and textbooks where classical orders were assimilated and interwoven with local traditions producing stylist inventiveness that referenced political, social, and cultural change. This included a relationship of design and proportion to numbers, for example such aspects as building corners and columns were specified as being of an even number, while the designation of apertures were always uneven. The numbers three and nine were also regarded as being privileged, referencing Dante's similar obsession.

Alberti regarded the "ideal" form of a circle as an example of nature, along with other centrally planned geometric shapes for sacred buildings—the square, hexagon, octagon, decagon, and dodecagon, all derived from the circle. Together with rectangles that exhibit the square and a half, square and a third, and double square, all of which have harmonic parallels in music. On an architectural level these can be combined to create a variety of floor plans, utilizing simple ratios that bind all elements of plans and elevations into a harmonic unity. Alberti came to favor a classical model of the square inscribed within a circle, reflecting Dante's philosophical interpretation of geometric boundaries. This in turn relates to the sequence of figures from the proof by Archimedes on the measurement of a circle by means of subdivision into an infinite series of polygons, first enclosing the circle with a square, then an octagon, and thereafter polygons, each with double the number of sides of its predecessor. The circle cannot, however, as Archimedes discovered, be precisely measured because of its arc, despite construction of a series of polygons having an increasing number of sides.

An emphasis on the centralized plan form set out by Alberti, and later taken up by architects such as Antonio da Sangallo, Giuliano da Sangallo, and Andrea Palladio as a circle within a square or octagonal form, emphasizes its uniformity from all sides, with a visual and symbolic balance between the interior and exterior. The centralized plan effectively dispensed with aspects that denoted inferiority or superiority, and sought to achieve humanism and harmony through regular proportions. This coincided with a new

concept of cosmology that reflected a philosophical transition from Ptolemaic astronomy to a post–Copernican universal structure in the early 16th century, which necessitated a reformulation of previous ingenious causal theories that had attempted to explain both the performance of the Cosmos and its many inconsistencies. Squaring the circle came to represent the concept of infinity, seen as both a valid and necessary means for assimilating mathematical knowledge.

The design of religious buildings in particular offered a means to celebrate the privileges of a supposed God-given universe rather than invoke fear of it. The figure of a human inscribed within a circle and square originally represented the view of Vitruvius whose centralized plan compositions for religious buildings were considered symbolic of a "perfect" relationship between humans and architecture, just as God was adjudged to occupy the center but also the circumference of the universe. This harmonious mathematical relationship that borrows from nature, is referenced by Alberti, Bramante, and Palladio and was famously illustrated by Leonardo da Vinci.

Perspective representation began to focus attention on architectural appearance and "fit." In effect, the vanishing point at the horizon, which allows for the visualization of infinity, was used to accurately represent a precise appearance of a three-dimensional structure from any number of viewpoints. Each then sets out the same information but in a slightly different way, relative to the position of each observer. However, the totality of views achieved from the sum of each perspective representation includes certain characteristics that are common to all and can be said to be invariant. Relativity is therefore at the core of what is being represented and allows observation of many complementary facets of the same subject, together with an interaction between subject and observer.

Alberti's last book *De Iciarchia*, written in the Tuscan vernacular and setting out his ideas on Florentine humanism, marks his key position as a monumental figure of the Renaissance. Vincenzo Scamozzi in *L'Idea dell'Architettura Universale*, published in 1615, 145 years after Alberti's death, supports Alberti's elegant mathematical treatise in defining architecture as both a science and a productive art, both theoretical and practical, to be assimilated systematically within all human pursuits. Such an approach adopted a maxim of Aristotle that grasping the "truth" behind an appearance, derived from a unification of geometry and proportion, echoed the evidently infinite mathematical structure of the universe.

The new technology of printmaking in the 16th century had a profound impact on appreciation and discussion of the emergence of art and design in terms of both aesthetics and high-Renaissance culture. The invention of the printing press facilitated the dissemination of knowledge, awareness, and education that actively offered urban-centered horizons but also an entirely new way in which populations could interpret the world around them. Humanist works also discussed not merely the making of art in a systematic way, but one that was grounded in prevailing religious texts, perhaps explaining the divine devotion of the artists themselves. A new conception of art therefore emerged in the Renaissance aligned with the significance of perspective and representation as a form of knowledge that stretched from the templates of cathedral design and the practices of craftspeople to maps of the heavens. The ramifications for both art and science led in turn to interacting networks of assimilation and theory, and therefore to new forms of interpretation, helping to fashion a longer term humanist narrative. It conforms to the notion of an immutable presence according to mathematically correct dimensions—the purposeful evocation of a Renaissance cosmology.

Alberti stated that, "When I investigate and when I discover that the forces of the heavens and the planets are within ourselves, then truly I seem to be living among the gods." Infinite space expresses the infinite life of the universe that cannot be ascertained merely through observation, so that the empirical reality of the Cosmos came to be characterized by unity reflecting a totality of interacting movements according to precise laws. A new generation of astronomers used the mathematical conception of the infinite in quantative determination, reducing geometrical figures to "definite integrals," which helped to penetrate the essence of the infinite as representing an entirely new concept of the Cosmos. Descartes took this analytical geometry a step further, with the concept of a universe in perpetual motion, reducing geometric shapes such as the curve to an ordered complex of elementary movements. Through an intuitive acceptance of the infinite Cosmos, Renaissance humans could confront the divine and express an abstract relationship with it, levering it forward to a greater level of determination over the following century.

The streets of Bologna integrate 40 kilometers of colonnaded arcades, the longest in the world, creating a well-used interface between private and public realms.

Colonnaded frontages alongside the Piazza Della Republica in Florence.

RELATIONSHIP OF BUILDINGS TO
THE PUBLIC REALM

Bologna was the first Italian city to restore and conserve its historical sites and integrate local heritage concerns into consideration in the building and zoning regulations. New urban design and layout initiatives have to establish a level of "fit" with heritage conservation laws, effectively shifting the focus of planning concern from architectural prominence to environmental concern for the city as a whole. Such initiatives have created a distinctive urban structure, effectively tied together through colonnaded frontages and porticoes which extend public space and enhance the experiences of a compact and walkable city while providing a continuous form of shelter throughout the historic center.

Piazza Grande, Arezzo. Arcades supported by rows of arches and columns along street frontages were widely incorporated in cities creating sequences of columned and vaulted pedestrian space. These established both covered walkways but also "thresholds" between private buildings and public spaces that could be used for a variety of uses and displays. This established a design "language" that became associated with certain Renaissance cities. Similarly colonnades made up of rows of columns joined at the top by an entablature, were used as a form of urban enclosure to define a public gathering area such as an important square or marketplace. Colonnaded frontages made up of columns spaced at regular intervals were also applied to classical building porticos.

The high-arched Rialto Bridge in Venice with its lines of shops was designed in 1588 by Antonio da Ponte, a master builder and hydraulic engineer, to replace an earlier wooden bridge over the Grand Canal. The intention was to make a symbolic connection at a major bend on the Grand Canal, and designs were submitted by well-known 16th-century architects including Sansovino, Scamozzi, Palladio, and Michelangelo. The bridge depicts, in relief, the city's patron saints, Mark and Theodore.

ASCERTAINING· HELIOCENTRISM

We do not ask for what useful purpose the birds do sing, for song is their pleasure since they were created for singing. Similarly, we ought not to ask why the human mind troubles to fathom the secrets of the heaven.
GALILEO GALILEI

ELESTIAL MOTION was a fundamental consideration of cosmology during the medieval and early Renaissance periods. The conception of the Cosmos was that the higher the four earthly elements of earth, fire, air, and water stood in the cosmic hierarchy the closer they were to the divine or "perfect" origin of being. This contradicted the reality of a single universe as a true "ideal." During the Middle Ages, heavenly bodies were frequently associated with some form of integrated union of intelligent life and the soul somehow connected with the cause of planetary motion. However, theological concerns in the late 13th century, coupled with the possible consequences of a belief in extra-terrestrial life for Christian doctrine, led to an emphatic condemnation of this notion by the church in 1277, which might of course even have strengthened medieval beliefs. The idea of an external intelligence, such as some kind of celestial presence—deputed to regulate the motion of the heavens—lingered as a common opinion for many years. The concept of infinity was too radical a concept for open acknowledgment, and scholars were largely confined to the Roman Catholic Church, which prudently skirted such revolutionary prognostications in favor of less problematic conceptions.

The design of Florence's Santa Maria del Fiore itself reflected the cosmic order, not in a literal sense but in terms of balancing the spiritual dimension to which all participants in the new astronomy subscribed, with the physical manifestation of this within an architecture that sought to reach far beyond physical space to the heavenly paradise. These two entities were deemed to be quite distinct, the earthly realm being associated with the transient but necessary earthly elements, while the heavenly realm offered the more promising prospect of eternity free from the afflictions of time.

The notion of spherical astronomy set out in *de Sphaera* by Johannes de Sacrobosco in the early 13th century, was doubtless influenced by the work of a near contemporary, Thomas Aquinas, whose mix of ancient philosophy and theology caught the attention of Dante. This theorized that the elementary part of the universe is divided into heaven and earth. Dante's astronomical prognostications made little guesswork as to what remote force lay beyond the elementary region, other than an ethereal realm where the "ninth sphere" was the *primum mobile*, below was the sphere of fixed stars and the firmament made up of the seven planets, and above this, corresponding with Dante's *Paradiso,* was the Empyreum—the intangible abode of God.

From the 15th century onward, however, both philosophical and scientific thought began to change with each set of advances in thought and discovery. The philosophical doctrines of the early Renaissance represented an impulse toward a new freedom of the human spirit that stimulated the senses, and through this encouraged a blossoming of the universal man who was essentially liberated from the medieval period through a series of scientific and artistic transformations rather than a steady growth of ideas, but whose emancipation frequently collided with disputes between faith and knowledge. At its heart was a continuous struggle between the empire and the papacy, where harmony and humanism frequently encountered the face of lingering scholasticism, which emphasized tradition and dogma.

All we know of the truth is that the absolute truth, such as it is, is beyond our reach.
NICHOLAS OF CUSA

Cardinal Nicholas of Cusa, more widely known as Cusanus, a German theologian, astronomer, and one of the most important speculative thinkers of the early 15th century, put forward certain principles for a new cosmology. As a disciple of Italian humanism and an exponent of conciliation in the religious debate on the spiritual-cosmic order, he perceived that any relationship of a god to the universe, and of the universe to human knowledge, should be recognized as a reconciliation between pure intelligence and heavenly powers. This presupposed the necessity of empirical comparison and verifiable observation, and had to be subject to the same units of measurement if it was not to be devoid of logic. Unconditional faith in the divine as a mere concept therefore required a new form of scientific knowledge based on mathematical logic, situated along the lines of Plato's vision and characterized by a differentiation between what was reasonable and what was intelligible.

The philosophical approach of Cusanus was based on the ascertainment of truth through a step-by-step approach. He insisted that all parts of the Cosmos had to be in equilibrium, each having its own intrinsic value, although this could not be determined with absolute precision at the time. Intellectual reasoning, which in itself resonated with new astronomical findings, led Cusanus to conclude that it was unnecessary to establish a central point for the universe as it possessed no obvious delineated geometric form. In theological terms if there was to be a god this must accord not with a central point, but with an infinite and indeterminate circumference. From this emergent philosophical attitude, religious thought began to embrace a new but not inconsistent notion of cosmology that moved toward a universal order—something that all religions could subscribe to in a multitude of fashions, rooted in the essence of human knowledge and the particularization of nature that could be expected to yield progressively more truth. Any sense of the divine then discloses itself in a unified rather than an absolute way, where all viewpoints must be necessarily included. This suggests a universal self with a spiritual extent that embraces all humanity, connecting and unifying both the finite and the infinite.

Cusanus enrolled at the University of Padua in 1417, absorbing himself in the humanist philosophy and mathematics of antiquity, and attempting to reconcile aspects that came to represent the central intellectual focus of the Renaissance. This ideally signifies an unfolding of knowledge in its multiplicity of expression, although the Reformation in Europe caused the Catholic Church to retreat into medieval dogma for a long period, with scientific thinkers whose views conflicted with those of the church hierarchy suffering ecclesiastical persecution. From the religious viewpoint therefore, a devout theologian had to resign himself to rejecting almost precisely what his intellectual side was revealing. Cusanus explained it as follows: "in order for the seed to blossom and bear fruit, it must be planted in the soil of a sensible world."

In Dante's *Paradiso,* written a hundred years before this, redemption signified an ascension and liberation from an earth-bound existence, creating a union between God and all creation through an overriding spirit of humanity. The argument of Cusanus suggests that the power of the mind is necessarily behind all creative activity, setting a direction for intuition and insight, something that we recognize in great art and scientific discovery. We equally ascertain this through the symmetry of architecture, the disposition and proportion of its components, and the harmony of musical tones, all of which require a receptive instinct where the intellect provides the means to resolve conceptual differences and realize a state of congruity. Creative freedom becomes the only way to represent the divine within the limits of human nature and the importance we place on the concept of time itself that ensnares humans in the particularity of any given moment. It also requires an intellect that motivates the power of judgment, as without it we can make no distinctions.

Cusanus was one of the first proponents of Renaissance humanism, and influenced later philosophical thinkers including Kant and Hegel. Alberti makes reference to the philosophical speculation of Cusanus, in particular the concept of achieving equilibrium and balance, both of which were treated as basic aspects of aesthetics. Knowledge was therefore pursued as understanding and interpreting the divine signs associated with nature, which led to the discoveries of Copernicus, Kepler, and Galileo. This level of perception and the absoluteness of their revelations took away the arbitrariness of simple opinion about the universe, progressively making it subject to definite rules and propositions.

Accordingly, since nothing prevents the earth from moving, I suggest that we should now consider also whether several motions suit it, so that it can be regarded as one of the planets. For it is not the center of all the revolutions.
NICOLAUS COPERNICUS

Born in 1473, Nicolaus Copernicus was one of the first mathematicians and astronomers to straddle the transition from the medieval age to the Renaissance, reinvigorating the Heliocentric model of the universe set out in the previous millennium by Aristarchus. Around the time of his birth, events in Europe were changing both the political and scientific landscape, which were to bring about longstanding conflict between Church and State. One of the problems to overcome was that his proposed heliocentric model appeared to conflict with the geocentric one, and his inconsistent assumptions on motion still attempted to follow classical ideas. However, his deductions were to bring about a new era of scientific thought.

In the early 16th century Copernicus formulated a model of the universe with the sun rather than the earth at its center, around which the planets revolved amidst a vast constellation, echoing the prescription for a well-proportioned universe drawn from a three-dimensional foundation fortuitously prescribed by Alberti. Polish by birth, Copernicus worked as an ecclesiastical administrator in Polish Russia. He was sent to Italy to study the regulatory mechanisms of the Catholic Church at the University of Bologna, but curiosity drove him more toward mathematics and astronomy. His continued observations led him to challenge the existing "finite" model of the universe espoused by Ptolemy.

Copernicus proposed in a paper known as the *Commentariolus* that the motion of planets took place within a heliocentric solar system. This set out a number of visionary axioms that included the fact that the known universe had no obvious center, and more critically that the perception of planetary motion was caused by Earth's movement, even suggesting that Earth held no privileged place in the universe. Not to be outdone, it took the Church 73 years from the date of its publication to ban the book that had been prudently dedicated to Pope Paul III. Matching the obstinacy of the Catholic Church it was also denounced by Martin Luther, a seminal figure in the 16th-century Protestant Reformation in Europe. What was really central to this disjuncture was the prevailing belief system of the Christian Church and its inherent promise of religious salvation. The emerging science of astronomy threatened the hitherto accepted metaphysical relationship between body and soul.

The final version of his work, *On the Revolutions of the Heavenly Spheres*, was first compiled in 1514 and circulated to colleagues, garnering a good deal of interest, but was only published in the year of his death in 1543. In the process, it attracted the attention of Pope Clement VII, who purposely allowed it to lapse into obscurity. However, it remained as an obstinate point of reference, and an irritant to the church throughout the 16th and early 17th centuries. The *Commentariolus* is made up of eight chapters, of which the first sets out seven postulates that form an explicit and systematic explanation for the motion of planets. These contain sections beginning with the order of the spheres and their periods of revolution, with the outermost spheres revolving round the sun, and the Moon's sphere revolving around the earth while moving with it around the sun. It is followed by sections on the apparent motion of the sun, the equinoxes, the Moon, the outer planets of Saturn, Jupiter, and Mars, with final sections on Venus and Mercury. In short, it postulated the Ptolemaic model of a spherical universe with no single center, and proceeded to justify the movement of celestial bodies in a uniform way, with a harmonious relationship between the motion of spheres and their size—something that was to be eventually disproved without necessarily detracting from the mathematical elegance of the frame of reference itself. Its revolutionary conclusion, however, was the implication that sprang from this—that the irregularities in the movement of heavenly bodies that Ptolemy had tried so hard to explain were caused by the motion of the earth itself. However, Copernicus did not entirely dismiss Ptolemy's theory of epicycles, which followed perfect circles at a constant velocity. His mathematical explanation was published posthumously just one year before Johann Gutenberg printed the Gutenberg Bible with movable metal type that was to create the means for an unprecedented dissemination of knowledge.

The detailed observations and mathematical calculations of Copernicus represented a revolutionary leap forward, certainly in terms of the prevailing Church doctrine, in its radical conclusion that Earth was in a constant state of rotation around the Sun thereby depriving its human population of assuming the central role in creation, and instead giving them the distinct impression that they had much to be modest about. At the time it seemed an affront to both the prevailing belief system and to religious teaching, but marked a profound turning point from abstract philosophical reasoning to precision, and from quite rudimentary theory to systematic analysis. It introduced a necessary new role for scientific theory, pronounced by Copernicus as being based on simplicity, order, and nobility. Clear principles could therefore be derived from this, which in effect represented a transition from "ideal" to "real." Copernicus also participated in a project instigated by the Church to synchronize the Julian calendar, which involved long astronomical and mathematical computations. Meanwhile, dissenters from the established Church doctrine were likely to be summoned to the Roman Inquisition.

The new cosmology, applied to the relational order of space under the intuition of Copernican theory, was dependent on the relativity of place and motion, and the conception of a homogeneous Cosmos. Replacing the geocentric with heliocentric theory explained the irregular movement of planets in relation to Earth's rotation and exemplified the methodical approach adopted by Renaissance thinkers, some of whom remained bound to medieval thought. A commonly held fascination with astrology went hand-in-hand with new directions of artistic and technical thinking that shaped new attitudes and approaches. In this sense the fragile line between science and myth was kept in check by a lingering medieval notion of God's omnipotence. Nevertheless, an empirical mode of thinking emanating from a new scientific and awareness began to permeate design and artistic practice.

Copernicus, who was a Church Canon, was requested to assist with the reform of the Julian calendar by the Fifth Lateran Council, and controversially went on to explain his proposal of the heliocentric model of the earth's motion as being a necessary part of this process. This eventually led to the Gregorian Calendar in 1582, which was conveniently accepted even if its implications continued to be questioned.

The diversity of the phenomena of nature is so great, and the treasures hidden in the heavens so rich, precisely in order that the human mind shall never be lacking in fresh nourishment.
JOHANNES KEPLER

Johannes Kepler, born in 1571 in Baden-Wurttemberg almost 30 years after the death of Copernicus, underwent a program of theological studies at monastic schools, but became interested in the classical theories of Platonic solids and the astronomical discoveries of Copernicus on the movement of celestial bodies. He also experienced much the same constraints and upheavals in promoting the heliocentric system in the face of the counter-Reformation, but eventually succeeded in demonstrating the actual elliptical trajectory of planetary orbits.

Kepler was a natural successor to his 2,000-year predecessor, Plato, and was unsurprisingly able to work at a more precise scientific level. At the age of 29 he published a book—*The Cosmographic Mystery*—which staunchly defended Copernican theory. His model of the solar system which purported to accord with the regularities of circular planetary obits, supported by Platonic solids, allowed him to frame the three laws of planetary motion that provided a foundation for Newton's later discoveries on celestial mechanics. Working with the mathematician Tycho Brahe in Prague in the early part of the 17th century, and productively utilizing Brahe's very precise tabulations of his planetary observations after his death, he produced the *Astronomia Nova* in 1609. This contained Kepler's First and Second Laws describing planetary orbits. A combination of laborious experiment, detailed observations of the planet Mars and mathematical process led him to realize that the entire range of planetary motions belonged to a special group of "curves" that could form circles, parabolas, hyperbolas, and, in particular, ellipses, moving at varying speeds. Collectively they became known as conic sections. He recommended his teaching career in Linz while completing his book *Harmony of the World* in 1619, based on Copernican astronomy. This comprised three laws about planetary motion and geometrical bodies relating to these orbits, which referenced Plato's representation of the five elements of fire, air, water, earth, and ether.

Turning to Euclidean geometry he examined the orbits of the six planets and claimed that they had the same proportions to each other as Plato's five geometric solids. On this basis he proposed a three-dimensional model of a polyhedron—a solid in three dimensions with flat polygonal faces. This purported to show the shape of the solar system, with planets propelled by the revolutions of the celestial spheres. Kepler's famous model positioned Earth as the internal sphere of the dodecahedron; Mars as the external sphere and at the same time the internal sphere of the tetrahedron; Jupiter became the external sphere of the tetrahedron and in turn becomes the internal sphere of the cube; Saturn was located on the external sphere of the cube; Earth on the external sphere of the icosahedron; and Venus on the internal sphere of the icosahedron, which acted on the external sphere of the octahedron with Mercury on its internal sphere. The polyhedron was a brave and imaginative projection, but deeply flawed in its conception without the knowledge of other solar systems. It became clear that Plato's intuitive and seemingly

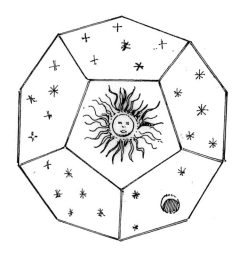

Kepler's Platonic solid model of the solar system from Mysterium Cosmographicum (1596), with a detailed view of the inner sphere.

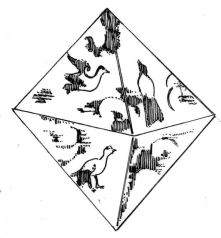

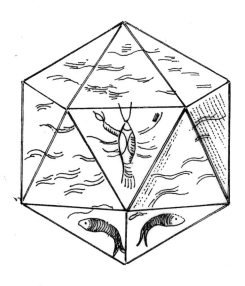

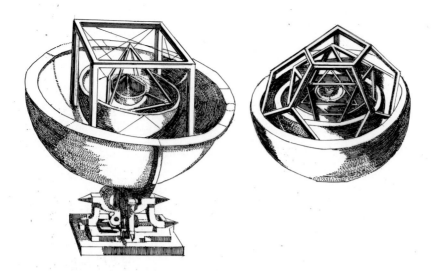

plausible theory of matter could not withstand more informed scientific analysis. It was, however, well fitted to Kepler's commitment to divine influence, based at least in part on his discovery that the Milky Way was made up of billions of stars. Kepler's work opened up an understanding that is still accepted as valid today—that the universe has a staggering diversity, and that mathematical symmetry is the basis of structure and therefore at the root of physical reality, whatever that turns out to be.

By 1627 Kepler completed a tabulated review, the Rudolphinian Tables, setting out the trajectories of all known planets, and a catalog of fixed stars. He considered that his Law of Planetary Motion was metaphorically in tune with the music of the spheres embodied in the "heavenly void." The three laws stemming from Kepler's work remain valid for all orbiting bodies. The first is that planets orbit the sun in elliptical paths; the second is the Law of Equal Areas inspired by Archimedes, which describes the speed at which any planet will move while orbiting the sun, and that an imaginary line drawn from the sun to any planet would designate equal areas in equal amounts of time; and the third is the Law of Harmonies which states that the ratio of the squares of planetary orbital periods to the cubes of their average distances from the sun is the same for each planet. The latter was formulated through a conviction that certain aspects of astronomy and mathematics could be linked with musical consonances through a geometric interpretation that related musical pitch to Kepler's previous work on planetary motion. He emphasized that his deduction of planetary movement was determined by the laws of harmony between the innate notions of numbers and beauty. That is to say, a determination that objects did not move according to constant velocity but at various speeds and pitch as they proceed in their elliptical orbits, producing changeable "harmonies" in relation to each other. Energy is smallest at the point of perihelion when a planet is nearest the sun, while velocity is highest.

Isaac Newton was to later formalize this as the inverse square law of universal gravitation, using data for the orbits of the moons of Jupiter produced by Galileo to provide an accurate rationale as to why planetary movements are in tune with each other. In turn this raised the possibility of an entire range of planetary motions that offered a new potential for a universe that was larger and more diverse than had previously been imagined. Increasingly sophisticated telescopes opened up an entirely new perception of the Cosmos and the enormity of the universe. Ironically, this heralded rather than reduced the earth's significance in the overall scheme of things.

To ban Copernicus now, when his assumption is proving truer every day and his theory more soundly consolidated as a result of many new observations and the activity of numerous scholars—what else would that be than contradict the holy scriptures in a hundred places that teach us that the fame and greatness of the Highest is miraculously revealed in all his works and can be read in a divine way in the open book of the heavens?

GALILEO GALILEI

Galileo's book *In Praise of Mathematics* was sent as a gift by him to Kepler in 1627. In this he makes the case for the importance of mathematical physics, which has been termed the science of proportionalities as the most direct means of objectively acquiring and synthesizing information on the natural world. This was consistent with what was actually occurring at the time through the rapid expansion of cities, new forms of building, and engineering inventions where a mathematical approach was essential. Galileo acknowledged that the scientific and the artistic have a common root. In this, Galileo's refinement of the telescope might equally relate to corresponding discoveries made through the fashioning of optics, which progressively revealed the microscopic world of bacteria and single-celled organisms that opened up the divine interrelationships at the extremes of the observable universe. Such an approach propelled inventive thought into unifying certainties that take discoveries in new directions—an approach that was later to be enthusiastically adopted by Newton who set out the laws of gravitation and mechanics that orchestrate the solar system.

Born in 1564, Galileo's family moved from Pisa to Florence some ten years later where he began his formal education at the Vallombrosian monastery before entering the University of Pisa in 1583 to study medicine. His natural inclination, however, was toward Euclidean Mathematics, taught by the redoubtable Ostilio Ricci, and he was adopted as a protégé by Guidobaldo del Monte, the Inspector of Fortifications for Tuscany.

Galileo was one of the forerunners of a modern science that by the mid-16th century was about to sweep across Europe. During a scientific and academic life, much of which was spent mulling over the ramifications and consequences of his pioneering astronomical and mathematical observations, he did not deviate, at least publicly, from an innate Catholic belief. However, this did not prevent a famous conflict with the church amidst accusations of heresy over theological interpretations of his work.

Galileo and Kepler discreetly shared an appreciation of the Copernican hypothesis, particularly after its telescopic affirmation by Galileo and the meticulous calculations of Kepler that established mathematical refutation of Aristotle's opposing doctrine, rooted in centuries of church orthodoxy. Of the two, Galileo was arguably the most cautious, on one hand taking an insistent stance on scientific evidence, while on the other covering himself from the prevailing conflict between science and the Catholic Church by quietly, but not determinedly, accepting the omnipotence of God.

Galileo was provisionally offered the post of professor in mathematics at Pisa in 1589, but was first requested to deliver two lectures at the prestigious Florentine Academy that had been established by Cosimo I de Medici. The subject chosen was the architecture of Dante's *Inferno*, drawing on a comparison of the models produced by Antonio Manetti, a friend and biographer of Brunelleschi, and by Alessandro Vellutello from Lucca—a traditional enemy of Florence. This somewhat innocuous comparison of two entirely imaginary interpretations compared and contrasted Manetti's extensive conical volume enveloping deep terraces for the seriously sinful inside the Earth, with Vellutello's cylindrical but constructionally questionable smaller volume at the earth's center.

As well as a familiarity with Dante's *Comedia* through his presentation of university lectures on the *Inferno*, Galileo's ideological approach might also have been influenced by the political philosophy of Niccolò Machiavelli, with his strong views on the weakening of political resolve in Italy at the time. While Machiavelli is also noted for the use of manipulative measures as a means to achieve political ends, his apparent lack of concern for conventional morality led Diderot to view his works as "the art of tyranny."

In 1587 Galileo produced a paper titled *Theory about the Center of Gravity of Solid Bodies* contradicting the theories of Aristotle through experiment and observation. He was not the first to address the motion of bodies, as its disputed philosophical ramifications had continued after the death of Aristotle, but Galileo was the first to systematically test them. In his first book *De motu*, written while he taught at Pisa, Galileo refined his theories on motion by comparing the relative weight of the four natural elements of air, water, fire, and earth, and concluding that Aristotle's notion was incorrect.

Galileo is famously said to have utilized the obvious advantages of the Leaning Tower of Pisa to measure the velocity of objects of different weight and material in the gravitational field, but is more accurately reported as erecting an inclined apparatus that allowed him to measure the speed of rolling balls made of different materials. He might equally have conducted many of his studies on stars, comets, and planets at the Observatory in Padua. By minimizing external influences he almost inadvertently exhibited the principle of acceleration. Galileo realized that it was this rather than velocity that affected forces acting on an object—otherwise as Newton later pointed out, the object would simply move in a straight line. Acceleration therefore had to be relative to the average distribution of matter, which is held in place by gravitational influence.

However, what became known as "Galilean Transformation" through formulation of the physical laws of inertia, were later shown to be true only for inertial systems moving more slowly than the velocity of light.

In 1592 Galileo was appointed to the chair in mathematics at the university of Padua, the capital of the Veneto area, which included Verona and Vicenza. From this authoritative position he began to attract large numbers of followers, which incentivized further astronomical investigations. The University of Padua had come under the aegis of the Republic of Venice and many of Galileo's students therefore came from the wealthy trading and shipping families who appreciated Galileo's enthusiasm for military architecture and fortifications. Galileo was not to forget the issue of scaling theory however, realizing that this was of particular concern as architects frequently built models to both indicate the design proportions and intricacies, and to provide builders with a basis for construction. The practical consequences of scaling up had been recognized by Brunelleschi in the construction of his cupola, but pointed to a greater reliance on the ground rules of structural and mechanical engineering, with mathematical calculation as a necessary part of the design process.

On top of his arduous teaching commitments at Padua he devoted himself to studies of mathematics and astronomy, referencing early works by Euclid, Sacrobosco, Aristotle, and Ptolemy. His familiarity with the observation by Pythagoras that sums of successive odd numbers act as squares is said to have inspired Galileo's parabola law. He used early references as the basis for lectures that ranged from astronomy and physics to military artillery and the mechanics of ship and machine building techniques. It was during this period that he began work on the motion and equilibrium of bodies, and embarked on a series of astronomical discoveries. In 1604 he developed earlier theories on motion, within a universal law on acceleration common to all objects. To assist his astronomical observations he refined and improved on earlier telescopic inventions that have been ascribed to Hans Lippershey and Johannes Kepler, who had neglected to take out reliable patents. He is said to have demonstrated his invention to the authorities who governed Padua from Venice in 1609, but they were unsurprisingly more interested in its use for identifying foreign threats, than in scientific

discovery. Having perfected his design, he constructed 12 such instruments for military purposes, and thereafter devoted himself to science and directed his telescope toward the heavens at the observatory that is still maintained by the University of Padua. It has been suggested that it was Galileo's knowledge of optical theory and perspective that enabled him to visually interpret his planetary observations in a three-dimensional sense.

During the course of the 16th and early 17th centuries, there occurred a long series of religious wars interspersed with various settlement treaties and brief periods of respite. These shaped the overall religious climate and the upheaval created by the Reformation in Europe. The growing conflict between Catholic and Protestant States, provoked by the intransigent religious disposition of the Grand Duke Ferdinand II in Italy, spread across Europe and changed its fundamental political landscape with allegiances in a constant state of change. Italy was also rapidly losing its economic primacy with the decline in the importance of its port cities that were necessarily directed toward the Atlantic trade in competition with the greater exploratory powers of Spain and Portugal in the New World and East Asia. The Counter-Reformation produced an even-more hostile situation for those who came into conflict with the dogma of the Catholic Church, with the "Holy" Inquisition handing out severe punishment to heretics.

In the meantime Galileo directed his attentions first toward the Moon and then at the other planets, observing the phases of Venus and Jupiter's four satellites that he energetically tracked, along with the myriad constituent stars that made up the Milky Way. In 1610 he was appointed as first mathematician and philosopher to Cosimo de Medici, Grand Duke of Florence, and in the same year he set out his findings in a short treatise, *Siderius Nuncius*, which cautiously supported the theories of Copernicus as to the structure of the universe. With appropriate finesse he contradicted Aristotle's long established position with recourse to his own observations and calculations, cleverly utilizing supporting arguments from past scholars rather than choosing to isolate himself in such a volatile political and religious context.

While Galileo was purposely prudent about the speculative implications of his astronomical findings, in particular its contradiction of Earth's supposed centrality within the universe, his annotations and descriptions formed the basis of debate with other scholars such as Kepler. *Siderius Nuncius* was dedicated to Ferdinand II the Grand Duke of Tuscany, and Jupiter's satellites were equally judiciously christened as the Medicinian Celestial Bodies. This was not only a popularly accepted gesture, but one that made its way through the superficial examination of the Holy Inquisition, and led to Galileo's appointment as a court mathematician to Cosimo II in Florence. This in turn led to a leading position in the Accademia della Crusca, a Florence-based society of scholars, and later membership of the Accademia dei Lincei in Rome. In publishing the results of his telescopic findings, including his discovery of sunspots on the sun's surface that were later found to be of magnetic origin, Galileo was careful not to be unnecessarily dogmatic. He wisely left open the validity of different opinions, including the tactic of diffusing arguments over chronicled biblical events that had a literal connotation or that implied contradictory scientific explanations. In communication with other eminent figures, he cautiously tested his theories and by 1614 felt sufficiently confident to confirm his discreet support for the Copernican model of the universe, although he seemingly ignored Kepler's findings that planets followed elliptical rather than circular orbits.

VITALIS LANDO PRAEF OPT HOROLOGVM RESTITVI

SENATVS VENETVS ANDREA GRITI PRINCIPE

161

Ptolemy's geo-centric theory served as a convenient model for the "universal truth," used to substantiate the authority of the Catholic Church, where challenging its religious and philosophical doctrine was tantamount to heresy. To openly disagree with this was to take on the entire panoply of religious thought. Challenges were dealt with condescendingly, and occasionally barbarically, until the onset of the Reformation, which led to increasingly independent thinking. However, at the time theological opinion still clung to the status quo that the Earth was the center of the Universe as affirmed by the scriptures. In 1616, despite the misgivings and attempted interventions of senior church figures, the Holy Office was instructed by Pope Paul V to politely summon Galileo and issue a warning against promoting his scientific views in support of the Copernican "hypothesis." At the time this did not seemingly prevent a series of friendly private discussions between Galileo and the Pope, and cordial exchanges with the College of Cardinals.

Sketch of Justus Susterman's 1635 portrait of Galileo Galilei, Uffizi Gallery, Florence.

The discovery of three comets in 1618 and the various contorted explanations put forward as to their celestial basis, provoked Galileo to publish a new manuscript *Il Saggiatore* several years later, dedicated to a new Pope, Urban VIII. It again underscored his stance that scientific deductions had to be based on sound investigations and verifications rather than biblical truths, but at the same time acknowledged that not all natural phenomena regarding heavenly bodies can be perfectly explained. While the manuscript toys with a number of aspects such as the relationship between heat and motion that were later to be refined and explained, it stimulated a variety of philosophical interpretations, some of which were incompatible. However, they position Galileo at the crux of a transition from one epoch to another—a passage from mythology to rationality and reason.

In 1624 Galileo was offered several private audiences with Pope Urban VIII at which he was encouraged to develop his theories of a universal order, and he proceeded to embark upon these with due reference to Aristotle, Ptolemy, and Copernicus. He cautiously, and with sensible foresight, shrouded this *magnum opus* into a supposed dialogue between several participants so that alternative expressed opinions could not be precisely attributed, in order to deflect any unpleasant repercussions. The Pope himself insisted on a suitably neutral title that evoked a comparison rather than a competition between the Ptolemaic and Copernican systems. However, when this was presented six years later, the authorities were left in little doubt that while the dialogue took into account all sides of the argument, it essentially constituted support for the theories of Copernicus. In fact, the tract also contained one unfortunate aspect in that it accredited to Copernicus an explanation of tidal movement caused by motion of the Earth, which was later discredited. Publication of the book, which was dedicated to the Grand Duke Ferdinand II, was held up for many years as those assigned to approve it continued to insist that the ideas remained incompatible with the ecclesiastical position.

The discourse itself reveals more than it hides, and centers on the division between proponents of the heavenly and the elementary, in effect the difference between the "perfect and unchangeable" based on its pre-set three-dimensional being, and the "imperfect and unstable" which must be subject to scientific observation and supposition in order to construct a sound explanation. After publication academic opinion was largely positive, but in religious circles and among his rivals less so. His established standing in scientific circles created a situation where the Church felt it necessary to contest further dissemination of the heliotropic system.

In October 1632 Galileo was summoned to appear before the Inquisition in Rome. He immediately wrote to Cardinal Barberini, the nephew of Pope Urban VIII, in an attempt to diffuse the situation, invoking both his ill health and the difficulties of prohibiting a text that had already been published. What transpired was a confiscation of all printed editions of the *Dialogo* and the convening of the Court of Inquisition in June 1632 where Galileo faced a charge of questioning ecclesiastical dogma and thereby attacking the accepted teachings of the church. The objective was to prosecute Galileo as a heretic, and if possible convert him. To assist this process, an Inquisitor had to be identified who at the same time acted as the judge.

The Roman Inquisition, as distinct but not too dissimilar to the Spanish version founded in the previous century, had been initiated by Pope Paul III in 1542 at the time of the Counter-Reformation, along with six Cardinals. A particular concern was the preservation of written propaganda against church conventions, and for this purpose an *Index Romanus* or Register of Forbidden Books, verified by church theologians, was kept for presumed reference by the permitted, the inquisitive, or both. Catholics who read any of these books without authorization were considered to have committed a grave sin that could lead to torture or excommunication.

Galileo's first interrogation began in April 1633, which centered on the authorship of the *Dialogo* and permission to have it permitted. He was then taken to prison quarters in the Palace of the Holy Office. During his second interrogation some two weeks later, Galileo, who had been given sufficient time to reconsider his original points of defense, conceded that parts of the *Dialogo* could be interpreted as support for the Copernican view. After this his place of imprisonment was switched to the palace of the Duke of Tuscany.

At the third interrogation Galileo was requested to submit a written defense, and during the fourth and final interrogation he withdrew support for the views of Copernicus almost completely, stating that these had never been affirmed and that the *Dialogo* was simply a means of systematically evaluating all the arguments. In one sense the case against Galileo raised a simple point that could well have been used in his defense, in that every scientific declaration must, until proven, be regarded purely as a supposition or hypothesis.

In summary, the verdict on June 22nd 1633 found Galileo guilty of heresy, forbade publication of the *Dialogo*, and replaced a long term of incarceration with a penance, reflecting a firm but sympathetic rebuke. After temporary exile in the Trinità dei Monti in Siena, Galileo was allowed to return to his country residence in Arcetri outside Florence, under house arrest and prohibited from any controversial appointments or teaching. His contacts were restricted and much of his correspondence with colleagues intercepted, although he was able to receive visitors, some of them very eminent.

Despite these inconveniences, Galileo almost immediately set to work on the *Discorsi*, as a set of mathematical demonstrations about new branches of knowledge that were published outside Italy as *Two New Sciences*. This was structured in a not dissimilar way to the *Dialogo*, as an informed discussion

Padua was the capital of the Veneto area, which included Verona and Vicenza. Galileo is said to have conducted many of his studies on stars, comets, and planets at the observatory using the telescope he invented. It is still maintained by the University of Padua.

between participating scholars. It was, however, markedly free from politically sensitive material, and concentrated instead on a series of "propositions" dealing with natural processes, motion, accelerated movement, and kinetic energy. It concludes with a series of mathematical theorems.

Toward the end of his life Galileo became blind, quite possibly from his prolonged use of telescopes to observe the sun and heavens. He referred to a number of potential projects but died in January 1642 and was buried in Florence. To prevent ill feelings within the Catholic Church, the tomb remained un-inscribed for 30 years.

In effect, Galileo presented a circumspect riposte to church teaching that was directed toward a commonly accepted understanding that humans have a preferred and special place in the universe. The fact that the Copernican principle states precisely the reverse introduced a contentious philosophical conundrum over the structure of the universe, and the fundamental laws of science that continue to have a bearing on life and meaning today.

MANNERISM, MONUMENTS· AND·MARKERS

Redrawn frontispiece from the original edition of *I Quattro Libri dell'architetture* (The Four Books of Architecture) by Andrea Palladio, Venice, 1570.

ANNERISM IS ASSOCIATED with the late Renaissance period. This partly reflected cultural and city-making advances, but ones that were gradually compromised by two main factors. The first was an increasing economic instability through competition over trading trajectories together with the loss of important territories that led to retrenchment; the second was the Counter-Reformation orchestrated by the Catholic Church in response to Protestantism that splintered the intellectual and belief structure of European populations.

By the 16th century, the Church had begun to assume a commanding role over both the spiritual and secular realms, and the papacy adopted the use of expressive imagery and monumental constructions to symbolize its power. In 1503 Pope Julius II began to restore the authority of the Church, which began an era of imperial association with a range of notable architects who were directed to articulate the increasingly triumphant program of building.

By the 16th century, the Church had begun to assume a commanding role over both the spiritual and secular realms, and the papacy adopted the use of expressive imagery and monumental constructions to symbolize its power. In 1503 Pope Julius II began to restore the authority of the Church, which began an era of imperial association with a range of notable architects who were directed to articulate the increasingly triumphant program of building.

Pope Leo X was born Giovanni di Lorenzo de' Medici, and became ruler of the Papal States from 1513 to his death in 1521. He encountered immense difficulty in implementing reforms agreed by the Fifth Council of the Lateran, but in 1516 a Concordat was signed between the Holy See under Leo and King Francis I of France. As an active representative of the Medici family, Leo was concerned to cement the relationship between Rome and Florence—the poetic association between the Tiber and the Arno. The Medici family itself rose to become Dukes of Florence with ceremonial trappings that consolidated their position as "first among equals." The Medici connection with Florence, and the opportunity to underscore its dynastic pretensions in this republican city, was further expressed through an architectural initiative for the design of San Lorenzo, the family's church in Florence and the burial chapel of the Medicis.

Leo was a strong patron of the arts, and he instigated the rebuilding of St. Peter's Basilica in Rome. Bramante was chosen as the initial architect for the new church, which was intended as a universal symbol of humanism. However, its combination of ancient and modern elements within a Latin-cross plan rather than a centrally planned one that proclaimed the absoluteness of theological teaching came at a time when, in certain quarters, absoluteness had come into question. Leo's death in 1521 and the election of another Medici, Clement VII as Pope in 1523, indirectly marked the end of the classical Renaissance, which coincided with a profound political and religious crisis associated with the Reformation and Counter-Reformation. The uncomfortable and often competitive relationship between Empire and Church that had so obsessed Dante some 200 years previously, came to a head in 1527. The emperor's role was essentially to enforce established doctrine and prevent outbreaks of heresy. However, the coming years were distinguished by the eclipse of imperial greatness and an increasingly powerful papacy.

Bramante was chosen as the initial architect for the new church of St. Peter's in Rome, intended as a universal symbol of humanism. However, its combination of ancient and modern elements within a Latin-cross plan rather than a centrally planned one that proclaimed the absoluteness of theological teaching came at a time when, in certain quarters, this was being questioned.

Progress of work on St. Peter's was slow. After the death of Antonia de Sangallo in 1546 Michelangelo modified the plan, based on Bramante's initial layout but with a monumentalized external expression. Michelangelo's proposal for a flat curve and a tall lantern for St. Peter's embracing an iconic image for "all of Christianity," was modified by his architectural successor Giacomo della Porta. The planning layout, shaped by the need for large assemblies and the visual axis of spectators, eventually took the form of a gigantic stage set, suggesting a familiarity with the work of Serlio. This formed part of a wider urban design that stretched to Rome's city gate, the Porta Pia, which formed the first part of later baroque city planning.

Pope Clement VII, alarmed at the Imperial power of the Holy Roman Emperor Charles V, formed an alliance with his great rival King Francis II of France, and a triumvirate of central Italian cities—Florence, Venice, and Milan. However, due to a lack of funds for the army of Charles V, more than 30,000 troops mutinied. A large force led by Charles de Bourbon comprising predominantly German, Spanish, and Italian troops attacked Rome on the 8th of May 1527. Despite a courageous "stand" by the Swiss Guard, 4,000 defenders were killed, and palaces, churches, and monasteries destroyed. After almost one month of fighting, Clement surrendered and paid a large ransom. As a result, the Emperor was able to exert almost complete control over the Catholic Church and much of Italy in the process, with strong repercussions for Italian independence and a prolonged pillaging of the gilded city by mutinous troops. This included the loss of the first globes of the terrestrial and celestial spheres, produced by Nicolaus Germanus, the German cartographer.

After a short period of enforced exile, the Medicis returned to Florence in 1530 under the banner of Charles V, vanquishing republican forces. After the 1537 assassination of Alessandro by his cousin Lorenzino in the Duomo, the young Cosimo de' Medici II began to exercise absolute rule over Florence and became increasingly influential on the world stage. He went on to regenerate Florence in various ways through remodeling of canonical sites across the city including churches, palaces, and public spaces, and construction of the Uffizi and the Mercato Nuovo.

It was left to Pope Paul III, elected in 1534, to instigate a program of church reconstruction and restoration over the next 15 years. He also convened the Council of Trent in 1545 that met sporadically until 1563, cultivated and prolonged through the religious upheavals of the 16th century. It represented the 19th ecumenical council of the Catholic Church, and was initiated in response to the Protestant Reformation in northern Europe. Its impact heralded an era of Catholic reconfiguration aimed at upholding the fundamental tenets of the medieval church, and to reform persistent corruption in its higher echelons. It included Imperial Diets that effectively redirected the long period of secular humanism along more doctrinal and theological lines, with the broad intention of providing a counter-force to Protestantism. Measures included large-scale exiling of Protestants from predominantly Catholic cities, a redirection of theological thought, and something of a return to traditional doctrinal practices, with religious education directed toward a more devotional foundation. It was persuasively reinforced by censorship of creative artists, writers, and philosophers, and led to the Roman Inquisition, which made humanism and scientific discoveries that contested the views of the Church acts of heresy. Senior members of the Church were empowered to zealously monitor all aspects of religious life for evidence of laxity and indiscipline. The council reaffirmed the devotional practices and sacraments, and the spiritual veneration of saints and relics, while pronouncing the Roman Catechism that was to form the basis of formal Catholic education until the late 20th century.

In the 1540s Cosimo de' Medici made major changes in the Florentine

170

government and began a process of territorial expansion. This led to both population growth at much higher densities, which induced a consolidation of agricultural tracts or wasteland for development with the urban perimeter defined by reinforced city walls that protected the populations within. It also necessitated sturdy city gates, which provided opportunities for imposing entrances or triumphal arches that added to civic status. Urban renewal intentions were influenced by the grand remodeling initiatives in Rome. His elevation to the Dukedom of Florence and Sienna in 1559 increased his ambition, and he began to play off both political and religious leaders against each other. After the death of Michelangelo in 1564, Giorgio Vasari and Vincenzo Barghini oversaw a number of new building and remodeling projects, including the renovation of Santa Croce and Santa Maria Novella, to the high standard of the Medici church of San Lorenzo, together with the construction of the Uffizi, driven mainly by aesthetic concerns. Other architectural masterpieces included the palazzos built by the Pitti, Rucellai, and Strozzi families.

The Council of Trent deliberately sought to emphasize a sense of awe and emotion in its religious architecture, employing the arts as a means to communicate its religious message to as wide a congregation as possible. A symbolic aspect of this was a central basilica illuminated by overhead light, together with lavish *trompe l'oeil* paintings on the high curvilinear ceilings of the cupolas, creating an illusionary perspective of apparently realistic heavenly associations. Plaques and alters, exquisitely carved out of fine marble, delivered sacred messages as well as fulfilling decorative objectives. One of the most influential Mannerist monuments was the deliberately dramatic intensity of St. Peter's Basilica and its soaring dome designed by Michelangelo, along with its gigantic square designed as a large-scale theater of assembly and defined by Bernini's quadruple colonnade.

Antonio da Sangallo, at one time an apprentice to Bramante, built a number of church domes in the early 16th century including that of Santa Maria di Loreto near Trajan's Market in Rome in 1507, and later oversaw the construction of St. Peter's Basilica. He incorporated Brunelleschi's design of cross-herringbone brick courses for the inner domes but adapted this to instead form double-helix brick skeletons filled in with horizontal brick courses.

As part of a strongly devotional agenda, both art and architecture were used to underscore the Counter-Reformation through religious imagery. This was, however, subject to restraints on its explicitness. Artistic representation focused on works with a strong religious basis such as decorative church altarpieces and in spiritual art by Mannerist artists such as Caravaggio and Bernini. These centered on distinctive aspects of Catholic dogma that encouraged piety and spiritual intensity such as the Transfiguration of Christ and the Saints, many of which held strong moral connotations.

The Piazza San Marco in Venice,
now an energized space of
activity and relaxation

The New Age of Venice

The amalgam of waterways, narrow streets, bridges and sudden culs-de-sac that make up the city of Venice relate directly to the history of its formation. The lagoon at the edge of the Adriatic became gradually filled by silt, introduced by the rivers that flowed from the Alps. The small islands and sandbanks were occupied by fishermen until larger settlements began to develop.

Venice, which was known as Venetia in Roman times, was subject to heavy siltation from the many rivers flowing from the Alps. An enormous wave of settlers arrived after the invasion of Rome by Attila in 452 CE, with the largest around today's Castello and Rialto areas. The islands in the lagoon were gradually developed through the political supremacy of Byzantium, which consolidated the island group into a city-state and a major power in the Mediterranean. In 828 CE the relics of St. Mark were transferred from Alexandria, in whose honor a church was constructed, which was later transformed into the Basilica di San Marco. This acted to unify the city, which continued to extend both its defense requirements and its trading interests. Sea trade and navigation were the foundations of Venice's wealth, and by the 12th century Venice had acquired trading posts throughout the eastern Mediterranean. The sack of Constantinople in 1204 marked the culmination of the Fourth Crusade, and after the city was plundered countless works of art were carried back to Venice to embellish the Basilica.

Extensive fortifications shaped the emerging city with wooden bridges linking the water-courses, with separate islands that housed virtually independent communities. As a direct result, Venice is divided into six self-contained districts known as *sestiere:* San Marco in the center, Giudecca in the south, Castello in the east, Cannaregio in the north, Dorsoduro in the west, and Santa Croco and San Polo in the northwest. Their individual morphologies were often developed around a centrally located church, with narrow alleys as a means of assisting local perambulation, while small boats served longer distances. Canals therefore assumed a greater importance than streets, and the lack of major bridge structures until the 19th century was never a concern.

The Chioggia Wars with the Genoese for trading supremacy lasted for more than 100 years, before finally succeeding in staving off the threat in 1380 and going on to increase the city's mainland possessions. However, in 1453 the Turks overran Constantinople and the economic foundation of the city's wars of conquest, together with most of the Republic's gains, were effectively lost.

In Venice the protective role of the lagoon and the expansion of its trading empire afforded the potential for elaborate decoration and symmetrical compositions, encapsulated by the Piazzetta, the Palazzo Ducale, and the Libreria Marciana.

In 1508 Venice suffered a decisive defeat to a joint army followed by the excommunication of the city by the Pope in 1509, while much of the new trading routes to the Americas were taken over by Spain and Portugal after 1492 to the detriment of Venice. This proved to be a catalyst for an epoch of extravagant building reflecting the aristocracy's investment in land, with wealthy families building palaces over-looking the Grand Canal. An unwritten building code, to which all owners subscribed, was that buildings had an overall consistency of form and none was built further out into the canal system than their neighbors, establishing an overall sense of uniformity.

While Alberti reformulated the principles of architecture during the Quattrocento, Bramante, Raphael, and Michelangelo represented the legitimacy of both papal power and secular society in the Cinquecento as a backcloth to an increasingly unstable political situation in the Late Renaissance. This was architecturally reflected in classical forms but with the potential for a wide measure of interpretation.

The savagery of Rome's invasion by Emperor Charles V's mercenaries, and the subsequent lack of patronage in both Rome and Florence, drew a number of architects and artists to Venice as a place of refuge, even though the city was largely a Byzantine one and continually threatened by an alliance of European powers. Among the new arrivals were Sebastiano Serlio, Michele Sanmicheli, Jacopo Sansovino, and Andrea Palladio. The city at this time had a population more than double that of Rome, and was the largest trading power in the world. Most buildings dated from the medieval period and were built in the Gothic style, which gave it an expressive but inconsistent identity. The ducal palace built in the 12th century, the Byzantine Basilica of St. Mark, and the Doge's Palace were symbolic of both the political and religious prominence of the city, where expressive imagery and monumental constructions came to symbolize its power. It was marked by the Serenissima Signoria system of government, which combined old-established representatives in the Great Council, aristocracy in the Senate, and monarchy in the Doge.

The aristocratic traditions of the city were elegantly substantiated by its architecture, with a connective system of bridges that accelerated the development momentum. During the 15th century intense redevelopment was an ongoing process as a result of periodic clearances. One of the largest was a plan for the re-building of the Old Procuratie in St. Mark's Square, which dated back to 1204 and housed the administrative offices of the city. The New Procuratie helped to formalize the spatial composition of St. Mark's Square and the Piazzetta, with its effective mix of public, private, and commercial uses, while its regular fenestration and colonnaded frontage acts to conceal its internal division into separate palaces for senior officials. The layout developed by Jacopo Sansovino helped create an important public space that offsets the elaborate detail of the Doge's Palace.

Filippo Calendario's sculptural depiction of Venetia symbolically embodies Justice, taken to be a virtue of the city-state, carved on the arcade of the Piazzetta. His sculpture of Noah and his sons is on the southern arcaded facade of the Doge's Palace.

178

Political power in Venice was associated with the Sestiere San Marco in the area around the Piazza. The administrative center of the city consisted of offices, official residences, the library, the mint and the prison. Prominent merchants and tradespersons had their premises on the Piazza and the Piazzetta that were used as intermittent market spaces. The Piazza San Marco is the central and major focal point of the city. Its traditional informal role was one of celebration in terms of reception ceremonies for dignitaries, processions, and parades. It remains as the most prominent gathering space in the city. The Basilica has dominated the eastern side of the square since its construction in around 830 CE, associated with the Doges' Palace. The present palace is the result of a rebuilding exercise and was completed in 1060, representing the wealth and power of the Catholic Church. At the height of the city's time as a ruling power in the Eastern Mediterranean, treasures and artworks originating from different periods were collected from conquered cities, and many were transferred to the Basilica. Its assembly of decorative features, multi-coloured mosaics and decorative marble incrustations, topped by an assembly of cupolas and turrets, is a result of different construction stages. These were inspired by Gothic and Byzantine interventions which combine together within a rich and uniquely ornamented composition.

Four gilded bronze horses were symbolically positioned above the main portal of San Marco. These were 4th century sculptures, plundered from Constantinople. They were erected in this prominent position to confirm the power of the Venetian state and the end of its status as a protectorate. The sculptures were removed by Napoleon in 1797 and transported to Paris, but returned in 1815 after the Battle of Waterloo. The threat of pollution led to the eventual removal of the originals to the Museo Marciano in 1982.

The protective role of the lagoon and the expansion of its trading empire afforded the potential for elaborate decoration and symmetrical compositions, some of them tipping their flamboyant hats in the direction of the Doge's Palace.

The Bronze horses of San Marco

Sebastiano Serlio, having worked in Rome for a number of years, arrived in Venice in 1527 and followed Alberti and Bernardi Rossellino in producing an architectural treatise of the Renaissance. Serlio's treatise of 1537 contained a large amount of illustrative material in seven volumes under the all-encompassing title *Tutte l'opere d'architecttura et prospetiva*, which was to be applied at an urban scale, helping to create "ideal city" forms related to geometry, perspective, and the five "universal" Architectural Orders from Tuscan to Composite. A further volume was devoted to the symmetry and proportion of facades derived from antiquity, with some stemming from the work of his teacher, Baldassare Peruzzi. The first volumes are dedicated to the "Euclidean heaven" composed of geometric planes, and the architectural embodiment of perfect form reflecting the use of the Orders in "temple" design. The second book, and one of the best known, contains three theatrical scenarios—comic, tragic, and satiric—together with cross sections that influenced urban planning as well as the theatrical scenes for which they were intended. Later editions were widely used as references for European Mannerist architects including Inigo Jones and Christopher Wren.

The island of San Giorgio Maggiore with its imposing church dominates the Venetian lagoon to the south. In 982 CE Benedictine monks settled on the island, which up to that point had been a vineyard. The monastery became one of the most important in Italy, and a new church was commissioned in 1565 from Andrea Palladio whose design acts as a visual counterpart to the Piazza San Marco and its campanile. The white frontage of Istrian marble forms an amalgam of two classical temple elevations. The plan form is based on a basilica with a transept and side aisles. The design also met the requirements of the counter-Reformation Council of Trent in placing the monks' choir behind the high alter, separated from the lay community.

Michele Sanmicheli and Jacopo Sansovino also left Rome for Venice. Sanmicheli was trained under Antonio da San Gallo, and was employed by the Venetian Republic as a military architect carrying out fortification works in the Venito. He is widely credited with introducing the High Renaissance style of architecture to northern Italy, in particular to Venice and Verona. His designs include the Porta del Palio and the Palazzo Canossa in Verona, and the Palazzo Grimani di San Luca on the Grand Canal in Venice marked by the orders that articulated the facades.

Jacopo Sansovino was a colleague of Bramante and for a time, working as a sculptor, he shared a studio with the painter Andrea del Sarto. In 1529 he was appointed city architect to the Procurators of San Marco in 1529 giving him enormous design influence in Venice. His most prominent work was the public Mint and Loggia at the base of the Campanile. Biblioteca Marciana, facing the Doge's Palace across the Piazzetta, echoes the Procuratie buildings, creating an open loggia for the ground level activities that have always characterized the square, using the form of a double arcade with an ornamented upper story. The adjoining Mint was intentionally designed to be necessarily defensive in appearance to protect the Venetian gold coinage. The result of the various buildings is that of a stage set with its pictorial quality offset by the backdrop of the lagoon, and its composition inspired the Venetian painting of Titian and Tintoretto. Andrea Palladio opined that this was the finest building of the Renaissance, creating the classically restrained but decorative architecture that later characterized his style. This included the Basilica in Vicenza, which referenced Sansovino's library and Loggetta. The library as a scientific institute became symbolic of the new Venetian classicism.

183

In 1577 the Doge of Venice commissioned a new church donated to the Capuchins. It was named "Redeemer" or Il Redentore, located on the island of Giudecca to commemorate the end of the plague that had devastated the population in the late 16th century. The island was notable for housing the villas of wealthy Venetians. It lies on the Canale della Giudecca, opposite Dorsoduro. Nearby is the church of Santa Maria della Presentazione, also planned by Palladio.

The Redentore became the focus of an annual procession, led by the Doge and senators of Venice, via a wooden bridge on top of boats, to ferry participants across the wide Giudecca Canal. The portico atop a flight of stairs is constructed of white Istrian stone, which accentuates and frames the main portal in contrast to the red-brick work on the main body of the church, and reflects Palladio's study of Roman temple design, in particular the Pantheon. Its interlocking vocabulary of columns and pediments on the facade formed a counterpoint to the similarly ordered composition of its streamlined bell towers and interior spaces that served the simple requirements of the Capuchin faith. The thin bell towers on the Redentore echo the form of minarets found on Istanbul mosques, reflecting the involvement of Marcantonio Barbaro, a Venetian diplomat to the Ottoman court who had a role in the church commission. The interior of the Redentore represents an equally unified organization of spaces through the arrangement of Corinthian columns that support the entablature.

The churches of San Giorgio Maggiore built in 1566 and the Redentore in 1577 designed by Andrea Palladio for sites in Venice herald a more stately assembly of forms within a unified whole. The church of San Giorgio Maggiore was designed in 1565 for the Benedictine community of Santa Giustina, across the Venice lagoon from St. Mark's Square. These exemplify Palladio's architectural transition from the circular "temple" structure that he favored, to the more functional and symbolic cruciform plan type arising from the Council of Trent that revitalized Catholic doctrine after 1545, prompted by the Protestant Reformation. The need for these churches to fulfill different ceremonial and votive demands indicated an opportunity to create harmonious but independent expressions of space that relate to the nave, the apse containing a high alter, and a presbytery under a central dome. In both churches this creates the opportunity for a classical facade frontage in the style of a triumphal arch that marks the central portal, and the use of white stone definitively expresses the virtuousness of the Divine Spirit.

Palladio's Venetian churches were designed to accompany the panoply of annual visits by the Doge of Venice. They signify a formal departure from Alberti's Early Renaissance design of S Maria Novella in Florence, creating a two-story classical composition with a tall central part, architecturally united with lower ones that extend over the side aisles. Both were used for the choral music written for St. Mark's, which required the use of separate choirs for its full effect.

The two churches represent not only the transformation of religious buildings during the 15th and 16th centuries but the refinement of architectural expression. In combination they admirably reflect Alberti's anthropomorphic principles of symmetry and proportion that trace an evolutionary course from antiquity. This encapsulates an essential beauty associated with an "ideal," designed to bring an increasingly secular population closer to the divine. Recourse to the classical style and spatial regularity inspired a new realm of church design, ironically referencing pagan temples described by Vitruvius. This applied not only to the facades but to the centralized plan form which was to have a long-term influence on church design as the ultimate perfection of nature, with the ultimate example being the Tempieto by Bramante with its circular configuration inscribed within a square, that served as the progenitor to the monumental Basilica of St. Peter's in Rome.

San Michele in Isola was the first Renaissance building situated on an island in the Venice Lagoon. It was initiated by Mauro Codussi in 1469 who also designed the campanile in St. Mark's Square. The island was donated to the Benedictine order by the Bishop of Torcello. The church is located in prominent corner of the S. Michele cemetery. The monastery was closed by Napoleon after France conquered the city in 1797, and its cemetery removed to the nearby island of San Cristofori. The canal between the two islands was eventually filled in, and the enlarged graveyard laid out as a formal park that contains the large mausoleums of wealthy Venetians.

Palladio's commitment to the theories of Vitruvius and Alberti produced a visual relationship between interior and exterior, utilizing a classically designed temple frontage that reflects the organization of internal elements. The rigor and geometrical refinement of Palladio's architecture exhibit a clarity of purpose along with an assimilated interpretation of forms and details from antiquity. Il Redentore and the palatine church of San Marco visually respond to each other with similar architectural credentials. It is said that the thin bell towers on the Redentore echo the form of minarets found on Istanbul mosques, reflecting the involvement of Marcantonio Barbaro, a Venetian diplomat to the Ottoman court, who had a role in the church commission. The interior of the Redentore represents an equally unified organization of spaces through the organization of Corinthian columns that support the entablature.

Palladio practiced mainly in Venice, the Veneto and Vicenza, with a range of buildings distinguished by an arrangement of entablatures, pediments, porticos, loggias, and "Venetian" windows made up of a central, round-arched opening and smaller side openings with small columns supporting the side lintels, encapsulated in the Basilica Palladiana in Vicenza, with prominent elevations modeled on Roman temple facades. His architecture was characterized by strict proportions with a strong reference to the symmetry of ancient "cruciform" temple architecture of ancient Greece. Its classical simplicity but dramatic sense of presence led to its stylistic incorporation on prominent church and public buildings, which lent these a refined but timeless quality through a consistent orchestration of architectural components reaching back to Vitruvius and his 15th-century follower Alberti that introduced a strong sense of balance and composition.

I Quattro libri dell'architetture (the Four Books of Architecture) was published in 1570 and set out Palladio's reinterpretation of architectural elements consolidated in refined residential compositions and villa designs. This draws on the work of earlier pattern books that in turn had been influenced by the Byzantine culture evident in the domed cross-type that formed the archetype of early Renaissance church construction. Along with *Vitruvius Britannicus* and *Alberti's De re aedificatoria* these helped to spread the refined classical style to wealthy patrons across Europe and America in the 18th and 19th centuries, in particular Britain.

The Grand Canal

The Grand Canal constitutes the main artery and thoroughfare of the city where trading ships once sailed to discharge their goods at the rialto. Its architecture displays a sequence of design development over 500 years

The design of the Venetian palazzi from the 13th century is notable for its mix of extravagant construction and its relative modesty of design, which contributes to a remarkable consistency of architectural form. This uniformity was expressed by Sebastiano Serlio in Regoli Generali di Architettura published in Venice in 1537. The organisation of the facade reflects the regularity of internal spaces and allocation of rooms. On the second floor is the piano nobile that represents the main reception room, or collection of rooms, marked by a group of tall window openings. These are flanked and offset by narrower private living rooms or apartments. In combination this contributes a sense of consistency and rhythm to the terraced facades. The mezzanine or "intermediate" floors above were generally designed in proportion to the reception floor and were used as residential accommodation, service and office spaces.

The earliest facades were built of plain brick with rounded arches framed by decorative elements such as bas-reliefs. During the Gothic period of the 14th and early 15th centuries, the pointed arch came to characterize the palazzi, possibly derived from Islamic trading connections. By the late 15th century stone inlays and tracery elements were added, an example being the Ca'Foscari stone facing that came into common use during the 16th century, although, to cut costs, facades were often painted. As all the structures were built on piles, these had to be driven through silt and into the solid canal bed, so in general building materials had to be of light weight.

Ca' Foscari commissioned by Francesco Foscari, the most prominent 15th century Doge, reflects the design of the Doges' Palace, and was supervised by Foscari himself. It has been suggested that noble members of the Great Council also copied its pointed arch symbolism in their own palazzi, an example being the Palazzo Giustinian, consisting of two identical buildings on either side of a central water gate.

The Palazzo Vendramin-Calergi was designed in the early 16th century by Mauro Codussi and fuses classical details with the standard Venetian form and restrained decoration breaking with the older Gothic palazzo. This represents a larger version of the Palazzo Corner Spinelli designed by the same architect who combined early Renaissance form with more lively Gothic elements such as the biforate windows topped by a common arch. Codussi was also responsible for St. Mark's clock tower.

Ca' Foscari

The series of palaces on the Grand Canal turned the city into a sequence of contrasting but spatially compatible facades. Their design took the form of a water-level floor with a gran salone located above the entrance and an ordered grouping of principal windows designed to represent the most distinguishing characteristics facing the Canal. While classical forms had become an accepted model for urban design in Florence, the prominent Ca'd'Oro designed by Marino Cantarini in the mid-15th century was a masterpiece of Venetian Gothic. Its name comes from the abundance of gold leaf that was used to decorate the facade.

Along the secondary canals apartment houses and institutional establishments were constructed, often for speculative purposes, grouped around a common internalized courtyard.

The connective structure of the
Venice canal network around
Calle de La Canonica.

The Dogana da Mar —the maritime customs office, sits at the entrance to the Grand Canal adjacent to San Giorgio Maggiore. At the pinnacle of the watch tower two Atlases hold a globe on top of which is a weather vane in the form of the goddess Fortuna, holding a steering oar which indicates the direction of the wind.

Santa Maria della Salute designed by Baldassare Longhena and constructed between 1631–87.

Other important buildings associated with canal frontages are the assembly halls of the *Scuole*, or brotherhood of laymen in the form of religious confraternities associated with the traditional guilds. These had an influential role in public life, and charitable donation to these organizations were collected as 'penance' to alleviate punishment and purgatory in the afterlife, but also to invest in the security of a favourable place in paradise. One of the oldest is the Confraternity of St John the Evangelist, founded in 1261, whose prestige was promoted by its supposed gift of a relic from the Cross in 1369. The last to be built was the Scuola Grande dei Carmini in 1594 and attributed to Baldassare Longhena. It was dissolved under the short rule of Napoleon but was re-established in 1840, and remains active. Admittance to the Scuole, and in particular to one of the Scuola Grande, was regarded as a great honour, and payments were made as a form of social security to the poor, elderly, and infirm. Members were ordinary citizens who did not need to support themselves but formally represented the community at public occasions and representations. Their communal status and fund management enabled them to build architecturally rich assembly houses containing splendid works of art by artists such as Tintoretto who was himself a member of the Scuola. It is recorded, however, that the assembly hall associated with the Scuola Grande della Misericordia designed by Jacopo Sansovino had to forego its intended impressive stone exterior when it ran out of funds.

A number of buildings relate to the artistic connections of the city. The Gallerie dell'Accademia originated in a structure belonging to the Santa Maria della Carità church, with an entrance designed by Giorgio Massari. Napoleon is credited with turning the private academy into a university where works of art purloined from churches and cloisters were relocated. The Accademia now houses one of the most important art collections in Italy. Work on the Palazzo Venier dei Leoni designed by Lorenzo Boschetti was halted and was later acquired by the Solomon R. Guggenheim Foundation as a modern art museum. The Gallerie dell'Accademia contains a number of exceptional overtly religious paintings from the Venetian School of the 14th and 15th centuries including the series of Madonna paintings by Giovanni Bellini. Artists also include Paolo Veneziao and Jacobello del Fiore from the 14th and 15th centuries; Giovanni Battista da Conegliano and Guorgione from the later 15th and early 16th centuries; Titian; Veronese and Tintoretto from the mid-to-late 16th century; and Tiepolo, Guardi and Longhi from the 18th century.

The Jewish Ghetto in the Sestiere Cannaregio dates from the late 14th century when Ashkenazi Jews from Germany and Eastern Europe fled to Italy at the time of the great plague. The term "ghetto" meant, at the time, a guarantee of safety and protection under a condotta or time-limited contract. At the beginning of the 16th century Jews were again permitted to come to Venice and were granted a dedicated residential quarter on the grounds of an old foundry. The Ghetto Nuovo was in fact not dissimilar to other merchant areas, but was subject to an independent jurisdiction where the community could practice its own religious traditions. As a result of population growth buildings were gradually built higher and more comfortable accommodation constructed. However, as the economy of the Republic began to decline the Ghetto began to lose its population, hastened by the action of Napoleon who burned its gated entry.

The Scuola di San Girolamo was constructed in 1592 for a community who accompanied prisoners that had been condemned to death, some of them across the Rialto bridge. Under Napoleonic rule in 1806 the building was converted to house the Società Veneziana di Medicina, which later became the Ateneo Veneto and houses a series of paintings by 17th-century artists.

The Arsenal, located in the Castello district, has operated as a complex of shipyards and armoires dating from 1104. It produced galleys for the battle against the Turks in 1570, and merchant ships during later periods. In pre-industrial times this depended on a sophisticated production and assembly process where tasks were undertaken as part of an orchestrated sequence from building of the hulls to fitting them out. Dante, who visited the site in the early 14th century, compared the intense activity, noise, and heat of up to 16,000 workers with Hell—something that perhaps inspired has later description of the *Inferno*. Security was clearly a major concern in terms of both the threat of invasion and construction secrets, so the Arsenal was surrounded by a stone wall and its entrance to the lagoon guarded by two tall towers. It is marked by a gateway designed by Antonio Gambello in 1460 along the lines of a Roman triumphal arch in Istria that was at the time under Venetian rule. The symbolic winged Lion of St. Mark placed above the entrance that became an indication of the city's military strength. In contrast to this is the nearby church of the Bishop of Venice, San Pietro di Castello, originally constructed in 1091 and rebuilt in 1596 by Francesco Smeraldi, to a plan by Andrea Palladio.

The recognizable form of the historical city can be seen from the landscape views of Venice by the redutisti painters, of which the most important was Antonio Canaletto who gained his knowledge of perspective through painting theatrical scenery. Many of these were sold to wealthy members of the English gentry who returned to Europe, guided by a classical architectural education, from which they set about reconstructing a new 18th century urbanism in the United Kingdom. Canaletto's paintings capture not only the architecture but the life of the city in precise detail, portraying both the gilded state ceremonies and the many traces of everyday activities on land and water.

From the early 17th century a more exuberant and decorative baroque style of artistry began to develop in Italy and other parts of Europe, partly as a deliberately flamboyant counterpart to the more austere styles associated with the Protestant Reformation. It was not universally accepted by aesthetically inclined commentators however, including the art historian Jacob Burkhardt who stated that the late Renaissance design product was a form of adornment rather than refinement and tradition.

The Pescheria, Venice's neo-Gothic fish market, was constructed in the 14th century to a design by Cesare Laurenti.

The Chiesa dei Gesuati originally constructed by a Venetian order of Jesuits who established a monastery on the Zattere in the 16th century. The order was later taken over by the Dominicans who constructed the church in 1668, which echoes the churches on the edge of the Giudecca. After the church was consecrated Giovanni Battista Tiepolo painted three narrative frescoes on the ceiling showing the history of the Dominican Order.

The Bridge of Sighs constructed in 1603, spanning the Rio di Palazzo, connecting the New Prison to the Interrogation Section in the Doge's Palace.

The Mores of Mannerism

Drawing is the necessary beginning of everything,
and not having it, one has nothing.
GIORGIO VASARI

Title page redrawn from the 1568 edition of Giorgio Vasari's *The Lives*.

What induces you, O Man, to abandon your home in the city, leave behind relatives and friends, and go to rural areas, hills, and valleys, unless it be the natural beauty of the world. Leonardo da Vinci, *Prophecies.*

Tomb of Galileo
Basilica di Santa Croce,
Florence

The Mannerist period can be divided into the early and late parts of the 16th century from around 1520, primarily associated with Florence, Venice, and Rome, was a broad reaction against the older artistic approaches of the early Renaissance. The later High Mannerism evolved more intricate and distorted forms that became a precursor to the emerging Baroque period. Both architecture and urban landscape during the period became subject to a flowering of popular imagery set against the Protestant Reformation and Counter Reformation that reflected a new realism associated with scientific revelations, new advances in printmaking, and voyages of discovery to the New World.

Mannerism extended the ideals of the classical high Renaissance that emphasized balance and proportion to more asymmetrical compositions that embraced architecture, art, music, and poetry. All of this brought social and artistic challenges to the previous "idealization" of subject matter. As a result, architectural and sculptural interpretation adopted more dramatic forms and juxtapositions, often with somewhat illusionary and ambiguous references. Architects such as Palladio began to experiment with the articulation and orchestration of the classical orders with "temple" porticos and pilasters that extended to two or more storeys. The Uffizi in Florence, planned by Vasari, broadened Mannerist expression through a virtuosic use of classical elements that required an astute concept of cultural intention. Palladio like Alberti was in many ways a theoretician and a master of superimposition, drawing on both the inherent art of antiquity while experimenting with a more pronounced arrangement of compositional forms. An acknowledged example of Mannerist architecture is the Palazzo del Te designed in 1524 by Giulio Romano, a pupil of Raphael, as a pleasure palace for the Duke of Mantua—Federico II of Gonzaga. Its inner garden was used as a private retreat with deep niches and "blind" windows producing a sense of visual decoration and depth, but also ambiguity.

The expropriation of land and properties in the San Lorenzo neighborhood of Florence associated with the Piazza della Signoria made way for Cosimo de Medici's requisition of the Palazzo della Signoria and its transformation into the Palazzo Vecchio as a grand residence in 1540. Both this and the adjoining Palazzo degli Uffizi, the city's administrative center, were carried out by Giorgio Vasari as an artistic urban design composition. The Uffizi, in the form of two parallel wings, provides a lucid example of Renaissance rejuvenation articulated through a classically ordered frontage drawn from Florentine precedents. A compositionally inspired cityscape forms an arcaded square terminating at the River Arno, establishing a coherent link between the political center associated with the Piazza della Signoria and the river, extending to the Ponte Vecchio.

Designers began to reject idealized depictions in favor of more exuberant and expressive forms that required a more nuanced interpretation and appreciation. In architectural terms it challenged conventional proportion in order to accommodate complexity and contradiction, heralding a move towards the embellishments of the Baroque period. This period also represented a time of discovery and dissemination of knowledge. This disrupted the more virtuous sense of harmonious proportion, just as astronomical advances began to disturb the hitherto accepted order of the "heavenly spheres" through the new cosmology of heliocentrism. At virtually the same time, the Protestant Reformation created both religious and intellectual challenges to Catholic doctrines. The artistic environment similarly became more confrontational, encouraging a new virtuosity. The church continued to promote a glorification of its sacred traditions that even cast aspersions on some of the leading artists such as Michelangelo who delighted in flaunting decorum, even in his fresco of the Last Judgement in the Sistine Chapel.

Artists of the period began to direct attention to a sense of figurative movement that emphasised a depiction of pictorial space that created interesting and often exaggerated gradations of depth. Of the late 16th century artists Caravaggio is best associated with a spontaneous realism, developing Leonardo da Vinci's mastery of chiaroscuro comprising tonal contrasts which helped to articulate and model the depicted subject material. This was coupled with a mastery of the dramatic possibilities associated with luminosity that came to influence the work of later 17th century artists.

In an artistic and critical context this originated from Giorgio Vasari who used the term *maniera* or "style" in an absolute sense that can be equated with "violations of the rules" governing the classical orders of the high Renaissance. It also introduces more elaborate combinations of features and treatment of surfaces. In many ways this represented a reaction against the rules of stylish classical perfection, blending its connections in a less conforming way that possibly reflected a crisis in the humanistic environment following the Sack of Rome in 1527. From the cultural confidence of the high Renaissance the period corresponded to a more precarious and irrational political state by opening up a more complex style with increasingly monumental and ornamental elements. Vasari was, throughout much of the period, an influential commentator on the development of artistic representation, technique, and invention, through his own work, scholastic ability, and important patronage—particularly that of the Medici family. He was a prolific artist and architectural practitioner, and under Cosimo de' Medici I he coordinated teams of artists, making the most of their individual strengths but reserving some of the most important projects for himself to ensure stylistic unity but constant variety and liveliness. Vasari's *Lives of the Artists* published in 1568 described this as a "modern" style that extended to social behavior and cultural expression, although its actual applications drew on a multitude of design references exhibited primarily in Florence and Rome.

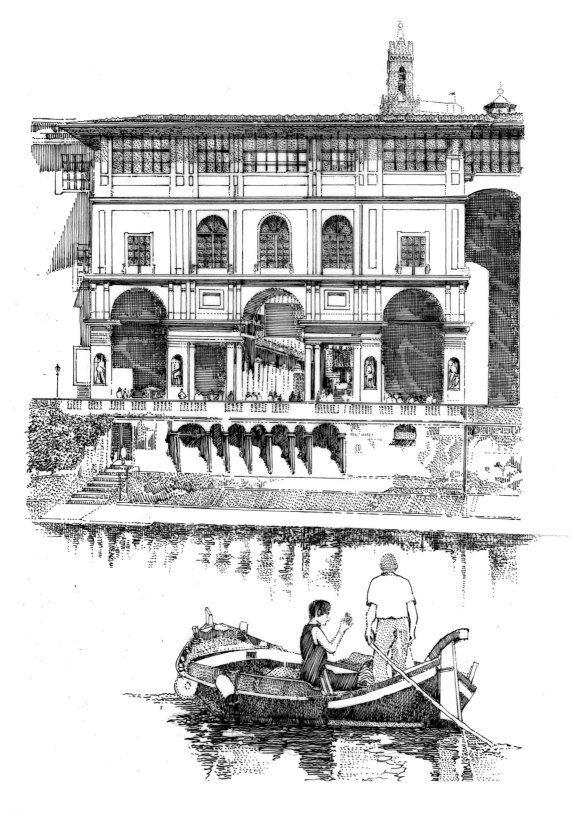

The Uffizi was created from the site of an old church together with adjoining sites, which were appropriated to facilitate a connection from the seat of government to the Palazzo Piti across the River Arno. A triumphal arch motif frames the view of the river, above which is a window, originally containing a sculpture of Cosimo de Medici gazing toward the Piazza della Signoria. Niches on each side were designed to accommodate sculptures of eminent Florentine personages, with Cosimo presiding over them as the head of an independent Grand Duchy in the guise of an imperial leader.

The Mannerist Kinship of Architecture and Urban Design

From the writing of Vitruvius in De architectura libri, and that of Alberti in *De re aedificatoria* both architecture and urban design are said to depend on symmetry and proportion in relation to building parts and to the whole. Mannerism however moved some distance away from the notion of an absolute or 'perfect truth' purporting to create an aesthetic of change while respecting an established historical style. Its validity during the late Renaissance reflected the changing character of society and the questioning of its standards, shaped by social, religious, political and scientific events, but also through changes in intellectual questioning of preconceived truths.

The Tempietto by Donato Bramante was constructed in 1502 as a memorial chapel commissioned by Ferdinand II to attract pilgrims to the site adjacent to San Miniato al Monte—the Spanish Church in Rome associated with the crucifixion of Saint Peter. This demonstrated a new conception of a centrally planned religious building taking on the classical appearance of a Roman temple, and referencing ancient history to underscore the legitimacy of the Church. Its circular form sits above the base of the cross in the crypt extending as a domed protrusion through a continuous entablature, and reflects the balance and symmetry of Rome's ancient temple designs. The meticulously crafted temple represented the expression of a culture close to neo-Platonism, merging together art and beauty, history and religion, pagan and Christian.

The sepulcher of Lorenzo, Duke of Urbino in the new sacristy of San Lorenzo, designed by Michelangelo who undertook both the architectural design and the sculptures.

Artistic expression overlapped with a growing architectural and theatrical extravagance that culminated with the grandeur of the Baroque. Young artists and designers sought to initiate and extend the impassioned style of painting and sculpture, following virtuosic role models such as Michelangelo, Leonardo, Andrea del Sarto, Raphael, and later Caravaggio who competed for patronage. In Florence the Piazza della Signora began to be filled with Mannerist sculpture, representing extravagant forms marked by serpentine figures that displayed both power and passion. In the process, art became increasingly commoditized and geared to the pretensions of a new, wealthy, and often powerful client body that extended to the court circles of Europe. This introduced a certain artifice in exquisite representation and sensibility that accommodated a striking resonance between artist and viewer.

A not dissimilar comparison to the architectural response of Mannerism to the High Renaissance style is that of the postmodern response to the paired-back conventions of modernism, that acted to reconfigure a new conception of cultural reference, complexity, and meaning in order to disarmingly recontexturalise building features and textures.

Much of the subject matter was closely related to a multitude of religious narratives and biblical scenes, often expressed by means of allegorical representation and elaborative symbolism as well as meticulous attention to detail that captures the impact of three-dimensional sculptural forms in two dimensions with extravagant and often erotic connotations. Michelangelo's extravagant Medici tombs express a historical sense of power just as much as they express sculptural finesse.

Giacomo Barozzi da Vignola, in a similar way to Brunelleschi, spent time drawing classical antiquities. From this he produced books on the Five Orders of Architecture, and encapsulated these values in the Villa Farnese at Caprarola and the Church of the Gesù in Rome. He also worked with Michelangelo on St. Peters Basilica. Vignola's Villa Farnese is a return to Bramante's simplicity and order, while his churches, in particular the Gesù, prepared for his patron Cardinal Farnese in 1568, was based on Alberti's simple oval and circular plans for a range of private chapels. Vignola's illustrated treatise *Regola delli Cinque Ordini d'Architettura* published in 1562 is a scholarly work that along with Palladio's *Quattro Libri* in 1570 spread an academic view of antiquity and Renaissance architecture to all points of Europe.

The Cinquecento's era of decorative embellishment, while incorporating graceful and refined gestures, was representative of a new way of interpreting the past. This is not only indicative of a change in the fashionable application of classicism, but to the almost spontaneous "enhancement" of work through inventive details, greater design complexity, and a diversity of building types.

Renaissance design itself placed an emphasis on humanism and truth in philosophical matters, and the value of human intelligence through an interchange of ideas. Thus the mathematical constructs of a harmonious universe imparted strong implications on design aesthetics corresponding to the role of man as the central focus of creation, with a pointed emphasis on glorification of the city. While the Church remained as the most important and immutable building type and a vehicle for some of the greatest artistry, an increasing amount of creative design was secular in nature. The Late Renaissance period became the recipient of a scholasticism that emanated from the late 15th century improvements in printing techniques and the accompanying dissemination of design knowledge. This encouraged a gradual move away from the perfection of classical forms, and the ideal proportional relationships and geometrical configurations advocated by Alberti, that Rudolf Wittkower stated as embodying "the perfection and goodness of God." Leonardo's church designs during the early 16th century for example reveal a new preoccupation with a gradation of spatial elements while retaining a dominant central dome within an inscribed circle, along with attached semi-circular chapels.

Some of the "ideal city" proposals of the period such as those of the Florentine architect Antonio Filarete, theorised strong geometrically oriented concentric forms based on radial organisation such as the star-shaped plan for Sforzinda and Palama Nuova by Vincenzo Soamozzi. In these plans placement of buildings and spaces fulfilled an astrological interpretation of hierarchy and unity, assisted by the necessary alignments of city fortifications and military technology.

The Villa Farnese at Caprarola is acknowledged to be one of the finest examples of Mannerist architecture, designed by Giacomo Barozzi da Vignola for Cardinal Alessandro Farnese in 1559.

The Villa Foscari designed in a monumental classical
style by Palladio in 1559 in Miva, Venice stands on the
periphery of the lagoon. The building was built on a high
plinth to keep out the water.

Roof turrets and arches with floral finials and multicolored mosaics establish the decorative magnificence of the Basilica di San Marco. The construction represents the result of several rebuilding exercises undertaken between the 11th and 13th centuries, each adding new phases of Byzantine inspired ornamentation.

The Council of Trent in 1545 introduced a tightening of academic freedom as Italy fell increasingly under the influence of the Spanish Hapsburgs. This was around the same time that the revolutionary theories of Copernicus began to instigate a new role for scientific theory and philosophical reasoning, under which corresponding changes in artistic directions helped to shape new approaches to design. The intellectual groundwork and even the ambiguities that stemmed from this cannot be separated from the expressive and experimental aspects of Mannerism, energised by a new individualism in the arts just as in the sciences. While the fundamental classical design vocabulary remained the same, the Mannerist approach encompassed both paradox and tension, disregarding the static remnants of tradition, at least to some extent, in order to evoke reaction and response. Building forms became more anthropomorphic and plans more elliptical, as designers responded to challenges presented by ancient belief systems that were, at virtually the same time, being overturned by scientists and astronomers.

This largely represented an intellectual process with the intention of shaking off formal precedent through constant change, unpredictability and spontaneity that reflected the political and religious uncertainty of the period. Historical associations could be merged with a more enigmatic vocabulary of signifiers that dramatized artistic and theatrical work, just as it expressed an affinity with a new architectural richness. Ovals rather than circular forms were used repeatedly in this work, and in the design of open space which helped to unify building groups. An example of this is the Piazza Di Campidoglio in Rome, designed by Michelangelo, which creates something of a spatial illusion through a manipulation of the adjoining building facades to emphasis the central position of the Senator's Palace from the stairway approach.

In terms of the Mannerist aesthetic, the more rigid approach is associated with Andrea Palladio, founded on humanist philosophy, albeit with deep roots in classical design gleaned from an early working partnership with Giangorgio Trissino, who in a similar way to Brunelleschi was inspired by the architectural remains of ancient Rome. His conception of architectural design has been referred to as a "gestalt-ideal" which acted to regularise and systematize the symmetrical planning of palazzos. His plans adhere to a basic pattern with some variation in response to specific requirements and site constraints. Wittkower has stated that Palladian principles held that floors and walls were sized according to mathematical rules, and rooms sized according to measured relationships with the perfect exemplification being the Villa Rotonda. In his church architecture the two elements of dome and nave interact, with short transepts and an extended choir, based largely on the more public requirements of a reinvigorated liturgy, but also to a strongly held Humanist approach.

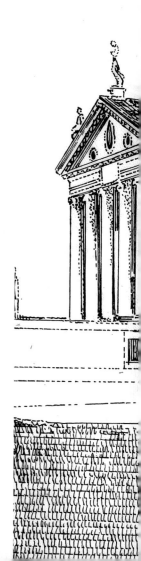

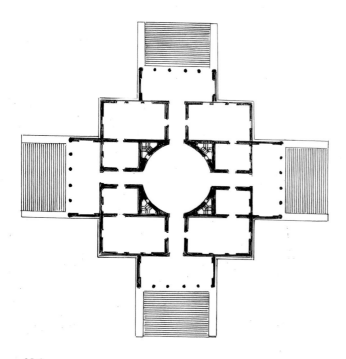

Outside the cities of the cinquecento period there was a growing demand for agricultural produce with a commensurate requirement for rural villas as the elegant centerpieces for large estates. Many of these came to represent the classical configuration set out by Vitruvius and the symmetrical proportions advocated by Alberti in De re aedificatoria. The refined villa designs by Andrea Palladio reflected his commitment to a symmetrical square plan as a compositional model for formal residential plans, occasionally with extended wings used for agricultural purposes. The Villa Rotonda, designed in 1567 is situated on a low eminence as a cubic form and dominates its rural setting on the outskirts of Vicenza. Its symmetrically designed rooms are positioned around a central, domed, circular hall, and is characterized by four identical colonnaded porticos based on a classical temple front.

The second and most influential figure was Michelangelo who configured a strain of Mannerist design, invoking his immense skills as an architect, sculptor and painter into the creative freedom that led to the Baroque period, and which matched an individualism based on constant experimentation. Part of Michelangelo's approach was the application of a giant order and scale on important facades such as the Conservators' palace on the Capitoline Hill, presaging a central aspect of the mature Baroque style. This led him to question an ideal unity and sense of proportion in favour of a more theatrical spontaneity applied to both spatial and decorative design approaches, often with a notable disregard for precedent or inhibiting preconditions. An example is the Laurentian Library in Florence which compells visitors to move through interior space in order to experience its spatial contrasts.

According to Nikolaus Pevsner one of the commonalities of Mannerists architects was to intensify the expression of movement and axiality. An imposing urban example is the Ufizzi Palace in Florence by Giorgio Vasari consisting of two tall wings that connect the Piazza della Signoria with the River Arno, proclaiming a spatial break from the static nature of the Mid-Renaissance period and combining the symbolic with the practical. This urban cleavage helps to create an axial and open-ended composition incorporating both visual perception and pedestrian connectivity along with intentional spatial contrasts and contradictions.

By the early 17th century Italy still retained the city-state polity of the Renaissance at a time of change through a period of constant scientific discovery and a noticeable increase in secularism, with an approach to faith based on salvation. The urban design of the city came to be seen as a backdrop to pageantry and display, encompassing design techniques which were used to achieve optical illusion, along with a reciprocal emphasis on grand effect rather than proportion. Architecture, sculpture and painting were combined, with an increased emphasis on the ordering capacity of public space. This was achieved by a gradation of scale, where urban composition and detail could be discerned at different distances. Building forms, and in particular their facades which were occasionally conceived with a curvilinear frontage, were increasingly designed for decorative emphasis or to define open space. They were also positioned as a backcloth for civic monuments, and this later became a feature of Baroque architectural composition in relation to adjoining spaces. Such aspects of cityscape also produced landmark foci in relation to patterns of movement such as the Piazza del Popolo in Rome, characterised by Rainaldi's compositional positioning of twin churches—S Maria dei Miracoli, and S Maria di Monte Santo.

Bernini's colossal double columned hemisphere that shapes St. Peter's Piazza in Rome creates an articulate monumentalist composition in its own right, but is nevertheless, not dissimilar to the combination of palazzos, waterways and bridges of Venice. The dominance of the Santa Maria Novella dome in Florence by contrast subjugates its surrounding cityscape within a dominant force field.

The Piazza del Campidoglio designed by Michelangelo forms a public plaza laid out between two summits of the Capitoline Hill in Rome

In terms of the Mannerist approach to urban design it is possible to elaborate on certain factors that helped to orchestrate an approach to city design in the 16th century which came to fruition in the ensuing Baroque period, coinciding with new metaphysical philosophies on space and time by scientific thinkers such as Galileo Leibniz, Descartes and Newton. This introduced aspects that structured the experience of urban space, helping to reconfigure an increasingly intelligible approach to the understanding of the Renaissance city.

Complexity and Contradiction

The notion of complexity that arguably stems from the Mannerist period materially relates to the cultural role of urban design in city making. It brings together symbolic qualities and occasional abstraction attuned to the basic attributes of the Renaissance city itself along with a recurring challenge to its representational qualities. In their 16th century incarnation, cities catered for a range of interactions including an emphasis on social and cultural rituals, overlaid by the political events that swirled around them. New forms of architecture in this situation related primarily to the reinforced role of urbanism to provide for a symbiosis of old and new development forms, where it is the role of the latter to achieve a necessary level of "fit" with the former.

In this sense the presence of commonplace elements, rather than overly contrasting ones, supply the main sources of vitality and variety that meet urban design objectives. It is equally important that the achievement of urban contrast as an adjunct to complexity adheres to certain ordained parameters. This is akin to the unwritten but responsive code that applied to residences on the Grand Canal that combined uniformity and order with variety of expression. This provides for different degrees of co-existence and overlap that can involve a range of design interpretations.

The Prato della Valle in Padua represents the largest public square in Italy, designed in an elliptical shape on land belonging to the Abbey of Santa Giustina. It contains 78 out of the original 88 statues installed between 1775 and 1883 in inner and outer rings around the perimeter moat. Statues of the Venetian doges were destroyed by Napoleon in 1797. The Palazzo Angeli built in the 15th century is now a museum.

The church of Trinità dei Monti in Rome dominates the skyline from the Piazza di Spagna. The Spanish steps were built by French diplomat Stefano Gueffier in 1723 to link the church with the square, which is named after the Spanish embassy to the Holy See.

Edges and Interfaces

Streets and canal frontages embedded within the city fabric tend to display a modulated visual affinity and divisional emphasis rather than rigid duplication. This helps to strengthen spatial boundaries through a harmonious dialogue between uses. In this context repetition is alleviated by patterns of correspondence that include materials, texture, color, and profile. At the same time the aesthetic beauty of the Renaissance city comes from diversity based on common principles. This represents a fusion of familiarity and novelty, where the overall pattern of the street or canal-side structures establishes an essential unity but where the parts exhibit some degree of contrast to create a "rhyming urbanism" blending complexity with pattern. The result is a recognizable totality that is both expressive and responsive. This is assisted in the Renaissance city through a practical standardisation of building plots but with an extravagance of roofscape where the building meets the sky—a characteristic of the Baroque. Buildings that make up the street are necessarily enlivened by the essential contributors to the urban environment—the users and observers themselves, who contribute an expressive array of market places and pavement cafes that comprise the ad hoc value system.

Imprints and Palimpsests

Older urban quarters are marked by cycles of regeneration and replacement which incorporate layered remnants of the past in the form of physical permanences. Historical signifiers promote symbolic meaning to different localities, where established street forms can be broken down into tangible heritage that represents recognizable architectural enclaves, and intangible heritage with expressive values encouraging urban activities that mark a sense of place through strong cultural and social associations.

The evolving impact of land values and ownership patterns, are continually shaped by an accretion of historical trace elements, both physical and metaphysical. Embedded persistencies and elaborate overlays inject an influential spatial presence related to time as well as use, inscribing the past into the present. This raises important questions on to cultural and aesthetic values associated with historic urban environments, and to functional diversity related to cultural consumption and visitation, while retaining "permanences" which reinforce distinctive localities and the "memory" of the city that accompanies this.

Diverse forms of representation formed a central part of Mannerism through an ability to sustain expressive qualities which reinforce the value of historic urban fabric to the community through patterns of association and economic interdependencies. The less specific the form and ownership structure, the more city fabric becomes responsive to localized improvisation, with overlapping functional configurations. Constant insertions invoke different qualities of uses which interact in ways that transcend time and place.

Compositional Organisation

During the course of the 16th century, a constant process of renewal and adaptation created sequences of new uses layered onto existing fabric. The cultural value of this, intermeshed with the diffuse narrative of growth and change, achieved an integrative urbanism where disparate parts were mutually reinforcing. Periodic insertions underscore the significance of historical associations that heighten the perception and understanding of the contemporary city through a co-existence of design languages. This establishes an affinity with wider qualities of use where aspects of familiarity, embedded within the fine-grained city fabric, reinforce urban identity and preserve "place" associations. In this context the concept of maniera can be said to encompass a variety of approaches including the asymmetrical as well as the elegant. In fact the degree of tension and "instability," which extends to Mannerist art and literature, establishes a bella maniera that combines the essential characteristics of the Renaissance city, synthesising both style and stimulation in its presentation. In this situation the irrational and contradictory complement the harmonious, and virtuosic grandeur can be experienced hand-in-hand with a new and atmospheric sensibility that extends to what seem to be cultural stage settings applied to place making in the late 16th century.

The fact that Italian Mannerism arose through political power, challenges to the Catholic Church and Copernican heliocentrism, cannot be separated from its departure from previously accepted conventions, where deliberate breaking of norms sought to overturn the older order and engage with an ambiguous future. It introduced a distorted but ultimately rich period of invention and extravagance that was to spread well beyond Italy.

Spaces of Convergence

Diffused patterns of movement within the late Renaissance city broadly emphasise the well-established and newly articulated medieval street framework where the relationship between public and private realms resulted in an urban design of delineated spaces and interfaces. An intensive mix of spatial situations lightens patterns of social and economic engagement in relation to activities and events and reflects long established settings for monuments and sacred places associated with cultural and behavioural rituals. These have forged a connective framework of fragmented gathering spaces that act to reinforce the identity of different urban sectors which establish an overlay of order out of the fine-grained morphology.

Building and spatial configurations that present an organic appearance in their present state are generally the result of early settlement imprints, regulatory regimes, land ownership and market imperatives. In their present state they help to sustain the older associations with urban 'places' occasionally at the expense of incongruity, helping to incorporate an undercurrent of unexpectedness and encounter as enigmatic additions to the urban narrative.

The diversity of the street realm reinforces aspects of cultural continuity that underpin public life. Points of transaction create "edge" places that focus on special types of activity and interaction. This is shaped and animated by a wide range of users and operators. Voids in the street matrix become positively changed with temporary interventions, responding not merely to what is there but what is lacking. As residential development generally forms an integral part of mixed-use urban neighbourhoods, commodification and commercial interaction become inevitable by-products of this process, establishing distinctive local identities to urban quarters regardless of territorial boundaries.

Monuments and Markers

The urban design language encapsulates distinctive spatial character that has, from the 15th century, encompassed many layers of meaning. In this sense Renaissance cities are expressive of their historical and cultural past. Monuments and markers act as expressions of durable city values helping to fix the identity of civic places through spatial emphasis. These are woven into the city fabric through public statutory, ornate fountains, and the domes and spires associated with religious edifices. The result is contrast and complexity within a highly intelligible pattern on which intense levels of visitation and economic activity have been superimposed over several centuries. Street buildings accommodate a diverse range of uses behind, new or upgraded facades that have changed very little in terms of overall design and proportion. The older cultural dimensions are therefore interwoven with revitalised development pockets reflecting constantly changing economic and visitor priorities. In these situation upgrading and gentrification relates not just to the economic health of the city with regard to asset values and changing needs, but to cultural attributes marking historical events and often contested territory. This induces a range of secondary benefits, safeguarding a range of qualities that matter to the community. New growth is directed to the urban fringe and beyond, re-fashioning the physical extent and capacity of the city while reinforcing the dimensions of its older core.

CALIBRATING·
THE·COSMOS

To me there has never been a higher source of earthly honor or distinction than that connected with advances in science.
ISAAC NEWTON

VER THE YEARS immediately following Galileo's *Dialogue*, despite the scholarly work of Tycho Brahe, Kepler, Copernicus, and others, Aristotelian treatises in Latin translation and in particular his *De caelo* on natural philosophy—along with Sacrobosco's *Treatise on the Sphere*—were largely followed through a lingering assumption that the Cosmos was in an eternal state of being. Aristotle had declared that no changes in the celestial region had ever been recorded, and that such a body was likely to be more perfect the further it was from the earth, so that the logic of human activity was at one with that of the Cosmos. This unequivocal observation was evidently accepted by Thomas Aquinas who similarly stated in *On the Eternity of the World* that God could have created the world without a temporal beginning. Copernicus, despite his revelatory calculations of planetary movements, not only referred to the sun as the occupant at the center of a spherical universe, he poetically called it "the lantern of the universe." Galileo stated that, "the circular motion of the heavens is of such a nature that it can be perfect in itself, for it is always the same in the beginning, the middle, and the end." Enthusiastic astronomers going as far back as Ptolemy could at best only record astral movement rather than provide an explanation for it.

Gottfried Wilhelm Leibniz, a 17th-century German logician, was a thinker rather than a scientist, and, while dismissing any aspect of metaphysics that was incompatible with the Eucharist, is credited with a philosophy that the metaphysical position on space and time, and in fact all subjective matter of mathematics, cannot have a reality independent of the human mind. Eminent scientific thinkers have generally been entirely satisfied that the beauty in a set of mathematical equations is in itself equal or even more important than the experimental process. The justification for this is that the generation of new knowledge relies on the certainty of mathematical demonstration and "fit." Mathematical equations are in fact a gateway to the workings of the natural world.

We might say that scientific discovery moves us on from the specious argument made plausible by unquestioning faith, to the more liberating possibilities associated with reason. And of course scientists must take either a rationalist approach based on sound logic and deduction, or an empirical approach based on verifiable knowledge, facts, and experience. These approaches are not necessarily coincident, but rely on the certainty of mathematical demonstration. The language of mathematics exhibits both symmetry and harmony that we see in nature's design just as it is evident in the structure of our DNA. Copernicus for example put forward his heliocentric model of the solar system on the basis of its mathematical fit. While this does not necessarily preclude essential observation, a proven mathematical formula facilitates further essential deductions about naturally occurring phenomena, which allows physical reality to be expressed in precise terms, even if aspects of our subjective experience and observations cannot be treated in such a way.

Kepler's laws of planetary motion paved the way for scientific insistence on precision and mathematical symmetry applied to the testing of hypotheses. While Galileo reconfigured Aristotle's concept of motion using quantifiable data, it was Isaac Newton who finally articulated this in definitive terms in relation to natural philosophy in *Philosophiae Naturalis Principia Mathematica*. In this he drew a distinction between mathematical truth and physical truth, while acknowledging the necessity of observation and experimentation in progressively refining the conclusions. The unification of the terrestrial and celestial realms was convincingly resolved by Newton who showed that gravity was the force that kept planets in orbit within a Cosmos comprising an unholy trinity of matter, space, and force.

Newton, whose birth in 1642 four years before that of Leibniz, also coincided with the death of Galileo, modestly acknowledged an indebtedness to his immediate predecessors by claiming that he was merely, "standing on the shoulders of giants." At the same time he raised a number of leading questions that suggest that he was open to philosophical speculation as well as scientific analysis. His three laws of motion were the final proof that gravity equally governed celestial as well as terrestrial dynamics, and led to his Universal Law of Gravitation. Galileo would have readily acknowledged the first law, which states that a body will change its state of rest if some force is impressed upon it, and in all probability would also have recognized the second law in which a body accelerates in free fall, in proportion to the impressed force. The third law states that for every action there is an equal reaction.

In chronicling the shadows of the sun to keep an accurate track of time in the rural English countryside, Newton was well versed in astronomy by the time he attended Cambridge University at the age of 22. As a result he developed many of his ideas on calculus, universal gravity, and optics as a young man. Although chiefly identified with the universal law on gravitation, his analytical experiments on the chemistry of light established that the spectral colors can be effectively formed from white light derived from the sun and passing through a second prism. The photons from sunlight can be separated allowing for beams of pure substances whose properties can be reproduced. Thus the periodic table of light can be arranged according to the chemical properties of the spectral color elements. Newton developed Galileo's telescope based on optical lenses to produce a reflective version using mirrors, which reduced chromatic problems. By analyzing light from a star, its composition could be determined, paving the way for new scientific discoveries.

The immediate relevance of the laws of motion was to ascertain the forces that might be at play in maintaining a planet's elliptical orbit around the sun. Edmond Halley, a contemporary of Newton, concluded that the force must vary inversely with the square of the planet's distance from the sun. From this Newton deduced that the force that attracted a planet to the sun also caused the same attraction toward its own satellites, implying a mathematical correlation proportional to the product of their masses. Newton proved that the forces of gravity and inertia was a universal property of all matter as a consequence of bodies adopting a direct path in space-time that was curved through mass and energy— something that could be verified mathematically.

His mathematical proof of the principles of gravitation was published in 1687, and established for the first time the relationship between realism and precision. The laws of gravitation, proportional to the quantity of matter in each body that governs the structure and motions of the Universe, became the basis of modern astronomy, finally explaining the orbits of planets, the action of tides, and the precession of equinoxes.

A belated scientific recognition that there was no distinction in apparently empty space signified an unsurprising erosion of belief in the existence of an identifiable heavenly realm, including Dante's graphic allusion of the Empyrean as the place in the highest heaven. It was still possible to hold open a spiritual perspective as the reason behind the gravitational force, but how it was transmitted and why planets acquired their orbital positions remained unknown, other than through a divine explanation of an apparently harmonious and stable universe. The more that science stripped away the heavenly adornments associated with divinity through lack of verifiable evidence, the more theology turned to abstractions and conjecture in order to explain, or even justify, the significance of human beings in what seemed to be an exceptionally large Euclidean void.

The *Principia* equations have a regularity and equilibrium that we can equate with a relationship between previously realized but unconnected characteristics of the universe that was to further the search for an underlying symmetry. Newton's Universal Law of Gravitation could in fact be applied to the orbits of light particles, as gravitational force was eventually found to be proportional to mass, and force to be equal to mass multiplied by acceleration.

Newtonian mechanics relates to the ways in which things change by opening the gateway to new possibilities, including an expanded field of natural philosophy. The force of gravity operates between all bodies in space and hold planets and moons in constant orbit according to the squares of their distance from the centers of the planets around which they revolve in space-time. The consequences of the laws of planetary motion can then be determined from mathematical analysis of the trajectories, which carry information derived from points along the curve. For the first time this reflected the exquisite elegance and mathematical order of the physical world, described through systematically synthesized principles. However, more than this, it allowed scientists to look into the past as well as hypothesizing, and to admire the regularity and order of the solar system. While Kepler's precise rules on planetary motion and the orbits of planets essentially describe "relationships," Newton's inference of the universal force of gravity reconciled common laws that unite Earth with the Cosmos. It also explains the shift in the orientation of Earth's axis in a cycle of approximately 25,000 years. However, his monumental mathematical advances and their physical implications did not detract from a belief in divine providence and preordained determinism with regard to the solar system.

Extrapolating Insights

Some people gain their understanding of the world by symbols and mathematics. Others gain their understanding by pure geometry and space. There are some others that find an acceleration in the muscular effort that is brought to them in understanding and feeling the force of objects moving through the world. It is the combination of them that give us our best access to truth.
JAMES CLERK MAXWELL

Descartes's philosophical intuition in *Principia philosophiae* published in 1644, exactly a century after the publication of *De Revolutionibus Orbium Coelestium* by Copernicus, extended the notion of a spherical Cosmos into an infinite universe with no boundaries. The indeterminate but solid and creative properties of matter were deemed to be the forces that formed the universe and held it together through its cosmic evolution. Immanuel Kant's transcendental claim that reason, independent of sensibility, could be applied to astronomy as part of the Enlightenment's scientific revolution, led him to propose a hypothesis in

1753 on star and planetary formations, which theorized that clouds of gas and dust matter in the Cosmos would collapse under the force of gravity, and form stars and planets. With planetary motion dictated by Newton's laws of gravitation this suggested to Kant a universe made up of individual galaxies, out of which came the theory of "island universes."

Taken together these theories, one leading to the other, freed up scientific thinking from the doctrine of religious dogma, the latter at almost the same time that Charles Darwin and Alfred Russel Wallace were about to produce a new theory of evolution through Natural Selection via inherited variations that increase the ability to compete and survive.

William Herschel, who discovered the planet Uranus in 1781, used a much-improved telescope and in 1784 was able, along with William Parsons, to clarify the "construction of the heavens," introducing a more informed investigation of the universe. In particular this identified the nature of nebulae, the clouds of dust and gas in space, and stellar clusters that had formed due to gravitational attraction that appeared to vindicate the notion of island universes. From his study of the Milky Way, Hershel's son John later published a catalog of these, some of which were in the form of spirals. After the discovery of the massive nebula of Andromeda in the 1860s the hypothesis of island universes gradually fell out of favor, but was resurrected through new observations in the late 19th century.

Michael Faraday was a 19th-century English chemist who was the first to produce an electric current from a magnetic field. He almost independently came up with the concept of lines of force from the two magnetic poles, and deduced that these could be traced to a set of curved lines that can be observed from the space filling pattern of iron filings induced by a magnet. His elucidation was that this revealed the visible materiality of the medium itself expressed through lines of force and included the rate of change of magnetic fields. Faraday explained the electromagnetic field as a new kind of physical entity rather than something that established a fit with previous hypothetical assumptions.

What might be termed "modern physics" commenced with James Clerk Maxwell, born in 1831, who assembled a series of four previously discovered "laws" from Carl Friedrich Gauss who combined mathematics with scientific discovery, Andre-Marie Ampere a founder of electrodynamics, and Faraday. Maxwell developed these ideas into a consistent mechanical model of the materiality of space. He ascertained that an arousal in electrical and magnetic fields could mutually exert these to a velocity that equates with the speed of light, leading to the obvious conclusion that light is essentially a type of electrical disturbance. These "Maxwell Equations" enabled him to theorize that the Cosmos acted as a tangible medium that possesses a materiality rather than being merely a void. They express relations between electric fields that change through time to induce magnetic fields and that produce a poetic and consistent accommodation of Faraday's Law, which envisaged lines of force across space.

Maxwell's mathematical equations opened the door to a new understanding of electromagnetic forces, light, and radiation. In the process it introduced a more pointed way of looking at space, from its prior conception as mere interstellar regions situated in a cosmic void, to more of a material "space-filling" medium. It successfully filled the gap left by Newton's law of universal gravity that had no answer to how the gravitational forces were actually transmitted. Maxwell successfully resolved the relationship of electromagnetism to the transmission of light, and in doing so proved that light had to be an electromagnetic wave. In fact, the oscillations between different fields led directly to pioneering work in the progressive discovery of radio technology, microwaves, X-rays, and gamma rays.

The Impact of Relativity

Relativity teaches us the connection between the different descriptions of one and the same reality.
ALBERT EINSTEIN

Albert Einstein's *Special Theory of Relativity* in 1905 references the unified theory of electricity and magnetism developed by Maxwell. The first principle drew on both the Copernican principle and Newton's laws of motion, proving that the laws of gravity and motion take the same form and hold the galaxies and planets in place. The second principle established that the speed of light is the same for all observers who move at constant velocity in relation to one another. However, modern cosmology began with his *Theory of General Relativity* some 10 years later, together with the studies of cosmological motion by Willem de Sitter in 1917, which best satisfied Einstein's field equations and that helped to determine the structure of space-time.

General relativity extended Isaac Newton's theory of gravity to also include a unified theory that describes a four-dimensional universe, equating to three spatial dimensions and a single dimension of time. Einstein's theory of gravity differed from Newton's in that it incorporated pressure as well as an object's mass, which gives rise to both attractive and repulsive gravity. Relativity was itself partly derived from Max Planck's earlier explanation of spectral-energy distribution of radiation, necessary for understanding the theory of atoms, nuclei, and elementary particles that was constantly refined and revised by new discoveries. From this the structure of space could be calculated through the distribution of matter, and paradoxically how its structure influences this distribution. Under general relativity three-dimensional space can be structured according to flat, positively curved, or negatively curved space according to different geometric models. Einstein showed that the forces of gravity and inertia were in the same ratio as a consequence of all bodies adopting a direct path in space-time that was curved through mass and energy, and could be verified by mathematical equations. The rule of general relativity is that matter tells space how to curve while curved space tells matter how to move the energy density that determines the expansion rate.

The four fundamental interactions of gravitation, electromagnetism, and the strong and weak nuclear forces affect different particles in different ways, and have different universal roles in holding particles together, while the gravitational interaction acts to assemble matter into planets, stars, and galaxies. We know that ordinary matter is composed of protons, neutrons, and electrons that in combination account for the structure of the universe. Neutrinos are necessary to help power the stars while electromagnetic interaction between charged particles requires the carrying ability of photons. There also exist countless elementary particles.

Einstein's insight was based on his intuition that the speed of light is constant across the universe, along with a calculated assumption that all states of motion are consistent with the fundamental laws of physics. Even light is deflected by a strong gravitational field such as exists in a dense concentration of mass—for example a galaxy of stars. The force of gravity represents a distortion or "curvature" of space-time, and as there is no universal "present" moment Einstein was given to remark that time itself is infinite as the electromagnetic field never ages. Essentially, what makes time flow is the asymmetry between space dimensions and time dimensions. In the early history of the universe there was a uniform distribution of matter and a low level of entropy before the amalgamation of matter into stars and planets. The continuity of time is defined, however, by an increase in entropy, its most extreme result being a stellar black hole predicted by Einstein, usually formed in the aftermath of a supernova explosion. This effectively represents an immense sinkhole in the fabric of space-time where time and light cease to exist.

Einstein's introduction of a Cosmological Constant in 1917 as a means to counteract gravitational contraction due to the density of matter and to achieve a static universe was an inspired decision that helped determine the geometry of the universe and would later be acknowledged as a fundamental factor in modern cosmology. It might, in its original application, be compared to a more profound version of the sea monsters or dragons portrayed by early cartographers when they were doubtful about the local circumstances. The "de Sitter universe" was dominated by the Cosmological Constant and corresponded with the discovery of distance dependent time, and the concept of dark energy present within the universe. It was not until the 1990s that two groups of astronomers concluded that as the repulsive action of a cosmological constant overcame the gravitational pull of ordinary matter, deceleration gave way to accelerated expansion. From this it was concluded that dark energy makes up around 70 percent of the total mass of the universe, spread throughout the Cosmos. In the process it confirms the prediction of inflationary cosmology.

Einstein's radical conception of curved space held the implication that the universe was static and spherical, while Willem de Sitter and Alexander Friedman adopted the notion that it was dynamic and expanding. Friedman extrapolated Einstein's laws of motion and gravity, and derived a set of solutions to the static universe altercation in a 1922 paper on the curvature of space while retaining the isotropic and homogeneous four-dimensional cyclic universe. This suggested a spatial curvature that could vary in time, and a cosmological solution that could expand, contract, or oscillate. In other words, this nicely symmetrical solution was dynamic rather than static, showing that the entire Universe is in motion, technically either in a state of expansion or contraction.

In 1926 Edwin Hubble estimated the mean density of galaxies in the observable universe and calculated that the velocity of spiral nebulae galaxies was related to their brightness, which indicated a linear correlation between speed to distance and a direct relationship between distance and "red-shift," a phenomenon where electromagnetic radiation from objects allows these to move closer or more apart in space, suggesting that the Cosmos was in a state of continual expansion. The rate of expansion later became known as the Hubble Constant.

The first scientific explanation of an accelerating universe utilizing Einstein's fundamental equations was made by Georges Lemaître, an ordinated priest, mathematician, and astronomer. In 1927 he formulated the robust cosmological theory that the universe began as a cataclysmic "big bang," which caused space to be filled with plasma from the heated hydrogen gas. This was determined by Lemaître through simple observation and mathematical corroboration, and established an important stepping stone in cosmology, unraveling the universal structure, and even the calculation of its mass. To resolve the long "static-dynamic universe" debate, Lemaître introduced a coordinate system where time flow was consistent at all locations, establishing the principle of homogeneity in space that corresponded with Einstein's closed, curved universe but with a radius of curvature that could change in time, for example increasing during a period of universal expansion.

Lemaître persuasively built the case for the decay of a primeval atom in a highly condensed state that contained all matter and energy, so that the abrupt termination of this state would lead to the creation of space and time. Both Willem de Sitter and Arthur Eddington acknowledged the breakthrough of Lemaître, and in January 1932 produced a joint paper *On the Relation between the Expansion and the Mean Density of the Universe*. Following this the Einstein-de Sitter model of the flat Euclidean universe became the standard cosmological model.

The cosmological principle, a term coined by the astrophysicist Edward Milne in 1935, essentially predicted that the distribution of matter is homogenous and isotropic throughout the universe, and from this the universe could be stated as being spatially flat. Forces act uniformly based on the outcome of the cataclysmic Big Bang from which distant galaxies are not simply expanding but accelerating toward the outer edge of space-time. This posed a central question as to whether an "in-built" fate of the universe has been destined from the beginning of time, or whether the active disintegration of the single atom is able to propel many different space-time scenarios, with destinies determined by providence. Lemaître maintained that disintegration was due to a disparity between two opposing forces: gravitation and dark energy, incorporated within the cosmological constant associated with vacuum energy. Under this scenario, evolution of the universe would then entail a rapid preliminary expansion where stars were formed through decaying primeval material, followed by a periodic stagnation or even contraction, and then a reinvigorated expansion stage. It also introduces into the debate the notion of indefinite periods of expansion and contraction, and raises the question as to whether the present universe is the preliminary version or one of a succession. In a representation of an expanding and spatially curved universe the result is a homogeneous sphere, where the forward movement of time relates to the expansion of space and a change in spatial curvature.

Despite fundamental advances in science and cosmology since Galileo, it cannot be categorically stated that the universe is as yet physically comprehensible in the sense that there is no unified theory based on empirically corroborated evidence through all possible applications, whatever their context

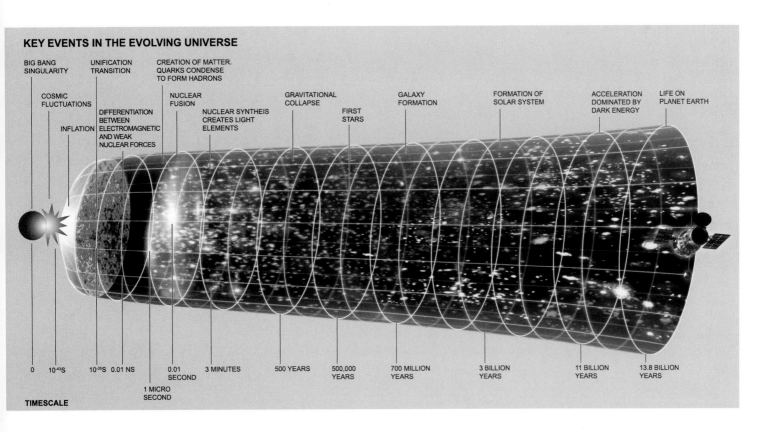

KEY EVENTS IN THE EVOLVING UNIVERSE

BIG BANG SINGULARITY

COSMIC FLUCTUATIONS

UNIFICATION TRANSITION

INFLATION

DIFFERENTIATION BETWEEN ELECTROMAGNETIC AND WEAK NUCLEAR FORCES

CREATION OF MATTER. QUARKS CONDENSE TO FORM HADRONS

NUCLEAR FUSION

NUCLEAR SYNTHEIS CREATES LIGHT ELEMENTS

GRAVITATIONAL COLLAPSE

FIRST STARS

GALAXY FORMATION

FORMATION OF SOLAR SYSTEM

ACCELERATION DOMINATED BY DARK ENERGY

LIFE ON PLANET EARTH

TIMESCALE

0   10^{-43}S 10^{-35}S   0.01 NS   1 MICRO SECOND   0.01 SECOND   3 MINUTES   500 YEARS   500,000 YEARS   700 MILLION YEARS   3 BILLION YEARS   11 BILLION YEARS   13.8 BILLION YEARS

and constitution. Unification relies on symmetry, precision, and progress in physical science, and is dependent on the accuracy of the assumptions used rather than on existing metaphysical ideas. Newton even found the essential notion of his own theory of gravitation to be "an absurdity, that no man who had a competent faculty of philosophical thinking could believe to be comprehensible."

The generally accepted explanation of the atomic explosion that generated all matter in the universe in a single stroke of creation has become directed toward the origin of the expansion process itself through inflation. Its dimensions have now stretched beyond spatial curvature to form a practically "flat" universe with a "bent" space-time geometry.

The entire observable cosmic structure was created from a supposed singularity through an inflationary process that incorporated density fluctuations via quantum effects, amplified through gravitational instability and scale invariance. The strange reality of our flat universe was in fact caused by the massive inflation process itself. The current phase of inflation now effectively doubles the size of the universe approximately every eight-billion years. The discovery of gravitational waves stemming from quantum fluctuations during the rapid and seemingly continuous inflation process might suggest that a single Big Bang event is not a beginning but an end to inflation in an infinite number of galaxies, indicating a continuing sequence of Big Bang events. This technically opens the door to a possible infinity of parallel universes or a "multiverse." Eternal inflation of space could, in theory, generate sufficient energy for quantum fluctuations to create completely different operational arrangements under these conditions, where the effective laws of nature might be of an entirely different order. A combination of three space dimensions and one time dimension encompassed within relativity theory is the only situation capable of supporting life as we know it, although the apparent laws of physics are only applicable in our universe, not necessarily in a multiverse of infinite space. In fact, space itself is not expanding uniformly, and the long spiral arm of the Milky Way galaxy is not expanding at all. However, before we breathe a sign of relief, scientists estimate that it is on course to collide with its nearest neighbor, the Andromeda galaxy, in the next billion years or so.

Einstein's insight into relativity was based on his intuition that the speed of light is constant across the universe, along with an assumption that all states of motion are consistent with the fundamental laws of physics. This marked a critical transition from classical to modern physics. The geometry of general relativity was concerned not with three-dimensional space but with four dimensions including time, establishing a connection with the distribution of mass. This brings into focus the seemingly infinite nature of space, and introduces a central question as to whether time actually existed before the universe came into being. However, a reconciliation between the requirements of special relativity and quantum mechanics leads to mathematical inconsistencies in fulfilling all the requirements of both theories along with a need for more accurate experimental material as to the forces of elementary particles. As there is no universal present moment, Einstein liked to remark that the distinction between past, present, and future is a persistent delusion, and further cosmological investigations have shown that distant galaxies are not merely expanding but that vacuum energy is accelerating the expansion of our universe toward the outer edge of space-time—if indeed there is an outer edge. What we recognize as the flow of time can therefore be said to represent an expedient way to order our world and our relation to it.

The Ouroboros is taken as a link between the microworld of fundamental particles (to the left) and the planets, stars, and galaxies (to the right).

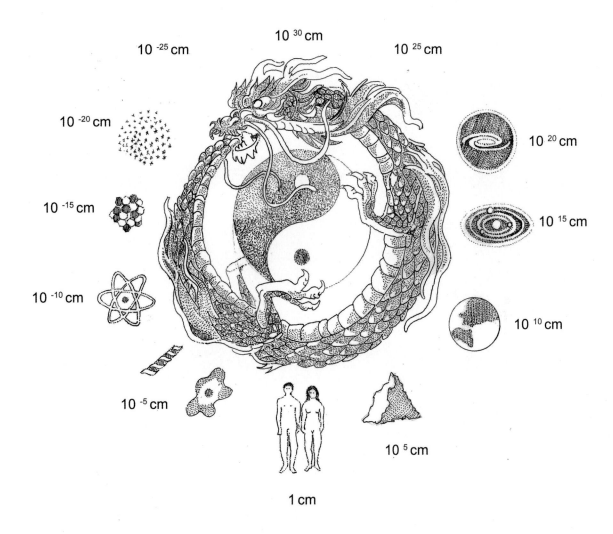

10^{30} cm

10^{-25} cm

10^{25} cm

10^{-20} cm

10^{20} cm

10^{-15} cm

10^{15} cm

10^{-10} cm

10^{10} cm

10^{-5} cm

10^{5} cm

1 cm

DECONSTRUCTING·
PARADISO

There is a theory which states that if ever anyone discovers what the Universe is for and why it is here, it will instantly disappear and be replaced by something more bizarre and inexplicable. There is another theory which states that this has already happened.
DOUGLAS ADAMS: *The Restaurant at the End of the Universe*

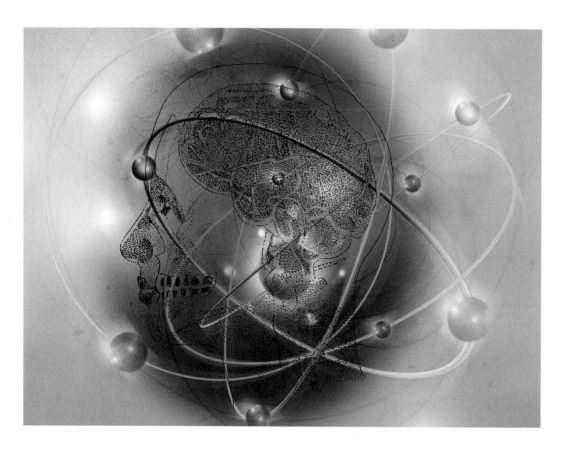

METAPHYSICAL INTERPRETATION of the Inferno, Purgatory, and Paradiso captures a cosmological significance in drawing together the intelligible, the abstract, and the creationist belief through an illusionary passage of events. To at least some extent the poem repurposes the literal interpretation of the Old Testament in prescribing a central impetus to the laws of nature and evolution, where scientific truth and religious truth are not in conflict. The process of Dante's poetic revelation is in effect rooted in a belief that moral justice and the omnipotence of God were part of the state of things as they exist in the Cosmos. The poet drew on the fabric of the visible Cosmos, manipulating its metaphysical features within a static configuration and unfurling them in a version of space-time that provocatively transcended an accurate interpretation of nature's laws that determine its underlying properties. In the world of Dante, the cosmic constants shift or become unstable, soliciting an illusionary narrative in time and space but with an inspired choreography and a determined sense of moral purpose. This of course flouts the traditional convention of the scientific method, whereby observable events in the natural world must be explained through natural causes.

In articulating the solar system as a set of spheres, including the sphere of the "fixed stars," Dante's 13th-century vision of its key characteristics, including of course its geocentric model with the earth at its center, clearly had no recourse to the revelatory astronomical findings that were to come. Otherwise the vertical trajectory to *Paradiso* might well have been rather longer. Dante's collection of terrestrial and celestial realms associated with planets also innocently bypassed the difficulties associated with their compositional characteristics. The Sun condensed through gravitational pull on its solar nebula of gas and dust, while Jupiter, Saturn, Uranus, and Neptune coalesced into "gas giant" planets. The terrestrial planets of Earth, Mercury, Venus, and Mars grew through a process of accretion of solid particles that amalgamated through electrostatic forces. Planet Earth in fact has an inner core of solid iron and an outer molten core thousands of kilometers thick, with a solid crust made up of six major and other minor crustal plates that have moved over 300 million years to create the familiar pattern of continents and oceans. Its atmosphere, made up predominantly of nitrogen, oxygen, and water vapor sustains the essential greenhouse effect whereby gases which include carbon dioxide, nitrous oxide and methane reflect back infrared radiation. This makes the planet suitable for life but vulnerable to global warming.

The main planets can be divided into two groups: the terrestrial planets that lie closest to the sun, and the gas giants beyond. The orbits of the major planets around the sun, including Uranus and Neptune, which are missing from Dante's model, were formed from an accretion of gaseous material some 4.5

billion years ago. The sun itself was surrounded by a solar nebula that gradually cooled and condensed, coalescing into planetoids. As this material fused together through gravitational attraction, protoplanets formed isolated entities, each occupying its own orbit, while the remaining material formed asteroids or minor planets. The Moon was in all probability formed by the fusion of protoplanetary material. Most planets in the solar system lie in virtually the same plane although there are variations in inclination, and they orbit the sun in a counter-clockwise direction, along with clouds of debris known as the Kuiper Belt, and the Oort Belt that gave rise to comets.

We can now examine various factors that seek to put Paradiso into a contemporary perspective, and in the process examine the nature but perhaps also the philosophical and scientific contradictions that infiltrate our divine Universe, and our relationship with it.

The Anthropic Interpretation

Observers themselves can only come about in universes that are conducive to their existence.
PAUL DAVIS, *The Goldilocks Enigma*

Space and time structure our experience and allow us to make systematic sense of the natural world. Nature itself appears to have established a seemingly perfect fit with human existence through the "anthropic principle" proposed by a physicist, Brandon Carter in 1973, partly in response to the fact that the universe changes significantly over time, and that most of space is uninhabitable to the human physiology. In its weak form, the principle is stated to be applicable only to exceptionally privileged locations within the universe, of which Planet Earth is the only known location compatible with our existence as observers. The strong anthropic principle involves the apparent tuning of the fundamental forces, and the constants of nature that are necessary for humankind to come into existence and allow intelligent life to develop to the extent that we can actually comprehend a participatory universe. However, the metaphysical notion that the universe was designed for such a pre-eminent purpose is at the heart of the creationist conundrum.

In fact a very delicate balance exists in nature. If the masses of elementary particles and the relative strengths of basic forces were even slightly different in terms of its fine tuning, the universe would have evolved in a totally different way. The fact that gravity is much weaker than the other three forces has allowed our solar system to evolve, and for stars, planets, and galaxies to form.

From a human perspective it is easy to view the central achievement of the Cosmos as humankind, representing the pinnacle of evolution. The communicative ability of *Homo sapiens* through both language and the symbolism of mathematics allow us to unravel the laws of physics and speculate on the creation and the far future of the universe.

An important question is what essentially introduced us into the planetary system apart from an assemblage of molecules known as proteins, suffused with amino acids that create the basis of molecular structures made up from atoms of necessary elements and primed by the appropriate genetic code. Life itself has evolved through any number of self-sustaining cycles, being endlessly re-worked through chemical processes and the assimilation of molecular carbon energy sources as part of a process known as endosymbiosis.

All living creatures on Earth are carbon-based, as the versatility of carbon atoms means that they can join together and uniquely link with atoms of other elements, notably hydrogen, creating chains of polymers that form the basis of complex organic molecules. A carbon-based life form clearly raises a fundamental question as to the means by which it was produced. The nucleosynthesis of the Big Bang enabled nuclear energy levels of helium to turn into carbon and all the other atoms that later became clouds of gas, forming new stars and planets. It might well have also contributed to the early life forms. The energizing outcome of combining the helium nuclei in the interior of a star boosts its carbon generating capacity. The universe has thus, in theory, a built-in propensity for the actual occurrence of life, although many other properties and relationships must also be present, in particular the presence of water. We are therefore quite possibly intimately connected with the heavenly forms according to physical laws that help govern the Cosmos, but cast in mathematical terms that would no doubt have given Dante cause for satisfaction. Of course the fact that extra-terrestrial life might exist somewhere in the Cosmos does not make us pre-eminent or even exceptional, let alone significant.

With an accelerating universe, and with an assumption of its critical density of matter and background radiation, scientists have calculated the approximate age of the universe at around 13.8 billion years. There is, therefore, much that requires a better understanding of nature's fine tuning. It was only through the discovery of radiometric dating in the early 20th century that the age of the solar system could be measured, and at an approximation of 4.57 billion years it far exceeded previous estimates. Scientific analysis indicates that macrobiotic life in the form of microorganisms commenced not long afterwards—around four billion years ago, using evidence from stromatolites found in ancient rocks. By this comparison, evidence of human life is quite recent. Fossil records posit this at around seven to eight million years ago in the late Miocene period. The earliest fossils of humans date from the Middle Paleolithic Period 200,000 years ago. If recognizable life forms are indeed to be found elsewhere in the universe, this would have to represent either primitive organisms requiring the presence of the most important molecules in cell biology, Deoxyribonucleic acid and Ribonucleic acid, or would require altogether different life-forming processes than those found on Earth.

This brings us to the paradox attributed to Enrico Fermi—the seeming contradiction between high estimates of probability for an occurrence, and the lack of actual evidence for it. It represents the essential conflict between the fact that probability would seem to favor the presence of intelligent life as being common in the Cosmos given the rate of star formation and the possibility of many theoretically habitable worlds, and the absence of reassurance for this other than on Earth. This of course ignores the multiverse theory where requirements for life in other universes might be very different.

The general consensus for this low level of probability is *abiogenesis*—an agonizingly slow and complex process by which life arises from non-living matter through self-replicating molecules and random chemical processes. This is the situation even before we come to the evolution of a brain capable of asking the question in the first place. The "Rare Earth" hypothesis in fact argues that this would require a massive number of fortuitous circumstances, and that advanced civilizations must therefore be a rarity in our galaxy if not in the universe. Some scientists, including Stephen Hawking, have argued that even intelligent life capable of knowledge production would also be likely to encounter the unstable and potentially self-destructive tendencies we have experienced on Earth. This might include warfare, resource depletion, climate change, virus contraction, extinction events, imaginative processes of annihilation, and even a lack of ability to properly manage its own technological inventions leading to increasing entropy beyond an ability to control it.

As facts about the Big Bang singularity emerge around the point where philosophy merges with metaphysics it raises a central question with regard to a creative force. There is little rational scientific evidence as to how or even why human life evolved on earth, which seemingly reflected a transition from chemical reactions to living ones. In all probability, life on Earth began through the transfer of complex organic material, possibly via electrical storms, comets, or meteorites that brought amino acids with them. An alternative scenario is that the synthesis of existing chemicals as part of a primordial soup constituted formative components of deoxyribonucleic acid or DNA. Amino acids, when strung together in chains, form proteins that have a significant role in forming the building blocks of living systems through enzymes that control particular biochemical reactions. The sequences of atoms in DNA spell out the genetic code of life, essential in the creation of new cells, and allows for the process of self-replication.

The complex interaction of atoms and molecules into a myriad of providentially directed chemical processes that somehow create the human beings challenges the opinion that this can be simply put down to fortuitous circumstances. However, theories of predetermination severely test our sense of credibility, and also raise a central question of purpose in relation to living organisms, and what the precise catalyst could have been on a small planet that is, as far as we know, unique in the solar system only for being conducive to evolution. Perhaps attempting to intuit cosmological significance is not so far removed from Douglas Adams's inspired notion in *The Hitchhiker's Guide to the Galaxy* that Earth could in fact be a giant computer, dedicated to ascertaining "the meaning of life, the universe and everything."

Science only barely helps us to understand our significance. Our confined place in the universe is not so much our reason for being, but what we do with it as intelligent organisms. We must look inward as well as outward to sustain the rules that underpin the dimensions of nature, just as we seek to understand the symmetries of the universe.

The seemingly hospitable biosphere of Earth appears to have no technical reason to exist, except to secure and nourish life forms. Following the impact of the Big Bang, protons and neutrons were formed from the ensuing plasma, giving rise to nucleosynthesis. Whether this can be harmonized or conveniently reformulated with the creative impulse set out in Genesis is open to speculation. However, within a single universe we can assimilate the laws and parameters that appear to be conveniently wired for the development of life, in such a way as to admit our existence, and, therefore, our consciousness. The anthropic principle sets out an unarguable, if simplistic, explanation for the presence of life on Earth, just as Darwinism satisfies our desire to describe the sense behind evolution that led us to invoke the workings of nature as a valuable part of human history and culture, and gave us an ability to live productively as part of generally balanced communities. The need to discover how this all works and fits together through theory, experiment, and observation is as much a part of evolution as the drive to propagate, which applies to nature and reality as a whole.

It is not that humans must assume a privileged central position in the universe, or that it is centrally directed, however, we have to build into the evolutionary equation the fact that natural selection has been responsible for a continual fine-tuning of life forms in response to a constantly changing environmental context. Darwin's theory of evolution satisfies this in relation to living organisms in accordance with the known laws of physics, the effective balance between chemical and biochemical environments, and Earth's climatic stability.

The double helix of human DNA is made up of around three-billion base pairs and between 20,000 and 25,000 protein-coding genes although only a very small amount is unique to humans. Half of the human genetic code is exactly the same as a banana, and more than 80 percent is shared with many other animals including 98.8 percent with chimpanzees. The default position of the human brain therefore appears to lie in the divide between mind and matter and the way we process information though the cerebral cortex.

The argument for gauging an anthropic interpretation is essentially that human's very existence on Earth must be in accordance with certain fundamental laws of physics that create conditions conducive to such a carbon-based intelligent life form and provides exactly the right ingredients for life with an abnormal precision. If the relative strengths of the many interactions were different, the Cosmos as a relatively ordered system would be well outside the evident balance that we experience today. A "Theory of Everything" must therefore rationalize, amongst many other things, how and why the creative universal properties have almost magically orchestrated such conducive conditions for life. Even slight differences in fusion, decay, or chemical structure would preclude this. It might be said to be an extension of Descartes's logical reasoning behind the nature of existence—*cogito ergo sum* (I think, therefore I am)—essentially a human's capacity to believe in a sense of knowledge and reasoning. This raises a fundamental question as to the means by which the appropriate conditions are produced. It was not until the 1950s that this problem was at least partially elucidated through the identification of nuclear resonance—the energizing outcome of combining the helium nuclei in the interior of a star, which boosts the carbon generating capacity of the nuclear reaction. The universe thus has a built-in propensity for the occurrence of some form of life, the so-called "Goldilocks Enigma," although many other properties and relationships must also be present. In another sense it might also be technically possible to establish the potential for any extra-terrestrial existence of life by examining and understanding the underlying properties of the Cosmos.

In essence, the universe must be sufficiently fine-tuned in order that we can discern it in terms of its physical nature. Our state of being interacts intimately with what we deem to be reality, in the sense that according to quantum theory the observer, the observed, and the process of observation are inseparable and each participates in the entire system of growth and change, creating a cosmic connectedness. Roger Penrose has noted that this issue involves various properties and numerical relationships that can be shown to exist between a number of known physical constants, including the gravitational constant. The astrophysicist and Astronomer Royal, Martin Rees, has advanced a proposition that just six pivotal numbers are required to specify all relevant properties of our universe, known as cosmological parameters. These are: N, which measures the strength of gravity to electrical forces; E, which defines the nature of atoms and how their atomic nuclei bind together; L, which controls gravitational repulsion; Q, which measures the strength of the fluctuations that initiated the formation of stars and galaxies; Omega, which measures mass-energy content; and D, which states the number of spatial dimensions in our universe. If the finely tuned values of these deviated even fractionally from their measured values life as we know it would not have arisen. Nor would our stars and galaxies, or Dante's *Paradiso* for that matter. And we would undoubtedly not be here to tell the tale.

We can anyway fall back on the lack of any convincing evidence to suggest the presence of intelligent life in our Galaxy other than on Earth. In fact, we might invert the Anthropic theory to suggest that the beauty and vastness of the universe can only be given meaning through our habitation of a planet from which we can observe this and perhaps even colonize parts of it during the coming millennium. It is likely that we live in the most probable of all possible worlds. If not for this we must return to the question of precisely why the universe is in any way meaningful.

Connecting Mind and Matter

The mind is not a vessel to be filled, but a fire to be kindled.
PLUTARCH

As all matter is derived from and exists by means of a driving "force," some scientists consider that consciousness or the "phenomenon of mind" is at the heart of our reality. Under quantum rules, as we both inhabit and observe our environment, our interaction also changes its state, introducing new particles into existence and creating a change in physical matter in terms of uncertainty and probabilities that provide not just for what we might be seeking but possibly what is necessary in achieving an infinite number of possibilities. From this we have an interesting and rather innovative way of looking at what we think of as reality, as simply a combination of mass and energy. But how much does uncertainty and randomness exclude grand design, grand purpose, and even meaning, which we assume to be fundamental goals of human life? The question comes back, in a rhetorical way, to the relationship between the human brain and the mind, and to the development of the cerebral cortex and central nervous system. While activity of the brain is in most cases quite orderly, it can be relatively unpredictable and capable of remarkable mental feats that we deem to be the result of high inspiration rather than predetermination.

The primary regions of the cerebral cortex are concerned with all sensory information and processed by tertiary regions that construct our relationship with the outside world. How this operation gives rise to thought, awareness, and retention of images is far from clear, and the seat of rational consciousness goes well beyond the brain stem and the hippocampus. This might operate through some form of internal algorithm that has evolved in the modern form of humans via natural selection.

Traditionally the mind has been associated with brain activity and the firing of neurons, but there is growing evidence that the "seat of consciousness" goes well beyond this. The complexity of the brain, together with its relationship with the mind's paradoxically ordered quality of reason, might also be linked to quantum processes. Perhaps in this way the strange logic behind a participatory universe leads toward the inference of a cosmic thought connection. Neurotransmission to all intents and purposes creates our relationship with reality, our sense of experience, and our ability to reflect and rationalize. We might well be wired for different levels of appreciation, likes or dislikes, but this might also be why we can so easily be taken in by the illusion created by a magician, or why we optimistically embrace a belief in miracles.

The term "qualia," which literally means a subjective quality, consciously perceived or experienced, might be extrapolated to include a deeper level of consciousness that embraces all dimensions of the universe in space-time, forming a connective structure between its many parts including the human mind. This then becomes, in effect, the basis of how we perceive reality, although this is open to a more focused discourse on neuroscience and our ability to transmit fine-grained conscious experiences.

The human cortex appears to have developed at an astonishing rate over some 40,000 years as opposed to the evolution of modern *Homo sapiens* over at least five times this period. This might possibly be synchronized with other genetic changes, including the relatively recent acknowledgment of a creative consciousness emanating from the mind, which appears to be associated with the brain but inconveniently detached from it. In fact our sense of reality is filtered through the brain and the mind perceives and evaluates this from its depth of experience that is encoded in our psyche. This is personal to us and gives access to a cognitive realm of images, feelings, and memory. While the brain is the central processing element, it is interlinked with the context of the mind through neural activity. However, the transmitting function of the brain cannot comprehend anything outside space-time, and as it processes raw information it has to filter much of it out so that the mind receives only a fraction of available data. There are also psychological and other reasons why the brain's sense mechanisms can be unreliable in terms of processing mental events, such as those that lie outside our normal sense of perception. Much of "reality" can be distorted by false expectation and selective memory, together with mood and emotion that personalize the "wired up" neural network, ignoring or discarding that which does not fit. We clearly need to comprehend the realm of information we receive, and if the brain is simply a transmitting agency then it is the mind that makes us part of a cosmic reality. Each one needs the other, and both matter and mind must combine to achieve this.

The limbic portion of the brain—which deals with sensory stimulation, behavior, and motivation—is part of the thalamus that creates a pathway of information to the cerebrum and, it must be assumed, acts as an elusive conduit to the mind itself. The process registers positively with the visual cortex, located in the occipital lobe of the brain, that processes visual information. Limbic value might therefore be said to be a property of consciousness that reinforces perception and our sense of place.

We know that the brain is able to form almost instantaneous connections between billons of neuron transmitters located in its different parts, seemingly coordinating our sense of reality with the brain's otherwise routine processes. But there has to be a mechanism that differentiates the wave function of quantum mechanics from our ordinary level of observation and our normal notion of reality and perception. Our brain facilitates our sensory experience and allows us to delight in pattern recognition through a realization that inherent geometric relationships define the state of things as they exist in the Cosmos, and that mathematical laws determine their underlying properties.

Alberti and others were aware that in designing Renaissance cities, opposite and complementary forces somehow formed a sensory coalition that continues to achieve visual satisfaction from apparently quite arbitrary compositions, where intuitive perception appears to ignite our inherent sensibilities. Compositional symmetry can be regulated at an urban level through a certain level of dissonance in ascribing a sense of balance between complex organizations of shapes, textures, and colors. This is not dissimilar to the way in which matter and antimatter find a way to coexist. In an urban sense this goes well beyond aesthetic awareness. It produces a sense of familiarity associated with novelty and complexity where pattern and likeness are tempered with difference. A rhyming urbanism acknowledges subtle variations at various frequencies rather than repetition just as it does in musical appreciation, and might equally be applied to many Renaissance cities where buildings, streets, spaces, and waterways articulate major and subordinate rhythms that appeal to the senses.

Gestalt psychologists affirm that the human brain is able to rationalize patterns of order and recognition out of complexity, so that the whole shape or form is perceived as more than the sum of its parts. It is common for architects to refer to the weight, strength, or symbolism of building features. Beauty might, on the other hand, relate more to a totality expressed by Palladio, in which nothing could be added or subtracted without sacrificing the harmony of the whole. The "golden mean" is, after all, known as the divine proportion that relates to the Fibonacci series and can be expressed mathematically and incorporated within the "Mandelbrot Set" discussed below, where a "biological architecture" occurs in many natural forms such as plants and seashells.

The relationship between mind and matter goes back at least to Plato, Aristotle, and Hippocrates, who were proponents of linking the mysterious working of the mind to physiological characteristics of the body, which involves an assumption that both physical and mental characteristics are simply the result of how particles in the body are arranged. Much of current thinking on cognitive science has to do with the definition of the mind and its relation to consciousness. At the heart of this is the question of how the material processes co-exist to generate conscious experience and how this is communicated. We know that certain parts of the brain such as the hippocampal complex are related to mental activity while other parts of the central nervous system are less so. Neurons are known to continually exchange signals, which affects the distribution of electrochemicals, but this is far from understanding the relationship between mental state and neuroscience. It is necessary to comprehend how this relates to the circuitry of neuron behavior, and its connectivity across the synapses of the brain which is subject to constant change. This might even reflect properties of an outer reality, which unfolds in our minds as a sequence of signals or events that link consciousness to information processing.

The mind can also be described as embodying a transcendental quality with a spiritual dimension, and belongs to a clearly linked world of thought, feeling, and imagination. Consciousness is in itself caused by brain activity in the prefrontal cortex and is therefore linked to the nervous system. However, the issue of mind remains partly a philosophical one, where we must confront its apparent interaction with the quantum world simply by its perceptive function, whether or not we entirely comprehend the implications or outcomes. It is in fact quite possible that quanta actually imitate the human mind and that they simply do not have specific properties until they are actually perceived, just as human thought would seem to have no actual properties until it emerges into existence. Change your mind and you change the universe. Technically, the instantaneous three-dimensional perception of the physical world is the result of the optic or cranial nerve transforming visual information from the retina to the brain via electrical impulses. The human body, with its cells, tissues, and organs is nevertheless, like the living universe of which we are a part, made up of electrons and particles so that the notion of a consciousness of self embraces the same components of space, time, energy, and matter. It is therefore just as able to change its state.

The intrinsic quality of our subjective conscious perception, which helps us to perceive external reality could well be a necessary ingredient to insight and even aesthetic appreciation. It is where Dante, Plato, Brunelleschi, Alberti, and Einstein come together in words, design, and mathematical thought. We must also not forget the concept of mind that sent Europe enthusiastically into the Enlightenment in the 18th century. The scientific conundrum as to the nature of humankind and the universe still reverberates in the 21st century with its quantum-inspired paradoxes that challenge our conception of physical reality, even with so much artificial intelligence at our disposal.

We might choose to regard Dante's *Comedia* as expressing simply a tangent of thought well outside logical interpretation, and more divinely directed toward the study of the soul, intended to bring a message to society. Dante indirectly attributed a supernatural intelligence to a celestial realm based on a purposeful conjecture that the soul is capable of a separate knowledge-based existence, but one that was ruled by an incorruptible heavenly being. If we assume this to be the case, we have to hope that he or she is a benevolent and non-interventionist one. Copernicus stated in a more direct way that the heliocentric model was based on "simplicity, order, and nobility," and that it was easier to move the earth rather than the heavens.

This in turn reinforces the notion of a possible, although much contested, cosmic connection, within a participatory universe that is constantly expressing itself through a prescient sense of purpose with mind and matter in a constant state of interaction—something that Dante would no doubt have found reassuring. For all our superficial knowledge of the brain's physicality, we cannot yet comprehend the link between the brain cell and its wondrous ability to act as a neurotransmitter, and the commensurate link between consciousness and the quantum world. In fact we steadily open up indisputable mathematical laws that might yet propel us to an acknowledgment of a cosmic "divinity." To paraphrase George Orwell, all divine events might be real but some are more real than others.

Creative intelligence in human form came late to the universe and cannot be held responsible for its design. However, neither can this be necessarily put down purely to chance, and it is the responsibility of both science and design to explain its critical working. This is also demanded of us through the outcome of natural selection and replication through evolution.

Human epistemology and the theory of how knowledge is filtered, articulated, and validated is what makes us self-aware. It might well be possible to reproduce the elusive activity of neurons, the brain's computational processes, in a future generation of super computers although this might posit a questionable scenario where software assembled by succeeding generations of highly intelligent machines might rapidly outstrip the capacity of humans to impose ultimate control of the process. It could be equally argued that a suitably benevolent superintelligence might embody a refreshingly new consciousness that would save the planet from its unfocussed approach to combatting climatic catastrophe, pandemics, conflict, and existential inequalities, where rapid environmental change over the course of only one century has arguably compromised the process of natural evolution itself. An amalgam of science and technology has streamlined a demand for information transmission related to instant convenience and amusement, and helped to shape a more beneficial future through such things as microprocessors, superconduction, and magnetic resonance imaging, all of which we have adopted, directly or indirectly, to make our lives better. While Einstein famously stated that the flow of time was merely a means of ordering the world, we can now use quantum theory to measure it. An alternative scenario is a continual merging of human and machine, that simply projects forward our now indispensable and intimate relationship with hand-held mobile devices that contain more realms of computing power than that which took humans to the moon in the late '60s.

The Quantum Conundrum

Those who are not shocked when they first come across quantum theory cannot possibly have understood it.
NIELS BOHR

Quantum theory posits indeterminate behavior of individual systems, allowing for alternative possibilities such as a participatory condition where the observer is inevitably absorbed into the essential fabric of quantum reality. In this situation some properties can change their state just by being observed, while other properties can simply disappear. The theory, originated by Max Planck, revolutionized the understanding of atomic and subatomic processes through Planck's constant, which led to Einstein's determination that light exists in quanta of energy, or photons. Only one perspective is therefore valid at any one time. This might be said to be central to the core of contemporary physics, and its philosophical repercussions.

An investigative approach to atomic phenomena in the 1920s by several scientific luminaries including Erwin Schrodinger, Werner Heisenberg, and Paul Dirac engendered a new description of the physical world that enabled a later application to problems involving the nature of observable quantities in the atomic realm. These are, by their very nature, subject to Heisenberg's Uncertainty Principle, which underlies quantum theory, and states that it is impossible to simultaneously measure identified pairs of quantities such as the position and momentum of a particle. It is therefore necessary to explore these in terms of probabilities instead of firm assertions. Heisenberg demonstrated that if something is confined to a small area of space then it will gain momentum and spread out so that it cannot simultaneously have a precise position and an exact velocity, and the "Heisenberg cut" effectively separates quantum events from our perception of them. Schrodinger's equation established a basic physical principle which described the state of a freely moving particle that he termed a *wave function,* whose ripples spread outwards in all directions like those from a sudden disturbance on the flat surface of a pond. The evident absence of space and time within the quantum vacuum demonstrates a bewildering and unexplained ability for a particle to be everywhere and nowhere at the same time. "Virtual" particles emerge into the vacuum and almost instantaneously cease to exist, while so-called vacuum fluctuations involve the creation and assimilation of particles. As the universe appears to react according to the subjectivity of the observer this leads to something of a confused reality, although the search for a unified theory that Einstein was so convinced existed, still goes on. Evidence of a "graviton," a hypothetical elementary particle without mass that mediates the force of gravity, would be an essential aspect of this theory. This has much to do with making sense of the universe through symmetries that describe the particular forces and patterns of nature.

The "probability wave" has clear implications for the nature of reality itself as it appears to suggest a randomness built into the underlying laws of nature. Various quantum interpreters have concluded that what causes the collapse of the wave function is quite possibly associated in a non-linear way with the nature of consciousness and the brains of observers. Photons and electrons if unobserved act like waves, but if observed they behave like particles, rather as a startled animal might adopt a form of camouflage at a sudden realization of a potentially intrusive or inquisitive presence. This represents a line of reasoning not far removed from the anthropic interpretation, that infers the universe exists because quantum observers and interpreters are looking at it, creating an elusive connection between energy, matter, space, and time.

The elementary particles are similarly fine-tuned for a habitable and distinctly atypical universe that seemingly mitigates against coincidence. In fact, with just one quantum reality governed by the Schrödinger equation, particles can strangely be in two places at once. This can be interpreted as a technical means of splitting the universe into two quantum parallel universes with an infinite number of dimensions, without actually violating any physical laws.

Paul Dirac, a distinguished precursor to Stephen Hawking in holding the Lucasian Chair at Cambridge University, had a skill at technical drawing and mathematics that helped him to investigate the statistical behavior of particles. Dirac attempted to join together special relativity with Max Planck's discovery of energy quanta and its effects through mathematical equations along with a visual sense of what these meant. The Dirac equation compiled in 1928 is a complex synthesis of mathematical ideas that forms a central truth about the universe, effectively unraveling what is going on in what appears to be empty space. It represents a powerful theory of the natural world from the expansion of the universe to the conundrum of quantum reality, which have contributed to both a zealous pursuit to reconcile these contentious aspects, and scientific attempts to resolve the apparent contradictions. His equations describe the electron, but offer proof that another electron could come into existence—an "anti-electron"—that could form part of an anti-atom or anti-particle. If the two meet they obliterate each other and turn mass into energy. This resolves the riddle of empty space, as it shows that matter can be created out of a vacuum and then disappear. What are now known as virtual particles in quantum field theory constantly appear and disappear, and are known as hidden fluctuations. A branch of physics called statistical mechanics relates to the properties of particles and the behavior of a system made up of these—that is to say, the probabilities as to the amount of energy being distributed among the systems.

Emmy Noether, a German mathematician of the early 20th century, perhaps telepathically echoing Alberti's insistent 15th-century design philosophy, produced a theorem that states, "Every conservation principle corresponds to a symmetry in nature," which can be applied to the laws of physics and their application to the Cosmos—for example, to the conservation of energy. The deeper we delve into elementary particles of matter smaller than a proton or neutron, the more difficult it is to establish order in the midst of apparent chaos caused by interaction and decay. Certain of these behave in such an outlandish way they were christened "strange particles" by Murray Gell-Man who formulated the hypothetical notion of "quarks," held together by gluons, which are massless and travel at the speed of light. These represent the ultimate building blocks of matter from which elementary particles, subject to the strong interaction, are composed. The curious name comes from James Joyce's *Finnegan's Wake*, "three quarks for Muster Mark," and was considered appropriate as the particles come in threes. Evidence for quarks was confirmed in 1968 through the Stanford Linear Accelerator, but they cannot be directly observed or isolated and can only be found within hadrons, which represent composites of subatomic particles.

While it is normally directed at microscopic systems, quantum theory also suggests that the evolution of the universe might involve a multiverse of Big Bang events giving rise to many different spatial dimensions, and quite possibly different laws of physics, only some of which would be likely to permit life in a bio-congenial way. However, Roger Penrose in *The Emperor's New Mind* makes the pertinent observation that the Big Bang might well have been the continuation of someone else's infinity, and therefore was not necessarily the beginning of the Cosmos.

The fundamental laws of nature are now well understood, but the search for its smallest building blocks has been the subject of intense speculation and experimentation for over 200 years, progressively unveiling atoms and subatomic particles. Modern physics has in fact largely been a somewhat "reductionist" process, revealing a chain of progressively elementary particles around which new theories are developed to explain the larger dimensions of reality. However, it appears that the more we delve, the more we find ourselves left with a quantum vacuum where we are forced to conject on probabilities rather than scientific measurement.

A paradox appears to exist at the heart of our mathematical rulebook, and the quantum process forces us to question what we think we know as reality. Time as we know it is part of the fine-tuned universe that suits life, but in the quantum world where particles have zero mass and can move at the speed of light, time can stand still or even move backward. Photons can move from one place to another instantaneously, bypassing time. Quantum theory allows for a multitude of dimensions including zero and infinity, making every state a virtual one, defying the rules of cause and effect. The surrounding space, full of virtual energy, allows for constant changes of state millions of times a second where every change is an act of creation at whatever scale.

Richard Feynman, who was awarded the Nobel Prize in 1965, realized that an interaction between an electron and an energetic photon sends the electron backward in time until it interacts again. A fundamental feature of quantum electrodynamics is therefore a continuous process of complex interactions surrounding every single electron in the universe. We might be able to explain the quantum nature of electrodynamics as waves moving forward and outward from a charged particle or in a reverse motion in time, converging on an individual particle. Each would convey specific information from one particle to another, making each aware of its position in relation to all others as part of an integrated electromagnetic network, much like that of neurons and electrons in the brain that contribute to our conscious self. Even general relativity, which accurately describes the solar system, breaks down at the quantum scale, so that reconciliation requires a "theory of everything"—something that could lead to simultaneous multiple states and an infinite number of multiple universes, where one universe can "give birth" to other universes.

The "many worlds" interpretation of quantum mechanics is supported by a number of cosmologists, as it possibly involves the simplest interpretation of quantum activity. This emanates from Schrödinger philosophical hypothesis, articulated by his mathematics, and can be restated as the choice at the quantum level where the universe splits into an infinite number of parallel copies, so that multiple versions of possible "reality" are forming at all times in interstellar space. Each observer therefore assumes they are inhabiting their own unique universe. The theory itself was first put forward by Hugh Everett in 1957, and explains the appearance of wavelike interference associated with the quantum system. It offers an interpretation through "decoherence"—effectively the means of rationalizing the interactions between microscopic particles and the greater macroscopic environment. This posits the existence of stable states consistent with the intuition that a single wave function of the universe could be interpreted in terms of a multiplicity of realities.

At the quantum level, all space contains an enormous amount of virtual energy, and the multiverse theory is based on the fact that a quantum change of state can enable an entire "baby" universe to come into existence almost instantaneously—a hypothetical but consistent interpretation of quantum reality. The central claim of the multiverse theory is based on all the known laws of nature being tied into the open-ended concept of infinity, although computing infinity also raises issues of probability and inevitability. The alternative is that the constantly changing and expanding universe follows a course that, if not actually predetermined, obeys self-regulating mathematical laws through processes of creation and destruction that are as yet unknown.

Quantum physics constantly unfolds its enigmatic traits, many of them associated with unpredictability and chance that underpin the very existence of life, as the process of electron entanglement establishes its biological reach. It has been posited by some physicists that quantum theory reflects aspects of Buddhism, Taoism, and Hinduism that disdain matter itself for a cosmic rhythm of creation and destruction, with a commensurate ebb and flow of energy. For example, birds use its essential workings to assist migration routes through quantum waves that act as a magnetic compass through sub-atomic particles in their eyes that detect tiny variations in the earth's magnetic field. Our sense of smell is derived from detection of chemicals in receptor molecules that, under the quantum process, vibrate at different frequencies, analogous to an acoustic event linked to an inner consciousness. Metamorphosis through countless chemical processes brings about our evolutionary transformation, speeding up reactions necessary for cell development through quantum particles.

The universe displays time-asymmetry with a Big Bang situation, and the "wave equations" of quantum mechanics might well provide the means by which particles have "knowledge" of their past and future states through positive and negative energy waves. This extends the concept of space-time to multiple dimensions where time becomes enfolded within the spatial matrix leading to a highly complex quantum reality. It represents the ghost in the machinery of the universe. Looking for an explanation of reality arguably calls for a rethinking of the universe itself—something that some scientific commentators have expressed as trying to describe the Cheshire Cat from its grin.

The existence of a cosmic web of galaxies with a string-like filamentary structure surrounding vast voids of empty space was discerned in the 1980s, and brought into question the assumption of a homogenous universe. The Higgs boson is a quantized manifestation of the Higgs field. As particles pass through a Higgs field they acquire mass, where even microscopic differences in its properties could have significant consequences for the fundamental forces and thus for the processes that have established our existing universe. Under this scenario it is equally possible that cosmic inflation could generate parallel universes, each with infinite spatial extents and different time scales. There are several notable but somewhat theoretical versions of parallel universes exhibiting different degrees of nuance, stemming largely from the bewildering ramifications of quantum mechanics, and that could technically emerge from inflationary expansion including, quilted, quantum, bubble, and holographic, all of which require greater levels of insight which might shift both our scientific thinking and our theology. The notion of "bubble" universes for example stems from the theory that a multitude of universes arose through inflation, drawing energy from the gravitational field, and then developing through an inflation period that occurred at all points in what is known as *de Sitter* space. Symmetry might well suggest a deeper truth—that a second universe might extend from the Big Bang in the opposite direction from our known universe, experiencing an equally flattening process, and creating a parallel space-time "cone." Even if these theories can be mathematically proven it is relatively inconsequential as we cannot actually observe or test it. Such a secular picture in relation to a mathematical construct of space, which as far as we know has no actual physical dimensions, exerts a strong question mark over the meaning of existence, which invites some interpretation as to its narrower implications.

In the formation process of galaxies, agglomerations of space debris and dust provided a critical density of mass that increased due to gravitational pull and the coalescence of planets. For the past seven billion years cosmic expansion has been accelerating because of repulsive gravity supplied by dark energy, which drives distant galaxies forcefully apart. In receding from one another, galaxies move in excess of the speed of light, as they are assisted by the overall distention of space intimated by relativity. The nature of inflationary expansion through quantum fluctuation and in the energy generated across space, stretches the cosmic fabric, and this together with microscopic quantum uncertainty gave rise to our known galaxies and cosmic evolution.

Cosmic inflation effectively transformed energy into matter in the early universe, and an accepted theory is that cosmic strings, which still pervade the universe, were responsible for slight ripples in space-time. These gravitational waves occurred through supernova explosions that helped to create more matter than antimatter, allowing planets and galaxies to come into existence. Progressive insights into quantum field theory have revealed a strong degree of unity between the three non-gravitational forces suggesting that these might be combined as a single force of nature. However, it was not until the emergence of superstring theory, with reference to supersymmetry, that the refinement of mathematical methods began to compel a reinvigorated evaluation of cosmic laws through quantum electrodynamics. Supersymmetry unites the two families of particles: bosons, which have whole-number spins such as photons; and fermions, where particles have fractional spins.

In mathematical terms, superstring theory points to different shapes of space-time but still requires answers to some of the deepest questions about the Cosmos. The strings are thought to comprise a symphonic ensemble of miniscule vibrating filaments, most probably with extremely convoluted profiles, that produce different properties in particles, much like vibrating patterns on a stringed instrument produce different tones. In this sense, particles are represented by the strings themselves, and the different symmetries of string theory all appear to suggest that this might represent the most promising means of explaining the complex fabric of the universe, and the "missing link" between relativity and quantum theory, offering a possible unified explanation of all matter and forces. In reconciling the mathematical problematics, string theory's equations indicate a universe with nine dimensions of space and one of time, as opposed to three and one under relativity, as the most optimum and consistent "problem-free" model. More recently "M" (or membrane) theory has raised the number of possible spatial dimensions to 10, providing a unifying connection between different string theories and the notion of a "braneworld" scenario. The braneworld multiverse suggests that universes could differ not merely in shape but in terms of different laws of physics. String theory has also given a mathematical grounding to a cyclic universe—the notion of continual repetition of birth and decay.

It must be stated that cosmology, whether in the form of an inflationary or cyclic model, still requires resolution of many compelling but conflicting features of the space-time reality we inhabit. We are now able to observe many of the stars and planets and seek to explain them precisely because they are part of our wider chemical structure and ecosystem. Scientific explanation and verdicts might differ and for now we can only navigate a probabilistic realm of enquiry. The complexity of physics and mathematics surrounding the "many realities" generated by the quantum world, opens a door of understanding to those capable of interpreting its workings and implications. Brian Greene, a theoretical physicist and professor at Columbia University, explains the conceptually difficult many worlds approach as having to make sense of quantum mechanics' predictions in a context that envisions all possible outcomes.

The concept of 'black holes' began with speculation by the Cambridge professor of geology John Michell, but was only expressed through Einstein's theory of general relativity. The result of the mathematics relating to relativity was the realization that an extreme curvature of space-time would inevitably give rise to an equally extreme gravitational attraction entrapping surrounding matter, and compressing it to an infinitesimal size. This would later be termed the most intense configuration known to physics. If we accept the collapse of physical matter into a black hole of condensed gravity, then as Einstein demonstrated, space and everything with which we are familiar must logically disappear with it, leaving only a persistent and largely illusionary impression—something akin to iconic memory that occurs as a result of a brief sensory stimulus.

Stephen Hawking stated that quantum theory is about what we do not know and cannot predict. However, Hawking recognized that the event horizon of a black hole increases over time according to the results of the uncertainty principle, whereby black holes emit particles, precisely at the event horizon. Under quantum theory, pairs of elementary particles exist and if this occurred at the event horizon of a small black hole, one particle would be drawn in and the positive energy particle would escape the gravitational pull and extend outward to form what came to be known as Hawking radiation. As negative energy particles that fall within the black hole decrease its mass, the measure of stored information could be shown as being proportional to its surface areas rather than its volume. Hawking then showed mathematically that the entropy of a black hole was equal to the number of Planck unit cells covering its event horizon, indicating that information was stored on its surface rather than within its interior. We might question what the antipode of this is that presently evades observation or experience but nevertheless has an existence. One theory described by Brian Greene is that instead of

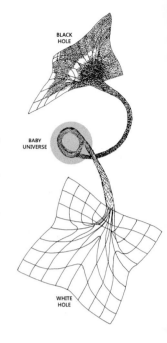

BLACK HOLE

BABY UNIVERSE

WHITE HOLE

Wormholes in space can link different regions of space-time. One end forms a black hole which draws in matter and energy while the opposite end is a white hole which emits matter. In principle, it is possible for this to emerge at an earlier stage than when it entered, literally moving backward in time. If a black hole exists for a long period, the wormhole itself could give rise to a 'baby universe' through an expansion of space—a self-propagating process that could continue indefinitely, technically creating an ability to give rise to new life forms.

matter disappearing entirely, the event horizon actually captures every quality, storing all information through an "inscription" on the two-dimensional space surrounding its outer edge. If these surfaces are connected through quantum entanglement, whereby two elementary spinning particles are connected in cosmic space even if they are far apart, the mathematics of string theory might then serve to explain the supposed threading of space and the presence of wormholes.

One insight that has been drawn by theoretical physicists using string theory is that within any portion of space the capacity of stored information can give rise to a holographic interlocking of parallel worlds. This is produced through a complementary combination of string theory operating within the curved area of 10-dimensional space-time, and quantum field theory operating on its "boundary." A mathematical translation between the two, borne out by experiments, explicitly indicates the correctness of the holographic principle, and can be applied to a black hole where all information in its inaccessible interior is ultimately available on its boundary surface.

The universe itself can only be fully comprehended by means of mathematics, which clearly limits a completely fulfilling appreciation of its nature, let alone a full understanding of the dark matter and dark energy that somehow fill the intergalactic voids. It seems that the more deeply we delve into the complexity of matter with its impenetrable sub-atomic inventory of quarks, gluons, neutrons, and protons, the overriding conclusion has to be that there is some artistic symmetry at work at its most basic level that exceeds anything poetically dreamed up by Dante in the *Comedia*.

This might be considered as a central challenge, but also an achievement of the mind in reconciling what we see and know with an implanted ability to query and question as a synthesis of rational thought, speculation, and conjecture. It necessarily follows that humankind has a seemingly central role in what we know as creative order, where the physical world we are familiar with might well be considered as only one aspect of a universe or even a multiverse.

So perhaps we have to regard *Paradiso* in the same way. By invoking a heavenly realm outside a conventional sense of attainment or unfiltered by the anthropic principle that makes it compatible with conscious life, Dante skirts around the laws and constants of nature, postulating a grander reality but one that is finely tuned to constitute evidence of a god-like creative intelligence with a strong sense of purpose. Max Planck himself stated that "all matter originates and exists only through a force behind which is an intelligent mind." If we accept this, then imagination is just as important as knowledge, and consciousness becomes more fundamental than matter. In fact, it becomes mind-like.

The mystery of time and reality comes down to the individual human being, and our transformational relationship with real time. This is synchronized in humans by means of the nervous system and regulated by its complexities. We are in fact all in motion relative to everyone else, so that the experience of time varies between observers based on the speed of light. Subatomic particles according to relativity theory bring time and space with them for the ride, so that their behavior allows for a range of actual possibilities.

It is apparent that quantum physics is directly associated with the uncertainty principle, which has determined that the universe is in many respects physically intangible and subject to unpredictable fluctuations—something that is inherent in nature. This implies that an apparent randomness must be addressed through probabilities applied to complex problems that attempt to balance order and chaos through mathematical rules. The multi-dimensional quantum process proffers a compelling although somewhat intangible ideal of harmony and structure in deciphering the ambiguities of elementary particles at the heart of the universe. It therefore pries open new opportunities for interpretation and a possible interaction with some form of cosmic connectedness. Our sense of reality, abstractedly tested by Dante's Inferno, Purgatorio, and Paradiso, therefore has both subjective and objective components.

The ultimate question, originally posed by Niels Bohr, is whether reality actually exists or whether we conjure it into existence by the act of imagination.

Chaos Theory and the Mandelbrot Set

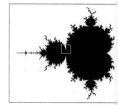

Clouds are not spheres, mountains are not cones, coastlines are not circles, and bark is not smooth, nor does lightning travel in a straight line.
BENOIT MANDELBROT, *The Fractal Geometry of Nature*

An underlying question with regard to natural form is how can inanimate matter create such geometrically intricate patterns? The answer is that this is determined through mathematical rules. Complicated shapes in nature outside the ideal of Euclidean geometry cannot be described by familiar symmetries, but when magnified a small piece of an object looks much like the whole. This is based on types of geometrical self-similarity. One of the simplest is the Sierpiński gasket—a triangle composed of ever-smaller triangles that can be replicated indefinitely with every part becoming a scaled copy of the whole. The importance of this was not recognized until fractals made it visible. Variations on self-similarity, when combined, produce computer-generated images of astonishing reality such as three-dimensional landscapes, cloud formations, and mountain ranges.

Contemporary ideas clearly run counter to some aspects of Newtonian science that once considered the universe as a massive mechanical machine where self-regulation happened independently of external influence. This came to be questioned through chaos theory—a system of mathematical equations that describes unpredictable outcomes. Immeasurably small variations can have an enormous cumulative impact that makes mathematical certainty illusionary, and indicates that unpredictability is inherent within the laws of physics. It suggests a cosmic connection where nature's power to self-organize must be balanced with potentially chaotic consequences woven into the pattern of the universe, and hardwired into the uncertainty principle.

The so-called "butterfly effect" out of which chaos theory evolved was a question posed by Edward Lorenz—"Does the flap of a butterfly's wings in Brazil set off a tornado in Texas?" Chaos theory showed that order and chaos are linked through mathematical rules, where their interrelationship creates spontaneous pattern formations that reflect the apparent irregularities that appear to permeate the universe.

The way in which time and space can be measured exhibits fluctuations that are scale invariant, showing that inflationary processes produce a fractal-like universe within the flatness of space-time. Even the distribution of galaxies have implications for symmetry, as uncovered by the German mathematician Emmy Noether from Newtonian cosmology, which was both homogeneous, i.e., it looks about the same in every location, and isotropic, i.e., it looks about the same in every direction. The clustering of galaxies, which are aggregates of dust, gas, and stars with the majority of their mass made up of dark matter, has much to do with self-similarity. Alan Guth, who put forward the original inflationary model of cosmology, describes how chaotic inflation could theoretically produce a branching of universes rather like a fractal structure enables a reading of nature.

Fractal geometry describes and models the complex forms found in nature through a process that is closely correlated with chaos theory. This does not lend itself to direct observation but can be seen in the Mandelbrot set, discovered by Benoit Mandelbrot in 1980, that can be interpreted through an infinite number of algorithms. Fractal geometry enables the observation of patterns that reveal the true complexity of nature and helps to establish a greater understanding through a visual interpretation via computerized imagery and iteration. Mandelbrot elaborated on how dynamic processes grow shapes so that a coastline is a story of rocks, waves, wind, and tides, just as the branching geometry of a snowflake is the story of temperature, dust particles, water vapors, and crystals. In the same way that mathematics can explain the poetics of literature, so the language of fractals can help us to visualize and exercise our curiosity as to the elaborate dimensions of the universe.

In a not dissimilar way to Pythagoras, Mandelbrot provided a visual counterpart to the musical proportion of theme and variation. In fact, it is a means of perceiving symmetry from chaos. This essentially results in a form of geometric repetition where copies of a pattern are "nested" within each other ad infinitum, based on the identical intricate shapes generated by a simple equation.

The Mandelbrot set has been called the "thumbprint of God," and represents a simple formula that feeds back on itself, with each output creating the input to the next set, thereby illustrating levels of increasing complexity. It incorporates the Fibonacci mathematical sequence with images created by sampling the complex numbers in the set through a predetermined number of iterations. The progressive level of recursive detail incorporates ever-intricate versions of the original fractal shape, and with the use of colored pixels in high resolution provides a sense of nature's infinite richness. This mirrors a truth in nature where complexity arises from simple rules relating to inanimate matter, so that every time the system is run for a particular phenomenon the results display minor variations.

Mandelbrot's "theory of roughness" examined the irregular aspects of physical phenomena in the field of fractal geometry—a mathematical principle that underpins the complicated forms, structure, and patterns found in nature. The applied fractals were called "Julia sets," named after Gaston Julia whose discovery was published in 1918 as the source of fractals that could only be explored to their full extent many years later via computers. Fractals are defined by their properties of self-similarity whose visualizations can be observed in such things as mountain ranges, shorelines, the dendritic systems of rivers, and even blood vessels. In Mandelbrot's words, "nature provides us with a powerful visual counterpart to the musical idea of theme and variation." It is also one of the most complex, and has been termed the aesthetics of mathematics. The Mandelbrot set has a large central region with a solid interior without any particular structure. It has a complex boundary with an infinity of different boundary shapes. The visual roadmap displays close-ups of its boundary containing small copies of the Mandelbrot set, but with each iteration displaying increasing levels of detail.

Plotting the topology effectively played a large part in introducing fractals into mainstream mathematics. The process of evolution builds on these patterns reflecting the refinement and shaping of existing systems according to iterations that equate with a cosmic time scale. Identical cells can self-organize into different organs and characteristics through a precise chemical process that causes the evolution of a given body. This allows for an intuitive and realistic physicality to be produced from the structure of plants to the clustering of galaxies, and in the process establishes a controlled unity to the knowledge of creative processes. It illustrates how complexity can be created from a simple equation that can be repeated endlessly to illustrate how natural forms evolve over time, and where outputs continually feed back to produce the infinite complexity that we find everywhere in nature. Fractal images can be produced using graphic computer code based on geometric intuition that is capable of simulating evolution, shaping and refining living organisms based on their reaction to unexpected events, and showing that infinite complexity spontaneously emerges from the power inherent in self-organization.

M.C. Escher used polyhedra in many of his artworks, here shown in a copy of *Angels and Devils*. He compi a number of "circle limit" artworks within a tessellate two-dimensional Euclidian plane or enclosure, throu repeated pattern of regular shapes that visually conn the abstract world with the real world. Escher captur realities and mathematical symmetries that coexist i multiple dimensions and morph into each other, with resulting transformation exploring and challenging t bounds of infinity. This is achieved through the adop of a recursive approach utilising the "Droste" effect where increasingly smaller versions are depicted thro repetition of the central image. He famously worked with the mathematical physicist Sir Roger Pencose ir the invention of aperiodic tiling using the golden rati of 1:1.618.

Melencolia I—a copy of the 1514 engraving by the Renaissance artist Albrecht Dürer. The central figure ponders the nature of beauty and creativity, represer through the humanist concept of melancholy and thought to be influenced by the planet Saturn. The p contains mathematical, geometrical and astrological references, with the central figure symbolic of a reflective quality that stimulates the mind's higher powers.

The engraving contains references to a 4x4 "magic square"—a grid of numbers that represented an ancie talisman of Jupiter. Configurations of columns, rows, diagonals, together with the four quadrants and the central quadrant each add up to the same number, while numbers that are symmetrically opposite add up to half this number. The date is set out in the bottom two squares, which can also be seen above Dürer's monogram. The Mannerist artist and historiar Giorgio Vasari described the engraving as "a technica achievement that puts the whole world in awe."

255

EPILOGUE

HE INSPIRATIONAL CITY building processes of the Renaissance that produced some of our most breathtaking urban environments, and the scientific breakthroughs that slowly unraveled the mysteries of the Cosmos, have certain things in common. Both represent human accomplishment and progressive understanding, and establish the necessary tools and techniques to proceed from one stage to the next, building on our acquisition of knowledge and perception. They also jointly recognize the essential qualities of symmetry, precision, and simplicity in expressing elegant solutions, be it in buildings or equations. Artists, philosophers, and scholars established manuals and handbooks that linked visual representation to the dissemination of knowledge related to the built environment. Alberti's *De re Aedificatoria*, Palladio's *I Quattro libri dell'architettura*, Vignola's *Regola delli Cinque Ordini d'Architettura*, and Serlio's *Tutte l'opere d'architettura* expressed an inventive creativity in city design, just as Copernicus' *Commentariolus*, Kepler's *Astronomia Nova*, Galileo's *Siderius Nuncius*, and Newton's *Philosophiae Naturalis Principia Mathematica* opened up compelling scientific trajectories that led to relativity theory and quantum mechanics. We can all experience the lasting static beauty of the Renaissance city, but the insightful understanding of space and time enriches the process and reconfigures our sense of physical reality.

In nature, symmetry reflects a regular correspondence between different things that achieves a pleasing and functional equilibrium. In physics it suggests something that remains unchanged even if it undergoes certain transformations. The physical outcome is therefore more or less the same—that external reality is perceived as more than the sum of its individual parts. Symmetries are in fact the foundation of relativity theory, and allow the physical world to be accurately described by mathematics. They are also the key to the way we construct urban space. The physical realization of the symmetrical approach to architecture and urban design set out by Alberti and Brunelleschi, notably advocated a necessary correspondence between the divine and human mind. This involves an articulated processing of information that takes us to the heart of reality but also access to fundamental knowledge about it.

Dante based his view of the universe, mediated through ancient philosophy and religion, on divine retribution, repentance, and reward, assuming that its purpose was at the discretion of a creator with control over free will. We can now state with confidence that knowledge of the physical world of things is governed by the principles of mathematics, which have been painstakingly uncovered on a piecemeal basis rather than invented. Each has helped to refine the work of its predecessor and unraveled features of the natural world that have met with no contradiction. There is, however, a separate world that deals with consciousness, comprehension, and feeling. We must therefore turn to a metaphysical vision of reality if we are to pursue a theory based on underlying unity. A divine hypothesis should presumably express unity in diversity, and, like Plato, equate ethical and moral values with aesthetic ones—a more subjective and abstract process than the necessary precision of science.

The rationalization of a supreme or "divine" underlying intelligence, in particular one that adopts a non-interventionist role in the continuing affairs of the Universe, is to follow Cicero's comparison with the invention of a timepiece that thereafter can follow its own independent but deterministic motion. A celestial creationist might therefore be given due credit for originating the Big Bang, the universe, or even a multiverse without necessarily incorporating any pre-destined follow-through to intelligently manage it thereafter. If we accept this then our combination of faith, knowledge, and scientific discovery needs to simply resort to the principle of sufficient reason put forward by Gottfried Leibnitz.

Dante's imaginative tampering with the particularities of the universe brought into play aspects that attempt to reinforce our significance. If it is life that gives the universe its meaning, rather than the other way around, then we can revisit Dante for his lofty appraisal of moral expectations and exactitudes, albeit ones that were assembled in an age when denying the reality of God was considered a crime against nature. The metaphysical states of Hell, Purgatory, and a Cosmic Paradise hold within them an assumption that human souls have an elusive capacity for immortality, but as Stephen Hawking observed, "the role played by time at the beginning of the universe might be the final key to removing the need for a Grand Designer."

Astronomical allusions take on a symbolic function in emphasizing the temporal quality of Dante's truncated itinerary that structures both the physical relationships between the three states, and their causal interconnection that represents a fundamental order. In Dante's work this is governed by the natural elements of earth, water, fire, and air, and a divine order under the auspices of a God—a fusion of natural science and scripture. It is perhaps why the strange and varied domains of Dante's classic poem reverberate through the centuries. It does not in itself have to reveal the expanse of reality, and this is just as well as it's physical dimensions should not be taken too literally. However, it compels us to explore a resilient path that can guide us to certain underlying truths.

An inspired take on the exactitudes of eternity seeks to project a ruthlessly moralistic Cosmos as some measure of its similarity to the stratification of society. It also questions boundaries, both of the conscious mind and the physical universe with its hidden inevitabilities, but at the same time it merely represents one of a myriad of projections that might apply to an infinite number of realities. The relationship between language and meaning is a challenging one for the interpretation of Dante's *Comedia*, based on the elusive stability of self and its relationship with the external world. The issue of infinity is itself something of a conundrum, in so much as it infers a limitless volume, a limitless number of spatial entities, and a limitless period of time. It therefore becomes something elusively situated beyond detailed observation, calculation, and prediction.

Both the artistic and scientific components of the Renaissance were caught up in a religious flux, which was either blindly followed for its supposed spiritual sanctity or contested for its questionable overtones and dichotomies. Either way, the balance between objectivity and subjectivity was delicately maintained in the face of a new knowledge-based frontier. Urban design and scientific method both emerged during the Renaissance as languages of pattern and symmetry that systemized an ongoing exploration for a well-reasoned and fundamental truth. Symmetry similarly underlies the laws of the universe, where

Streetscape, Verona.

balance and order change through evolution while maintaining a certain uniformity. In mathematics a quantity exhibits symmetry when it remains the same under the action of a transformation. In a spatial interpretation it implies the presence of harmonious proportions and a sense of balance, where similar parts face each other on or around an axis in a consistent way, just as the visual appeal of Renaissance design challenges us to reflect on the true veracity of the Italian city. What we should gain from both is the inspiration and motivation to embrace a consistent artistry and sense of exploration that might accommodate a symmetry of the parts but nevertheless with a sense of clarity and composition.

Certain scientific observations can be ascertained from the *Comedia*, including references to a spherical earth, the various time zones, and the visibility of stars. Students of Dante's cosmography and astrology, even in the rational context of the modern age, have made claims as to his anticipatory references on the discoveries of modern science, extruding the medieval a-priori foundation of the work and its lack of empirical objectivity. Dante's use of symmetries based on numerology display a familiarity and preoccupation for an ordered whole, drawing on a realm of knowledge that ranged from astronomy and alchemy, to meteorology, medicine, and mathematics. In many of the cantos, Dante displays an almost musical sense of alliteration, rhythmic ratios, rhyme, and resonance that relate back to Pythagoras.

Einstein's 1935 papers on quantum entanglement between distant particles, and "tunnel" threading between regions of space, create lines of theory and conjecture that tests our depth of understanding with regard to the working of the Cosmos, but also its meaning. The purposeful anti-symmetry of Dante's three spatial realms similarly postulated an entanglement in the fabric of space, forcefully probing a mystical connection between immortality and divine retribution. Such a notion tests our conception of impermanence and time itself, which can only be measured by change in relation to what we assume to be the finite nature of everything. The mathematics of quantum physics can be modeled but the deeper truth seems forever several steps away, engendering further levels of complexity.

While Dante conceived his *Comedia* in three-dimensional space and a condensed dimension of time, he might also have inadvertently stumbled onto the notion of quantum immortality in a parallel universe without recourse to our painfully assembled laws of cosmological interpretation. This would appear to have the extravagant potential for divine events to happen through quantum superimposition where realty conveniently diverges into different poetic states, helpfully propelled by the wave function. This suggests that Dante, an accomplished mathematician himself, might have innocently perceived a rudimentary mathematical basis to a then unknowable universe that scientific evidence later corroborated in relation to the natural world. A number of later scientists and mathematicians such as Copernicus, Galileo, and Newton were devout believers in a divinity based on eternal salvation, just as their theories and findings suggested a new cosmic order that created an opportunity to question the ordained balance between body and soul. If we view Dante's masterwork in four-dimensional space-time rather than as a complex illusion, the simulated realms of Inferno, Purgatory, and Paradiso within an "External Reality" would feel quite authentic to its subject inhabitants, and probably also to its fascinated observers. Their particular circumstances could, in our 21st-century world, be handily encoded within a mathematical structure, albeit with resource to an appropriate level of fine-tuning. For example Dante's notion of a terrestrial Inferno below the surface of the earth signified little knowledge of its liquid core, where plate movements are apt to cause fissures and raise mountains.

The notion of whether cosmic consciousness necessitates the presence of an omnipresent God is an open question. In the sense that this introduces a supreme divinity as a source of all moral authority, it is probably necessary to defer judgment. We might perhaps be more favorably inclined toward a modestly abstract cosmic presence, consciously and connectively plugged into its evolving universal creation, whether or not this is, or was, purposeful. We must anyway be ambitious for its problematic future, sensitive to its purpose, determined as to the quality of existence, and benign as to the humanized way it is experienced. The human being is, to the best of our knowledge, the measure of universal creation, precisely because every aspect of nature on our lonely planet supports human existence, and both mind and matter appear to be part of a universal consciousness. Dante most certainly had a divine imagination, but what was poetically described in the entirely fictitious *Inferno* erupted into reality in the world wars of the 20th century, and the furnaces of Auschwitz and Belsen. As the Greek philosopher Heraclitus stated rather resignedly, "A man's character is his fate," and Dante makes little distinction between each of Inferno's sinful categories; they are equally judged as being damned, and their condemnation inscribed across the portals of Hell—"Abandon all hope, ye that enter."

Dante might, at the very least, be gratified by Einstein's well known retort that "God does not play dice with the universe"; the confirmation of which is affirmed with the elusive Higgs boson, informally known as the "God particle," and the Mandelbrot set based on chaos theory, commonly referred to as "the thumbprint of God."

The Cosmic Mandate

Nature is written in that great book, which is ever between our eyes—I mean the universe—but we cannot understand it if we do not first learn the language and grasp the symbols in which it was written.
GALILEO GALILEI

The Copernican Principal, buttressed by Newton's suggestion that we hold no privileged place in the universe, carries the implication that our solar system and therefore Earth, cannot be assumed to be atypical. The estimated minimum diameter of the universe as far as we can determine it is 78 billion light years. Our Milky Way galaxy alone is around one hundred thousand light years across, contains as many as 400 billion stars and 100 billion planets, and our relatively undistinguished solar system is actually located, less than prominently, in one of its long spiral arms. The number of galaxies might, however, be reduced somewhat in the far distant future, as astronomers have recently discovered a black hole in the Milky Way, only 1,500 light years from Earth, with a mass 70 times greater than the sun. By comparison, the Andromeda galaxy beyond the Milky Way contains more than one trillion stars in 883 galaxies within a super cluster 520 light years across. We also know that there are many such galaxies, and scientists can therefore postulate, although with little actual evidence, that there might well be other earth-like planets lurking among them. Quantum theory, however, introduces concepts and definitions, such as perception and sensation that tend to be isolated from mathematically closed sets that are subject to different forces. These underlie human reality and make us respond to art, architecture, and music that arise from a positive interaction with the world rather than a necessary adherence to formal rules. As Heisenberg noted, the processes of art and science are not so different.

We are left to reflect on such abstract issues as energy and dark matter, where expression of density returns us to the cosmological constant. Expanding galaxies exist in clusters that range from the spiral to the elliptical, and are composed of several trillion stars whose trajectories are subject to constant gravitational forces. A large number of these are in the process of exploding and expelling energy and matter, while others are surrounded by planets that may or may not present conditions for life.

We now know that the universe is made up of approximately 4.9 percent atomic matter, 26.6 percent dark matter, and 68.5 percent dark energy, which establishes almost exactly the right amount of matter and energy within a universe with no spatial curvature. Atomic or "baryonic" matter forms part of the filamentary 'cosmic web' that connects galaxies. It can be measured according to temperature fluctuations in cosmic microwave background radiation. This was identified in 2020 by measuring highly energetic pulses of radio emissions emanating from distant galaxies and calculating how much matter the radio waves passed through before reaching earth.

The "dark knowledge" enveloping the universe is recognized by scientists but its properties are not fully understood. It is created as the universe expands, and while the proportion of dark matter is dropping, dark energy can travel more rapidly than light and is being created more quickly than space itself. The implication of this is that as the universe continues to expand indefinitely through cosmic inflation, it will eventually collapse into a singularity along with space-time, perhaps to re-emerge as an entirely new universe. Dark matter is an eminently transparent material that does not interact with electromagnetic radiation. Its composition is indeterminate, but is most likely made up of currently undiscovered subatomic particles necessary to hold galaxies together. It contains more than five times the mass of atomic matter, and can only be inferred from its gravitational capacity and from its effect on cosmic microwave background radiation.

Even the big bang singularity lacks full scientific agreement. The most accepted theory is that this represents the instantaneous creation of space-time and the existence of matter, while an alternative is that this appeared within an existing space-time vacuum. Its obvious conflict with accepted conservation laws of mass and energy suggest that all matter existed and was concentrated at a single point with infinite density, and that an explosion was triggered by a quantum fluctuation. Mathematical rules and patterns infiltrate everything in the universe, but while these describe the world with which we are familiar, they do not necessarily explain it. Underlying truths exist in a disembodied state and simply wait to be discovered. Things can either be unknowable or unprovable but while we have to accept certain rules there are some things that we cannot yet prove, and that have to be taken on faith from the limited evidence presented.

While different and legitimate mathematical structures and their relationships are widely accepted, the phantom theory of everything that unites general relativity and quantum mechanics, and that explains our physical reality, still eludes us. This might in itself suggest that a neat symmetrical solution could well have to give way to a more radical reality that is intrinsically indeterminate, incorporating an infinity of space beyond our cosmic horizon. This would somehow have to equate the many elusive aspects of quantum physics with an underlying mathematical structure, or several such structures, subject to forces that extend our familiar laws of physics. Inconsistency does not however rule out the existence of new physical realities, although describing them might entail an infinite amount of information commensurate with the underlying symmetries that support all known mathematical structures.

The search for a grand unified theory continues through the principle of super symmetry, which assumes that each particle must have a super-symmetric counterpart that satisfies the standard model. A further issue is how gravitation connects not just in terms of the properties of space-time, but with other fundamental interactions. It is possible that string theory, which postulates the quantum mechanics of space-time where particles act as miniscule filament loops, could model the four fundamental interactions of gravitation, electromagnetism, and the strong and weak nuclear forces, making it compatible with general relativity and super symmetry.

The embryonic universe can now be glimpsed in detail via computer simulations along with the irregularities in the quantum vacuum, where clusters of galaxies make up the universe. In 2014 astronomers at the Harvard-Smithsonian Center for Astrophysics created a virtual universe called *illustris* that could reveal almost 14 billion years of cosmic evolution from a singular origin, and in 2019 a holographic model of this was conceived. This gives rise to an important revelation, that the universe itself could have sprung from a vacuum, creating vast amounts of matter but also equal amounts of anti-matter, or could equally have been the rebirth of a previous universe. In either situation, the universe has experienced continual entropy since it exploded into existence, balanced only by gravity as it seemingly expands toward infinity. This raises a presently unanswerable question as to what is on the other side and whether there are other bubble universes stemming from what Stephen Hawking termed the initial space-time singularity.

What we see now comes from what was left from the explosion and the commensurate annihilation of matter and anti-matter, although if we wish to quibble, the bang itself only describes the expansion of space that happened in the split second after creation—not the inflationary cosmology that might have set it in motion. Galaxies 300 million light years from Earth are moving outward at around 16.5 million miles an hour, due to a stretching—or swelling—of space itself. The void holds within it the mysteries of the Cosmos. There is in fact a profound connection between the nothingness from which we originated and the seeming infinity which engulfs us. Empty space is defined as a collection of quantum fields that exhibit fluctuations arising from the presence of zero-point energy in space, the lowest possible energy for a quantum mechanical system, although physics still lacks a full theoretical model for this.

It took almost a hundred years from the discovery of gravitational waves, predicted under relativity theory, for these to be captured in 2015 by the LIGO Observatory, emanating from the collision of two black holes around 1.3 billion years ago. The first image of the creation of a black hole was captured by linking together radio dishes around the world using a network of atomic clocks to align the first observations in April 2019 via the Event Horizon Telescope pointed at the heart of a giant elliptical galaxy called Messier 87 in the Virgo cluster, which contains several trillion stars situated more than 50 million light years away from Earth, with a mass 6.5 billion times that of the sun. The biggest explosion ever observed in the Universe was announced by NASA's Chandra X-ray Observatory in February 2020. This occurred in the Ophiuchus cluster around 390 million light years from Earth through an eruption generated by a black hole equivalent to the size of 15 Milky Way galaxies.

The perpetual tension between science, religion, and design has persisted on the part of many because of the perceived contradictions between the assimilation of proven but often extraordinary truths, and an evident need to engage in a deep seated spiritual connection with the external world. This might be said to extend the realm of association beyond the travails of life on earth toward the reassurance associated with a more exalted realm. Such a transcendent quality inspires veneration, just as in mathematics it encourages a limitless challenge to investigate and explain the sublime in the universe, and also allows artists to convey the sublime in nature. As human beings we strive for freedom from "determining influences" and generally claim responsibility for our own actions. However, we also strive for knowledge and experience that influences our consciousness and also our behavior. Our freedom to make our own decisions means taking a position outside reality and beyond our horizon as we experience it, in order to explore its deeper truths. As Robert Browning stated in his dramatic paean to Andrea del Sarto, the Mannerist painter, "Ah, but a man's reach should exceed his grasp, or what's a heaven for?"

We can only pursue a precise universal truth in terms of the behavior of the physical world, sometimes called platonic reality, if we venture far beyond the realm of mere observation and enter a separate world of mathematics, inspired by insight and exactness. This lifts a metaphorical curtain on what might be invisible as opposed to Dante who imagined it. But Dante also necessarily stepped beyond the dimensions we are familiar with, to discern a more moralistic version of the Cosmos that continues to reverberate. Science is not beyond such measures—Einstein essentially invented the cosmological constant to make credible the logic of a static universe.

The notion that something carries on into eternity is a powerful force that binds together society in seeking purpose and meaning. This in turn justifies protection of society's interests and affiliations, and it is then only one small step to associating this with Dante's notion of retribution and reward as part of a grand design. Science helps to unfold physical reality on the basis of experimentation, prediction, and testing. It can identify the strange behavior associated with quantum theory even if it cannot readily explain it.

Wherever a pursuit of the elusive quantum inventory takes us we must keep in mind the science of thinking and knowing applied to the different orders of nature derived largely from a philosophical perspective. The term "Noetic" is derived from the Greek nous, meaning a focused state of insight and perception which might, within its many facets, include the role of a universal and pervasive consciousness in creating a communion between the "self" and the outside world. It is knowledge itself, which might well include that derived from ancient spiritual texts, which has contributed to the transformation of the mind across the millennia, rather than merely the development of intellectual prowess.

The mathematics that describe the quantum world have called into question the notion of material order and unity of nature in terms of absolute space and time, where chaos, chance and randomness are also brought into play. The asymmetry but also the complementarity we find in the arts and music, and in the liveability of our cities, reflects a still unknown configuration between the brain and the mind as to our appreciation of these attributes. Dante put his capacity for knowledge and reasoning into words, elegantly conveying a compositional structure and syntax that tethered language to an underlying meaning. The suggestion of a spiritual unification of heaven and earth through a metaphysical ordering of beings within the cosmos, linked

Dante directly with later philosophers such as Martin Heidegger who poetically termed science "the theory of the real", and whose work was largely associated with ontology and phenomenology.

If the mind does indeed exist at least partly independent of the body, it can be argued that its properties, including its mental processes, cannot be readily explained in physiological and cognitive terms but through more elusive electrochemical and neural processes, refined through evolution.

Mental and emotional states such as delight, fear or melancholy cannot simply equate with information processing, nor can the sense of reason depend entirely on the possession of knowledge. Volitional processes which commits us to particular courses of action must complement purely analytical functions but are shaped by more subtle processes. This in fact represents the human predicament set around the concept of "self" which might be seen as a coalescence of miscellaneous and immutable experiences.

Spirituality should not be cast aside for its incompatibility with science. It is necessary to feel the universe in a way that contributes to human experience. It is why the beauty and the underlying coordinates of the Renaissance city equally matches the beauty of the stars.

Neither religious beliefs nor scientific orthodoxy, in their continual search for hidden truths, can ignore questions as to observation and verification. The mandate of science is to identify regularities in the workings of the universe that explore and clarify the underlying laws of nature. However, this is not to minimize the role of insight and imagination in pursuing promising trajectories and creative scenarios, in particular those that might help to frame and invoke pertinent questions, however much they might defy our instinctual sense of reality. Quantum theory takes this level of abstraction even further, with the probability wave facilitating predictions that go well beyond categorical experience or direct observation. In our ruminations about the Cosmos, the main point of investigation is on how it operates rather than how it is defined so that we can comprehend its ramifications. Taking this as a standpoint we must continue to calibrate its properties in order to ascertain underlying truths.

Given our existing knowledge of the universe, and assuming it to be comprehensible, it would seem to be within our means to generate further empirically progressive programs of research toward the identification of a unified theory of space-time and matter, under which all phenomena can be explained, free of myth and superstition. However, it might just as equally remain unknowable.

ACKNOWLEDGMENTS

Dante's Divine Comedy is one of the most translated poetic texts of all time that continues to both inspire and provoke changing theological, natural science and ideological interpretations. Its ninety-nine cantos plus an introductory canto is termed a "comedy" only in the medieval sense that the poet's spiritual journey culminates in both discovery and meaning, but represents one of the most remarkable single works of Western literature. The uncompromising architypes of vice and virtue, together with repentance and reward, veer from a constricting sense of darkness infiltrated by a strong sense of mysticism, to a moral exultation at its culmination. Written in the early 14th century over a twenty year period it was translated into many European languages well before its first English translation by Henry Boyd in 1802. It is said that this long gestation period reflected its imposing Catholic theology, considered to be heretical to those of a Protestant persuasion.

The poem's encapsulation of spiritual ideals, drawing on both the political and religious fervour of the times, signalled the symbolic incubation of a new humanism that flowered during the various stages of a Renaissance over the next three centuries. This in turn opened up new avenues of philosophical thought, design rendering and scientific discovery that still engage us through metaphysical interpretations applied to cosmic revelations which continue to illuminate our understanding of the universe - divine or otherwise.

The Divine Comedy is difficult to translate into English verse, partly because of its often ambiguous symbolic representation, but also because of the rhyming style of terza rima in which it was written. However the language constitutes an instrument intended to convey an elevated message of harmony applied to a singular understanding of the universe. I have therefore referenced the fine translations by Allen Mandelbaum and John Ciardi, and the precedent set by a line of those authors who critically describe aspects of the poem in an eminently accessible way such as Robin Kirkpatrick, Marguerite Mills Chiavenza, Joseph Gallagher, Robert Royal, and the public and political vision of Joan Ferranti.

Further sections of the book extrapolate the philosophical legacy of the *Comedy* through the early pioneers of Renaissance design and its many cultural dimensions. I am indebted to a range of authors who ably reinforced my preliminary knowledge of the period and its theoretical and practical architectural applications over some 300 years. These include Jacob Burckhardt's *The Civilization of the Renaissance in Italy*, Leon Alberti's *On the Art of Building*, Anthony Grafton's book on *Alberti, Master Builder of the Italian Renaissance*, Giorgio Vasari's *The Lives of the Painters, Sculptors and Architects*, Diane Bodat's *Renaissance and Mannerism*, and Ross King's *Brunelleschi's Dome*.

Similarly the range of authors on the medieval cosmos along with volumes of work on contemporary philosophy, mathematics and physics, open up a visionary perspective on an astonishing range of enlightened tours across the heart of scientific pursuit and the timeless quest for truth. Cosmic observation clearly pre-dates the *Comedy* and there is strong evidence that Dante had access to ancient astronomical sources along with philosophical theories dating back at least to Plato and Aristotle as a basis for religious rituals. Among many others who have successfully surveyed the principles of relativity, cosmology and quantum physics, some of the most fascinating and ground breaking are Roger Penrose's *The Emperor's New Mind*, Brian Greene's *The Fabric of the Cosmos*, and *The Hidden Reality*, Frank Wilczek's *A Beautiful Question* and John Boslough's *Beyond the Black Hole: Stephen Hawking's Universe*.

There are many more excellent publications, and these are set out in the Reference section, by the name of authors in alphabetical order.

I would finally like to record my appreciation to Gordon Goff, publisher and managing director of ORO Editions, and to Jake Anderson, managing editor of ORO, for his constant assistance with this publication and for his valuable editing skills from which the book has greatly benefitted. I would also like to thank Pablo Mandel for the graphic layout and design, and for his many positive suggestions.

In conclusion a big thank you to my long-time friends and colleagues at URBIS for their constant help and support. I am particularly grateful to my assistant Lily Tam for her invaluable help in typing and coordination of manuscript drafts and her patient assistance with the compilation and editing process. Thanks also to Chu Yuen Ming and Pauline Ng for their periodic graphic help and advice.

REFERENCES

References are set out in alphabetic order relating to author rather than subject matter

Ames-Lewis F (Ed). *Florence*
Cambridge University Press, 2012

Anderson, Christy. *Renaissance Architecture*
Oxford University Press, 2013

Argan, GC and Robb, NA. *The Architecture of Brunelleschi and the Origins of Perspective Theory in the Fifteenth Century*
Journal of the Warburg and Courtauld Institutes, Vol 9, 1946

Adams, D. *The Hitchhiker's Guide to the Galaxy*
Pan Books, 1979

Adams, D. *The Restaurant at the End of the Universe*
Pan Books, 1980

Alberti, Leon Battista. (Translated by Rykwert J) *The Ten Books of Architecture*
MIT Press, 1991 (Originally published in 1485)

Barbour, J. *The End of Time*
Oxford University Press, 2000

Barrow J D and Tipler F J. *The Anthropic Cosmological Principal*
Clarendon Press, 1986

Battisti Eugenio. *Filippo Brunelleschi*
Electa, Milano, 1976

Baxter Jason M. *A Beginners Guide to Dante's Divine Comedy*
Grand Papals – Baker Academic 2018

Bell, J S. *Speakable and Unspeakable in Quantum Mechanics*
Cambridge University Press 1987

Berger D. *An Important Resume of the Anthropic Cosmological Principle*

Blunt, Anthony. *Artistic Theory in Italy, 1450-1600*
Oxford Clarendon Press, 1956

Bodart D. *Renaissance and Mannerism*
Sterling NY and London, 2005

Borsi F. *Leon Battista Alberti. The Complete Works, Electa*
Rizzoli, New York, 1977

Boslough J. *Beyond the Black Hole: Stephen Hawking's Universe*
William Collins & Co Ltd, Glasgow 1985

Boyde P. *Perception and Passion in Dante's Comedy*
Cambridge University Press, 1993

Brown, David. *God and Enchantment of Place: Declaiming Human Experience*
Oxford University Press USA-050 2004

Brunelleschi. *Studies of His technology and Inventions*
Prager, F D and Scaglia, G
Dover Publications, NT 2004

Burckhardt, Jacob. *The Civilisation of the Renaissance in Italy*
Penguin Books
London, 1990

C S, Lewis. *The Discarded Image*
Cambridge University Press, 1964

Canniffe, Eamonn. *The Politics of the Piazza*
Ashgate 2008

Cassirer, Ernst. *The Philosophy of Symbolic Forms (in three volumes)*
Yale University Press 1965 Amazon.com: Books

Cassirer, Ernst Translated by Mario Domandi. *The Individual and the Cosmos in Renaissance Philosophy*, Dover Publications 2011 (originally published in 1927)

Cast, David. *The Delight of Art: Giorgio Vasari and the Traditions of Human Discourse*
Pennsylvanian State University Press 2009

Cast D J (Ed). *The Ashgate Research Companion to Giorgio Vasari Ashgate*
Publishing Limited, 2014

Chiarenza, Marguerite Mills. *The Divine Comedy: Tracing God's Art*
Boston Twayne Publishers, 1989

Ciardi J. *The Divine Comedy* (Translation)
Berkley, 2003

Clark J O (Ed). *Maps that Changed the World*
Batsford 2015

Coffin D. *The Villa in the Life of Renaissance Rome*
Princeton University Press, 1979

Cox B and Forshaw J. *The Quantum Universe And Why Anything that Can Happen, Does*
Boston: Da Capo Press, 2012

Crum, RJ and Paoletti, JT. *Renaissance Florence: A Social History*
Cambridge University Press, 2016

Davis P. *Space and Time in the Morden Universe*
Cambridge University Press, 1977

Davis P. *The Goldilocks Enigma*
The Penguin Press, 2006

Deutsch D. *The Fabric of Reality*
London, Viking Press, 1995

DeVorkin D. Beyond Earth: Mapping the Universe
National Geographic D.C. 2002

Elkins J and Williams R (Ed). *Renaissance Theory*
Routledge NY & London 2019

Fanelli, Giovani. *Brunelleschi*
Scala Istituto Fotografico Editoriale, Firenze, 1977

Fanelli G and Fanelli M. *Brunelleschi's Cupola: Past and Present of an Architectural Masterpiece*
Mandragora, 2004

Forgan, D H *'Solving Fermi's Paradox'*
Cambridge University Press, 2019

Ferrante, Joan M. *The Political Vision of the Divine Comedy*
Princeton University Press 1984

Finocchiona, M (Ed). *The Essential Galileo 1564-1642*
Hackett Publishing Company Inc, 2008

Frame M and Urry A. *Fractal Worlds: Grown, Built and Imagined*
Yale University Press, 2016

Gadol J. *Leon Battista Alberti: Universal Man of the Early Renaissance*
University of Chicago Press, 1969

Galileo Galilei. *Two New Sciences*, translated by Henry Crew and Alfonso de Salvio
Dover Publication NY, 1954 (Originally published 1638)

Galileo Galilei. *Sidereus Nuncius*. Translated by Albert Van Helden
University of Chicago Press, 1989 (Originally published in 1610)

Gallagher J (foreword by John Freccero). *A Modern Reader's Guide to Dante's The Divine Comedy*. Liguori/Triumph Publications, 1996

Garrard, M D. *Brunelleschi's Egg: Nature, Art, and Gender in Renaissance Italy*
University of California Press, 2010

Gingerich O. *The Book Nobody Read: Chasing the Revolutions of Nicolaus Copernicus*
NY: Walker and Company 2004

Goldthwaite, R. *Building of Renaissance Florence*
The John Hopkins University Press, 1982

Gott J R. *Time Travel in Einstein's Universe*
Boston: Houghton Mifflin, 2001

Grafton A. Leon Battista Alberti: *Master Builder of the Italian Renaissance*
Harvard University Press, 2002

Grant E. *Planets, Stars and Orbs: The Medieval Cosmos 1200-1687*
Cambridge University Press, 1996

Greene B. *The Fabric of the Cosmos*
Random House, Inc New York

Greene B. *The Hidden Reality*
Alfred A Knopf, NY 2011

Gregory, S. *Vasari and the Renaissance Print*
Ashgate 2012

Gribben J. *Schrödinger's Kittens and the Search for Reality*
Weidenfeld and Nicolson, London 1995

Guth, A. *The Inflationary Universe*
Reading, Mass: Perseus 1997

Hall, AR. *Isaac Newton*
Cambridge University Press 1992

Hawking S and Penrose R. *The Nature of Space and Time*
Princeton University Press 1996

Heisenberg W. *Physics and Philosophy: the Revolution in Modern Science*
Penguin 1990

Hendrix S.E. *How Albert the Great's Speculum Astronomiae was Interpreted and Used by Four Centuries of Readers*
Lewiston 2010

Hollingsworth M. *Patronage in Renaissance Italy*
John Murray Publishers Ltd 1994

James, C. *Dante: The Divine Comedy*
Pan MacMillan, 2015

Kahn, CH. *Anaximander and the Origins of Greek Cosmology*
Hackett Publishing Company Inc, 1960

Kauffman S. *At Home in the Universe: The Search for the Laws of Self-Organisation and Complexity*
NY: Oxford University Press, 1995

Kay, R. *Dante's Christian Astrology*
University of Pennsylvania Press, Philadelphia, 1994

Kenelm F and Boyde P (Eds). *Cambridge Readings in Dante's Comedy*
Cambridge University Press, 1981

King, R. *Brunelleschi's Dome: How A Renaissance Genius Reinvented Architecture*
Chatto and Windus, 2000

Kircher T. *Living Well in Renaissance Italy: The Virtues of Humanism and the Irony of Leon Battista Alberti*
State University of New York, 2012

Kirkpatrick, Robin. *Dante: The Divine Comedy*
Cambridge University Press, 1987

Klonsky, M. *Blake's Dante*
Harmony Books, 1980

Krautheimer, R and Krautheimer-Hess T. *Lorenzo Ghiberti*
Princeton University Press, 1956

Kuhn T S. *The Copernican Revolution: Planetary Astronomy in the Development of Western Thought*
Cambridge, Mass: Harvard University Press, 1957

Leon Battista Alberti. *On the Art of Building in Ten Books*
Cambridge, Mass, MIT Press, 1988

Leon Battista Alberti. *Ten Books on Architecture*
J Rykwert (Ed) London: Alec Tiranti, 1955

Mandelbaum, A. Translation of *The Divine Comedy* with explanatory notes by Armour, P
Everyman, London, 1995

Markschies, Alexander. *Icons of Renaissance Architecture*
Penobscot Books, 2005

Mazzotta, Giuseppe. *Dante's Vision and the Circle of Knowledge*
Princeton University Press, 1993

Mazzotta, Giuseppe. *Reading Dante*
Yale University Press, 2014

Millon Klonsky, M. *Blake's Dante*
Harmony Books, 1980

Milne E. *Modern Cosmology and the Christian Idea of God*
Clavendron Press, 1952

Murdin PG. *Secrets of the Universe: How we Discovered the Cosmos*
Thames and Hudson Ltd, London 2009

Murdin PG. *The Secret Lives of Planets*
Google Books, 2009

Murray L. *The High Renaissance and Mannerism*
Thames and Hudson, London 1977

Naess Atle; Anderson, J. *Galileo Galilei: When the World Stood Still*
Springer, Berlin Heidelberg, 2005

Najemy J M. *A History of Florence 1200-1575*
Wiley 2006

Natarajan P. *Mapping the Heavens*
Yale University Press, New Heaven and London 2016

O'Rourke Boyle, Marjorie. *Pure of Heart: From Ancient Rites to Renaissance Plato*
Journal of the History of Ideas
Jan 2002, Vol 63 (1)pp41-62

Osterhage, W. *Galileo Galilei. At the Threshold of the Scientific Age, Osterhage*
Springer International Publishing, 2019

Peitgen, Jurgens, Saupe. *Chaos and Fractals*
Springer, Verlag NY 2004

Penrose R. *The Emperor's New Mind: Concerning Computers, Minds, and the Laws of Physics* Oxford, UK: Oxford University Press, 1989

Peterson, Mark A. *Galileo's Discovery of Scaling Laws*
Cornell University, 2002

Peterson, Mark A. *Galileo's Muse: Renaissance Mathematics and the Arts*
Harvard University Press 2011

Pickering A. *Constructing Quarks*
Edinburgh University Press, 1984

Pinker S. *How the Mind Works*
New York: W.W. Norton and Company, 1997

Rees, M. *Just Six Numbers: The Deep Forces that Shape the Universe*
Weidenfeld and Nicolson, 1999

Repcheck, J. *Copernicus' Secret: How the Scientific Revolution began*
NY: Simon Schuster, 2007

Ronan, Colin A. *The Natural History of the Universe*
Doubleday, 1997

Royal, R. *Dante Alighieri Divine Comedy, Divine Spirituality*
New York: Crossroad 1999

Rubin, Patricia Lee. *Giorgio Vasari: Art and History*
New Haven: Yale University Press 1995

Santagata, M. (Translated by Dixon, R). *Dante: The Story of His Life*
Belknap Press of Harvard University Press, 1987

Scharf S. *The Copernicus Complex*
Scientific American/Farrar, Straus and Giroux, 2014

Schütze S and Terzoli. *William Blake: Dante's Divine Comedy*
Taschen GmbH, 2019

Servida, S. *The Story of Renaissance Architecture*
Prestel Random House, 2011

Shaw, P. *Reading Dante: From Here to Eternity*
W W Norton & Co, 2015

Smolin L. *Time Reborn: From the Crisis in Physics to the Future of the Universe*
Boston: Houghton Mifflin Harcourt, 2013

Sobel, D. *A More Perfect Heaven: How Copernicus revolutionised the Cosmos*
Bloomsbury, 2011

Stanford Encyclopaedia of Philosophy. *The Role of Decoherence in Quantum Mechanics*
April 2020
Susskind L. *The Black Hole War*

Little Brown and Company, 2009

Tegmark M. *Our Mathematical Universe*
Penguin, Random House UK, 2014

Travena, A and Soren, B. *Recent Advances in Cosmology*
Nova Science Publishers Inc, 2013

Turner AR. *Renaissance Florence: The Invention of a New Art*
Download, 1997

Vasari's Florence. Artists and Literati at a Medicean Court
Cambridge University Press 1998

Vasari, G. *The Lives of the Artists*
Oxford University Press 2010

Vasari, G. *The Lives of the Painters, Sculptors and Architects*
Franklin Classics, 2018

Vigdor S.E. *Signatures of the Artist: The Vital Imperfections that make our Universe Habitable*
Oxford University Press, 2018

Vitruvius. *De Architectura*
London; William Heinemann, 1931

Vollman, W.T. *Decentering the Earth: Copernicus and the Revolutions of the Heavenly Spheres*
NY Norton c2006

Wade N. *The Art and Science of Visual Illusions*
Nicholas Wade, Routledge and Kegan Paul, London 1982

Weinberg, S. *The First Three Minutes: A Modern View of the Origin of the Universe*
New York: Basic Books, 1993

Wilson, R. *Vertical Readings in Dante's Comedy Vol 2*
Cambridge, UK: Open Book Publishers 2016

Wilczek F. *A Beautiful Question: Finding Nature's Deep Design*
Penguin, Random House, 2015

ORO Editions
Publishers of Architecture, Art, and Design
Gordon Goff: Publisher

www.oroeditions.com
info@oroeditions.com

Published by ORO Editions

Text by Peter Cookson Smith
Illustrations by Peter Cookson Smith
Managing Editor: Jake Anderson
Book Design by Pablo Mandel @ CircularStudio.com
Typeset in Galliard, TT Norms, and Esmeralda

10 9 8 7 6 5 4 3 2 1 First Edition

ISBN 978-1-951541-53-8

Color Separations and Printing: ORO Group Ltd.
Printed in China.

ORO Editions makes a continuous effort to minimize the overall carbon footprint
of its publications. As part of this goal, ORO Editions, in association with Global
ReLeaf, arranges to plant trees to replace those used in the manufacturing of the paper
produced for its books. Global ReLeaf is an international campaign run by American
Forests, one of the world's oldest nonprofit conservation organizations. Global
ReLeaf is American Forests' education and action program that helps individuals,
organizations, agencies, and corporations improve the local and global environment
by planting and caring for trees.